NATIONALISM WITHOUT A NATION IN INDIA

Nationalism Without A Nation in India

G. Aloysius

OXFORD
UNIVERSITY PRESS

OXFORD
UNIVERSITY PRESS

YMCA Library Building, Jai Singh Road, New Delhi 110 001

Oxford University Press is a department of the University of Oxford. It furthers the
University's objective of excellence in research, scholarship, and education
by publishing worldwide in

Oxford   New York

Auckland   Cape Town   Dar es Salaam   Hong Kong   Karachi   Kuala Lumpur
Madrid   Melbourne   Mexico City   Nairobi   New Delhi   Shanghai   Taipei   Toronto

With offices in

Argentina   Austria   Brazil   Chile   Czech Republic   France   Greece   Guatemala
Hungary   Italy   Japan   Poland   Portugal   Singapore   South Korea   Switzerland
Thailand   Turkey   Ukraine   Vietnam

Oxford is a registered trademark of Oxford University Press
in the UK and in certain other countries

Published in India
by Oxford University Press, New Delhi

© Oxford University Press 1997

ISBN-13: 978-0-19-564653-5
ISBN-10: 0-19-564653-3

Printed in India by Ram Printograph, Delhi 110 051
Published by Oxford University Press
YMCA Library Building, Jai Singh Road, New Delhi 110 001

To the memory of my Father

Preface and Acknowledgements

The study of nationalism—ideology, organization, movement etc.—in India, has long been the exclusive preserve of the historians. In its external dimension, the discussion ranged between sheer xenophobia, on the one hand and sacred patriotism, on the other. Internally, it hinged around the axis of Hindu-Muslim harmony or disharmony. Sociologists however, have been pre-occupied with movements of all other kinds, considered mainly as instances of status or social mobility, Sanskritization/Westernization or protests/transformations. Though these movements, the 'national' as well as the 'social' were contemporaneous, contributed to, and together constituted the formation of modern India, the 'totality' itself was not problematized in either, leading to the 'rarefication' and eventually 'reification' of the 'grand national' within history. The 'national' became isolated, insulated, elevated and far removed from the 'social' which was often delegitimized as communal/casteist. Concepts such as nationalism and communalism along with colonialism became self-evident categories endowed with almost magical powers to reveal the mysteries of modern India.

In the course of a changing and changed socio-political situation, these master-concepts lost their usefulness. In fact, their functions became reversed and instead of opening up to social reality, they began to block its understanding. This was realized early enough. The seventies pointed out that ideology was often enough an excuse for 'plain pursuit of power'; the eighties discovered that despite the shrill claims of nationalism, the 'nation itself failed to emerge'. These dissenting voices from within modern Indian historiography are indeed significant. However, they could not proceed beyond a certain limit due to disciplinary constraints, narrow data-base and non-problematization of the basic concept—nationalism. This is precisely where sociology of nationalism seeks to step in.

Sociology brings to the study of nationalism two specific perspectives: one, that nationalism is not unlike other social phenomena, occurring repeatedly in different regions, cultures and contexts. Various nationalisms are capable of being classified and analysed systematically and that, it is possible to develop at least, the rudiments of a general theory of nationalism. In other words, it is not necessary to consider every nationalism as a 'unique construction'. Instead, each case can be viewed as a particular instance of the general class of nationalism. Two, is contextual, according to which nationalism—the ideology, organization, and movement—of a given region or culture is to be studied in the context of the structure and change of that society as a whole. Social structure and social change are the two central themes of sociology providing the framework for investigating different spheres of the corporate life of a society and nationalism is no exception.

Viewed sociologically then, nationalism in India, is likely to appear different from what it does within traditional history. The present study is one such attempt. It needs to be taken for what it is: exploratory in nature and tentative in conclusion. However, the study is an attempt at a departure of a major kind. If the issues that have come up in the course of the study are taken up, contested and carried forward by greater minds, its objective will be fulfilled.

Professor Randolf David of the University of the Philippines introduced me to critical sociology; Professor Dipankar Gupta, of the Centre for the Study of Social Systems, Jawaharlal Nehru University, stimulated my interest in the study of nationalism; Dr Avijit Pathak supervised the dissertation out of which the present study grew; Professor C.N. Venugopal was an ever-welcoming resource person. Professor Manoranjan Mohanty of Delhi University examined my work and suggested improvements. Professor Dawa Norbu of Jawaharlal Nehru University read through the manuscript and offered recommendations. Among my colleagues M. Kiran was always there to discuss the numerous issues and assist in documentation. However, none of the persons mentioned, and scores of others with whom I have been interacting in the course of the study are to be held responsible for the views, arguments or formulations articulated in this study, which are solely mine.

The study was carried out mainly in the library of Jawaharlal Nehru University and Nehru Memorial Library. I am grateful to the staff of both these institutions for their help. I am also thankful to the Daryaganj second-hand booksellers for providing me with several important books at affordable prices.

I also thank Murali and Anoma for typing the manuscript, and Rasna Dhillon for preparing the text for publication.

Finally, the study could not have been completed but for the constant support and accommodation of Josna. To her I owe much more than I can express in words.

G. Aloysius
New Delhi

Contents

I

Introduction
Historical Sociology and the Study of Nation and Nationalism in India

CHANGE IN THE AGENDA

Nearly two generations have passed since the tumultuous events surrounding the most important organizing principle of the Indian polity occurred in 1947. Sea changes have taken place during this period within and without the country that warrant a fresh look at what was once an all-consuming passion in public life—nationalism.

The mass enthusiasm generated in the wake of Independence and the subsequent engagement in nation-building activities in the early fifties, seemed to have overcome the fissiparous tendencies visible earlier and gave us the illusion that nationalism had indeed invented the nation. But illusion it proved to be, for as mass euphoria over the British departure receded into collective memory and as the economic front began to stagnate, exacerbating the problems of unemployment, poverty, corruption in public life, tenacious illiteracy, population explosion etc., centrifugal and disruptive forces reoccupied the centre-stage with unprecedented vehemence. Nationalism, instead of giving birth to one national society, seems to have delivered a whole litter of communities divided from one another in terms of language, religion, region or caste.

The response of the centralizing state to this bizarre phenomenon has been predictable. True to its colonial inheritance, it has been arming itself to the teeth, not so much against the external enemy as against its own citizens, becoming increasingly nervous about even minor and marginal struggles against any form of exploitation.

That the pan-Indian polity no longer attracts the allegiance of the majority of the masses and is increasingly being replaced by smaller entities is clear from the emergence and struggle of nationalities often denigrated through charges of regionalism, linguistic chauvinism and separatism. Communalism and communal violence is spreading to newer areas with increased intensity, becoming more frequent and engulfing more and more sections of people. India seems to have become, instead of a nation-state, one powerful state system, comprised of multiple warring communities. The only way out of this impasse appears to be Hindu communal nationalism, for more and more fence-sitters, secularists and even leftists are being drawn irresistibly into this whirlpool. The fact that this is nothing but a whirlpool leading to an early demise of the nation-state itself is indicated in the contradictory nature of its ideology. It is a communal nationalism in a double sense; it is communal not only *vis-à-vis* other religious communities but equally so *vis-à-vis* the large mass of lower castes within the Hindu fold. It is therefore more appropriately termed uppercaste Brahminic nationalism.[1]

The changes in the world at large during the same period have been equally devastating. If the birth pangs of the new 'nation-states' are scarcely over in Asia and Africa, the very heartland of the 'ideal nationalisms', has now begun to show signs of disturbances. Ethnic revivals in England, Spain, Canada, and elsewhere have challenged the liberal, secular nationalisms of the nations that ostensibly taught us nationalism. The development of the concept of internal colonialism in the writings of Tom Nairn, Michael Hector and others are present in these advanced nationalisms.[2] The collapse of the Soviet Union,

---

[1] There has been much squeamishness within academia in using Brahminism as an explanatory category in macro level political studies. Instead, Hinduism is used, resulting in mystification. That Hinduism itself is a problematic category, a colonial, collusive construct by power groups, native and foreign, referring mainly to the Brahminical form is being increasingly realized; see R.E. Frykenberg (1989, 1993), A.T. Embree (1989), B.D. Metcalf (1992), G.J. Larson (1993), P. Vander Veer (1992), D. Gold (1993), P.M. Biardieau (1980). Within the country however, 'Hinduism' is largely treated as a religion such as Islam or Christianity. The single exception would be R. Thapar. It is important to point out that Brahminism refers here not to the people who comprise the Brahmin community, but rather to the ideology of the Brahminic way of life. See chapter 11, n. 13.

[2] For a survey of and discussion on the recent ethnic revival world-wide, see A. Smith (1981).

and along with it, the well-nurtured communist paradigm of thought, has thrown out of gear several precariously balanced relations; both of theory and praxis. Liberal nationalism appears different and diffident now; its ideological cloak is unable to cover its nakedness anymore.

The direction of change in the world scene is not only towards smaller and culturally homogeneous politics. Counter-tendencies can be observed at the economic level, in the attempts at globalization. Multinational corporate empires, with scant regard for national sovereignty have become the order of the day, and world finance bodies more often than not operate as super-states; regional level unification attempts too (e.g., ECC) are taking place. At the global level, thus, we see on the one hand, demands for political segmentation based on a new understanding of the relation between culture and power and on the other hand, the pull towards economic integration or standardization across multiple/diverse politics and polities. These currents and cross-currents at the world level and the developments within the country demand a review and reassessment of established notions of nation and nationalism, both Eastern and Western.

Historical Sociology

Such attempts to review and reassess the established understanding of nation, nationalism and the relation between the two, have been made possible by certain changes within the social sciences. We are referring in particular to the new developments within the disciplines of sociology and history.

Since the mid-sixties, significant shifts in emphasis have/taken place in the conceptions and objectives of these disciplines. In both, a movement towards the other is evident with respect to perspective and scope, which points to the possibility of a mutual domain. The extrication of sociology from the largely ahistorical mould cast by the dominant functionalist paradigm has been slow and tortuous. In both its meta-theoretical and micro-empirical variants, sociology had reached a deadend, especially on complex modern social issues. The compulsions of macro-level and multi-dimensional present day problems such as war, revolution and state-formation have made sociology take a significant turn in its progress. Historical explanation is being restored to its former significance within sociology. The past an explanation of the present, and it is recognized that the genesis of a social phenomenon is an important aspect of its present situation. Paul Sweezy sees sociology as an attempt to write 'the present as history' (C.W. Mills 1959: 146). With history as its vast canvas, sociology with its conceptual and analytical tools can now create and recreate small or large diachronic social pictures.

The advance of sociology towards history has been amply rewarded by the latter's own warm response. History is no more a chronological record of kings and queens; its realm has been considerably expanded and terms like 'social history', 'history from below', 'subaltern history' indicate the variations available today within the discipline. Another important aspect in which the linkage between the two disciplines has been strengthened is the changed understanding of truth and objectivity in history. The monolithic concept of one ideologically neutral truth which is central to liberal historiography is no more accepted (R. Guha 1989: 214). If history is primarily historical explanation, then several explanations of one reality are not only possible but also desirable, given the awareness, as expressed by Hayden White, of an 'irreducible ideological component in every account of historical reality' (ibid: 214).[3] Washbrook is more forthright: 'History is...invented by historians in the present for their own purposes and is ultimately a function of ideology' and 'objectivity lies only in the conventions of common logic and evaluation of evidence by which the community of historians agree to abide' (1985: 94). With this pluralistic understanding of historical truth and the expansion of history's domain into what hitherto had been the exclusive preserve of the other social sciences, the alliance between the two is sealed. The nascent sub-discipline of historical sociology is indeed better equipped today to scan the large time-frame required to understand, interpret and assess macro-phenomena such as nation and nationalism.[4]

New Forays into Modern Indian Historiography

History-conscious social scientists and sociologically-minded historians have been taking a fresh look at modern Indian history since the late sixties. Earlier, the 'stale fare of Indian historiography' was either imperialist or nationalist (J.H. Broomfield 1966: 279). The former

---

[3] 'Past and present illuminate each other reciprocally' (F. Braudel 1980: 83).

[4] Not all historians are uniform in welcoming this influence of social sciences on history, see T. Raychaudhuri (1979).

recorded the activities of the rulers of colonial India and the latter depicted the anti-imperialist movement and the different stages in its development till its successful conclusion with state-formation.[5] Dissatisfaction with either kind of historiography and the search for a more meaningful framework has resulted in what could broadly be identified as the Cambridge, the Subaltern and the Regionalist approaches.

The first step these new schools of modern Indian history have taken is a thoroughgoing criticism of the dominant nationalist historiography. Discounting the role of ideology, the Cambridge School traces the mainsprings of political action under the Raj to localities, local interests and their networks formed under the impetus as well as constraints of the overarching colonial administrative structure, for the purpose of advantage, power and profit. Nationalism is of little relevance here; rather its seamier side—factions-cliques, patrons-clients, and other struggles for power stand exposed.[6] Clearly the school has moved away from the idealistic appreciation of nationalism as the motor force in modern Indian history. The explanatory principle here is competition and collaboration of factions that are organized under some ideology convenient for the time being.

If power and profit-mongering by groups and cliques is what is at the core of the Indian national movement according to the Cambridge School, the Subaltern School finds the movement exclusively elitist, in sharp contrast to the struggles and aspirations of the subaltern masses, whose interests were distinct and different from those of the imperial or national elite. According to R. Guha, "...the numerous peasant uprisings of the period, some of them massive in scope and rich in anti-colonialist consciousness waited in vain for a leadership to raise them above localism and generalise them into a nation-wide anti-imperialist campaign...it is the study of this failure which constitutes the central problematic of the historiography of colonial India" (R. Guha 1982: 6-7). Clearly the Subaltern School too has distanced itself from the traditional nationalist perspective. Again, in contrast to the unified vision of anti-colonialism of the

[5] For an extended discussion on the different schools of history of Indian nationalism, see chapter IV.

[6] T. Raychaudhuri (1979) calls this 'Animal Politics'; and H. Spodak (1979) provides an extensive review of major works of the Cambridge School.

earlier school, the Subalternists posit an episodic pattern to study the struggles.

The Regionalist School of modern Indian historiography as exemplified in the works of A. Low (1968), J.H. Broomfield (1966, 1968) and others, moves in yet another direction away from the dominant pan-Indian historiography. For these authors, the interaction between Britain and India is not a single encounter between two great monoliths; it is only at a 'rather rarefied level that modern Indian history may be said to comprise a single all-India story' (A. Low 1968: 5). Needless to say this rarefication is ideological in both intent and character. Regional variations in the interactive processes between the British and the Indian according to this view, would provide a better framework for the study of Indian society of the time. Broomfield has thus utilized the concept of regional elite—Bhadralok—to study Bengal politics (J.H. Broomfield 1968).[7] This approach has yielded a rich harvest of regional social histories with a wealth of detail, and subtle nuances of meaning of contexts and relationships.

All these new ways of looking at the history of modern India are first and foremost a critique of the monolithic, un-contextualized and rarefied reading of the Indian response to British rule under the unified title of the nationalist movement. The nationalist historiography is viewed as elitist, false and insensitive to regional variations. The net result of this critique is that pan-Indian nationalism can no more occupy the central place it did uptil now, in both history as well as historiography (A. Low 1968: 18; A. Seal 1968: 351). The proposed directions are fairly clear: for the Regionalists, while one cannot get away from the unifying colonial structure, historiography should be much more sensitive to regional variations; for those of the Cambridge School, professed idealism and ideologies are not to be taken at face value but are to be examined with particular reference to the intense manipulative politics that goes on underneath for selfish group-ends; and finally for the Subalternists, a severe critique of the received definitions of nationalism, imperialism and colonialism should be followed by a search for the genuine kind of nationalist aspirations and anti-colonial struggles, especially among the subaltern peasant groups.

A rigorous contextualization of the pan-Indian nationalist movement,

---

[7] The Cambridge historians too, to some extent share this regional approach.

in other words, a reconstruction of the historical conjuncture of the ideology and movement as one among several such taking place contemporaneously, will reveal the true nature of the nationalist movement itself.[8] It would also shed new insights into what have been contemptuously called casteist, communal and chauvinistic movements. These labels of course have been part of the weaponry of the traditional nationalist discourse accepted *in toto* by academicians of all hues. The newer historiographical schools contain the vital uneasiness with nationalist histories, and they also point out the several possible leads. However, the hesitations or the difficulties of breaking with the overwhelming paradigms are also there.

Thus the impetus towards a change in the agenda of colonial Indian historiography, particularly where it concerns the question of nationalism, is from two complementary sources, as we have tried to delineate above: one, the changed productive and power relations of groups and forces within and without the country; two, the changes in the realm of theory both historiographical and sociological, as explained below.

Drawing profusely from the insights generated by these modern Indian social historians and rejecting at the same time their extreme formulations, it is proposed in what follows, to look at the colonial period of Indian history, not within a single undifferentiated rubric of nationalism on the one hand, or as scattered fragments (locality, peasant struggles or regions) on the other, but within a spectrum of categories: nation, nationalism and nationalities. What these differentiated categories within the spectrum mean specifically and how they are related to one another are questions to be addressed to the recent theoretical elaboration on the subject within sociology.

THE SOCIOLOGY OF NATIONALISM

The study of nations and nationalisms until recently has been the

---

[8] S. Sarkar (1983) is acutely sensitive to this non-contextualization of the national movement and accordingly his 'Modern India' contains several other responses to British rule. However his idea of contextualization seems to be limited to mere juxtaposition of different movements while wholeheartedly subscribing to the nationalist categorization of them all as caste, communal, etc. Washbrook's (1985) criticism of 'Movement studies' is indeed directed against this non–contextualization. Our own approach is akin to that of A. Touraine's (1985) 'movement–counter movement approach' to the study of entire social reality (See Touraine 1985).

exclusive preserve of either political theorists or historians. The former
spoke of the doctrine or ideology of nationalism, at par with liberalism
or socialism etc., the different aspects of it, its diffusion over the
globe, its progressive or regressive impact on world politics, international relations, etc. (E. Kedourie 1960, 1970; J.H.C. Hayes
1931). The latter on the other hand, narrated the story of the nationalist
movements in different regions leading successfully to the formation
of nation-states either spontaneous or forced, open or closed, humanis-
tic or xenophobic, and largely as western or non-western (H. Kohn
1965; H. Seton-Watson 1977). Both these approaches to the study
of nationalism concentrated on the movement of power between
political units or states as the key to the understanding of nationalism,
which was considered to be primarily the power-politics of state-
formation. Nationalism was here an attachment to the nation-state,
even more specifically to the territory as distinct from the nation
as a community. The roles of pre-existing national, cultural and
ethnic differences, common history and other similar objective factors
were sharply discounted. In this sense nationalism and nation-state
were considered specifically modern phenomena and creations of
modern politics. Max Weber could be considered as the theoretician
par excellence of this approach towards the study of nationalism. For
Weber, national consciousness was in no way dependent upon objective ethnic or linguistic realities and the decisive factor was conscious
participation in the process of deciding on the power-status of one's
own state.[9] This predominantly political or statist approach to understand the problem of nationalism is still the dominant trend within
non-sociological theories of nationalism.[10]

Sociology proper is a late entrant to the field of nations and
nationalisms. The founders of modern sociology, preoccupied as they
were with macro-level social transformations of European societies
in the wake of the Industrial and French Revolutions, paid scant
attention to the emerging phenomena of nation and nationalism,
which first became a problematic largely in the non-West European
contexts. Durkheim concentrated on the transition of societies from
mechanical to organic solidarity; Weber's interest was riveted by

[9] 'If the concept of "nation" can in any way be defined unambiguously, it certainly
cannot be stated in terms of empirical qualities common to those who count as
members of the nation' (M. Weber 1978: 922).

[10] See J. Breuilly (1982: 1–2).

the expansion of bureaucratic/capitalist rationality; and for Marx, it was the transition from feudalism to capitalism and from there on to socialism that mattered most.[11] The post-classical development of the discipline either as variations within structural-functionalism or as the search for meaning within micro psycho-social relations did not improve the situation. The phenomena of nations and nationalisms were too complex, being spread over long periods of time and encompassing large masses of people in vast areas, to be tackled by ahistorical theorizing.[12] On the Marxist front, despite lively early debates, Stalin's reflections followed by Lenin's policy statements on self-determination of nationalities seemed to have settled the question, at least for the time being.[13] However, in the face of tumultuous changes in post-war geo-politics such as the national liberation movements, the crises faced by ossified Marxism, and by the well nurtured liberal-democratic paradigm, the challenges to national sovereignties both from below and above and more specifically, the ascendancy of all forms of primordial loyalties, world-wide sociological theory has been forced to reckon with macro-history and the significant outcome is the new sociological approach to the study of nations and nationalisms. The writings since the mid-sixties, of Ernest Gellner (1964, 1973, 1983, 1987), Benjamin Akzin (1964), B. Anderson (1983), John Armstrong (1982), Walker Connor (1972), and Anthony Smith (1981, 1983, 1983a, 1986, 1988) represent such a sociological approach. The attempt here is to be analytical and thematic and yet to operate within the historical data at different levels. The contribution of these authors to theory building has been differential; successive reviews have pointed out the merits and demerits of these writings and in general have noted the quite underdeveloped nature of the theory as a whole because definitional, classificatory and other serious problems still beset these works (G. Stokes 1978; A. Waldron 1985). In spite of all these shortcomings, it is possible to identify within these writings a distinct sociological approach to the study of nations and nationalisms and to mark out certain shifts

[11] A. Smith (1983a) suggests that though the founders of sociology were not directly concerned with nationalism, their own vital concerns could throw a number of cues and insights to theory-building on nationalism.

[12] See A. Smith (1983a) for a discussion on the reasons behind the 'sociological neglect of nationalism'.

[13] J. Stalin (1913); See also C.C. Herod (1976), W. Connor (1984) and R. Debray (1977) for a critical introduction.

in emphasis and consensus in orientations, relevant to the present work.

The New Approach: Convergence and Divergence

The recent theoretical proliferations by sociologically oriented writers, on questions of nation and nationalism are largely a reflection of the fast developing crisis within both communist regimes and liberal-democratic nation-states in the wake of ethnic resurgence (A. Smith 1981: ch. 1). The numerous political challenges demanding re-distribution of national territories both in the West and the East have predicated a drastic theoretical review of the received and hitherto largely non-problematic notions of nationalism, nation, and nation-states. The first contribution then, of the new sociological approach to the subject, is the problematization of the concepts related to nationalism. The ambiguity of nationalism as a concept, used as it is to refer to a multiplicity and diversity of phenomena far removed from one another in space and time, meaning different things for different individuals and groups both within and without a nation or state, has been noted even by earlier writers (L.L. Snyder 1954: ch. 1; E.H. Carr 1939: xvi). However it is only recently that systematic attempts have been made to extricate the several meanings of nationalism and its cognates on the one hand, and to highlight the fluid nature of their interrelationships, on the other. Nationalism may refer to the doctrine or ideology of an aspiring class, or to the policy orientation of a state, or to a praiseworthy sentiment of attachment to one's own nation or state. Nationalism may also refer to a socio-political movement for state-formation or any anti-imperialist movement, or to the nation-building activities or mobilization of a government or class. Both as ideology and movement the concept could be used either in speaking of a state, a group of ethnic communities or a single ethnic community. The meaning of the term 'nation' is no less uncertain. It may refer to an entity forming part of the compound concept nation-state, or to a linguistic ethnic community struggling for its own statehood; again it may refer to a relationship that exists or is presumed to exist between individuals and groups with either equality or common cultural bond as the basis of common political consciousness. In the compound concept of nation-formation the reference may be to the complex process either of the slow emergence of meta-local cultural homogeneity or to the politicization of such a cultural community or even both. Ambiguity is doubled with the use of the term nation-state; the connotation of both parts, given the term is substantial, which is the primary and leading part? Does nation correspond to state or the other way round? Is it merely an appellation that could be used indiscriminately for all existing political units or does it refer to a particular kind of state system in which certain minimum conditions are fulfilled? Can one nation have several states? Or one state, several nations? Finally we have the term 'nationality', which may mean either legal membership in a nation-state or an ethnic community in transition.[14]

The conceptual kaleidoscope of nationalism has been in vogue for about two centuries, in the different continents in scores of languages, to express a bewildering variety of ideas, situations, events and forces and has had its own history or histories. The concept itself being contested, the different sub-concepts are all highly value-laden and defy all definitional and classificational attempts.[15] And finally, the inter-relationship between the various phenomena indicated by these related concepts—nation and nation-state, nation and nationalism—are neither pre-determined nor fixed. As categories of crisscrossing political discourses, they are ambivalent both as weapons with their own dynamics as well as playthings at the mercy of groups and forces in conflict. Therefore, while it is too early to expect either consensus or even consistent usage among the different writers, the sociological attempts to deal with the varied manifestations of nationalism have brought to the surface the complex and problematic nature of the terminology as well as the phenomena in their interrelationships.

The second contribution of the new approach to the study of the national phenomenon is the focus on nation as a distinct social category, deserving of attention on its own basis. The 'nation' is a new entity, a socio-political community in modernity. It is not a mere by-product or an afterthought of nationalism either as an ideology or a movement. It is a new kind of collectivity in which 'some deep, permanent and, profound changes have taken place in which society is organized'. Nation here precedes nationalism at

[14] See A. Smith (1983) ch 7 on 'definitions'.

[15] A.J. Motyl (1992) has recently rightly pointed out that definitions of nationalism reveal more about the definers than about the defined.

least logically if not also historically. The emphasis, therefore, is on the being and the becoming of a nation as a new form of society conceived in terms of either culture, as a meta-local homogeneity or of power, as a new politically equitable community, rather than ideology or organized political movement (E. Gellner 1983). This analytical disjunction between nation and nationalism problematizes the relation between the two—society and ideology. Nationalism, here is critically viewed in relation to the nation, in the aspect of the latter's being and becoming. While the ideological articulation of nationalism through the agency of a conscious political movement inevitably contains a sectarian or class-like character, nation in the sense of a cultural or political totality seeks to transcend this potential interest-based cleavage. Here lies a serious source of ambiguity in their relationship.[16] Another side to this emergence of the nation in sociology is the simultaneous movement away from the statist approach. The awareness that national boundaries rarely coincide with those of the state and that confusion between the concepts of state and nation is indeed a hindrance to the understanding of nationalism itself is evident in recent writings. This shift away from the state in the study of the nation has thrown up a serious challenge to the existing notions of nationalism which by and large tend to take for granted all the present state-formations as nations.[17] What Paul Brass terms 'end-state bias' in the studies of nationalism has almost subverted the autonomy of the academia into apologists for status quo ideology of the state (P. Brass 1974: ch. 1).

If nation is a new and modern social collectivity, then what was society like in its pre-modern or pre-nation stage? What were the specific ways in which the pre-nation characteristics of a society were transformed, or not transformed, and continue to exert influence today? What were the forces within pre-nation society that gave birth to the new ideology of nationalism? What are the senses in which nation can be considered a continuity or break with history?

[16] 'The best kind of party is in some sort of a conspiracy against the nation.' Ostrogorcki quoted in B.B. Misra (1976) p. 1.

[17] 'Loyalty to [an] ethnic group therefore should be called logically nationalism. But nationalism as commonly employed refers to loyalty to the state (or to the word "nation" when the latter has been incorrectly substituted for state)... with the term "nationalism" thus pre-empted, scholars have felt compelled to offer a substitute to describe loyalty to the nation. Regionalism, parochialism, primordialism, communalism, ethnic complementarity and tribalism are among those that have been advanced.' (W. Connor 1972: 334); see also S.Z. Nagi (1992).

Questions such as these have brought to the fore, the study of pre-modern culture and society as the potential raw material out of which nations are shaped and ideological movements arise and form, or fail to form, nation-states. This is the third characteristic of the new approach. At the heart of all nationalisms, defining themselves either territorially or culturally, there lies a 'persistent cultural core' problematically defined as ethnicity. This is increasingly becoming clear both within world politics and the new sociology of nationalism, much to the chagrin of the mostly poly-ethnic nation-states whose boundaries are determined largely through accidents of modern history.[18] While it is premature to predict the demise of the liberal idea of nation-state, ethnicity turning political is what nation and nationalism is all about. This appears to be the increasingly favoured view within the new approach to the subject (J.A. Armstrong 1982).

With the problematization of concepts, shift in emphasis from state, ideology and movement to nation as a distinct social category and particularly in the aspect of its becoming, i.e. the transition from pre-modern to the new cultural/political totality, the new sociological orientation to the study of nationalism seeks to situate the complex phenomena within the overall context of social change in keeping with the tradition of the discipline. The search now is for a new form and formulation of transition of societies. As a theory of cultural power, sociology of nationalism is a study of social change from such a perspective—the movements of power and power positions within society affecting its structure and culture. This internal approach to the study of nationalism as a specific form of social change is the most important contribution of the new sociological approach.[19]

If the above mentioned tendencies represent the emerging area of convergence, the area of divergence is no less wide and crucial: periodization of waves of nationalism, categorization of nationalist movements, the nature of social change that could be considered minimal and characteristic of the transition to nation, the role of different cultural factors such as language and religion, the potential

[18] See particularly the writings of A. Smith.

[19] This is particularly true of E. Gellner (1983). See A. Smith (1983) chs 3 and 4 for a review of sociological theories on nationalism within both the consensus and conflict traditions. C. Hah and J. Martin (1975) have attempted a synthesis of these two traditions.

reach of nationalist politics, the relationship between nation and nationalism, the modernity of the nation, etc. These issues are beset with disagreements and contested at all levels. As most writers generalize over a differential group of actual nationalisms, biases of all kinds tend to creep in and charges and counter-charges of Euro/ethnocentrism are freely traded. Questions of nationalism are highly value-loaded and are expressions of interests and power positions of individuals, groups and even nation-states. Therefore to expect a consensus on contested political realities or a single, overarching paradigm explanatory of all manifestations of the national phenomena is illusory, at least for the time being.

Congruence between Culture and Power

Nationalism, in the felicitous phrase of Ernest Gellner, is the 'congruence between culture and power'. Indeed, most of the differences and disagreements on the subject could be viewed as elaborations of the two crucial terms of this pithy phrase—culture and power. Most definitions of nation, for example, emphasize either the so-called objective cultural factors or the subjective (consciousness) political factors. The instrumentalist or primordial approach too, could be termed as a power or culture perspective to the problem. The debate on modernity or otherwise of the nation is but another formulation of the same power-culture dichotomy. Yet, it is the congruence between the two that constitutes nationalism. The consciousness of the imperative for such a congruence between culture and power is the ideology; the attempts to bring about this congruence, the movement; the actual congruence, the nation. And the juridico-legal approval of this phenomena by the community of nations, the essence of the nation-state.

If congruence between culture and power is what nation and nationalism is all about, was culture apolitical in the pre-nation or pre-modern stage ? While scholarship is divided on this point, the idea that culture resents being ruled over by another culture but seeks to set up its own power, is not entirely modern. Certain forms of fusion between culture and power could be identified even in ancient times.[20] In the modern phenomenon of nation a particular

---

[20] For instance, wars between groups in pre-modern times were largely known as wars between ethnic or racial groups.

form of congruence between culture and power as transition and social change is being indicated. The modern consciousness of the imperative for a fusion between culture and power and the conscious concerted attempts to bring this about, that is, nationalism both as an ideology and a movement, has two referral points, one external and the other internal. The external reference is to other cultures, nations and nation-states, which are perceived as obstacles in the way of one's own nationalism. This obstacle need not always be actual control by another culture as under imperialism, but could be a graded one. Under this aspect nationalism seeks to liberate one's own culture from the determinative influences and interference of other cultures. While this consciousness and concern was not entirely absent in ancient times, it came to be established (as the right of self-determination of nations)among the community of nation-states only in modern times. The internal dimension of the culture-power fusion is what constitutes the specifically modern element in the notion of the nation. Here the reference is to the culture's own past as the other. Nationalism seeks to move away from the notion of the past or pre-modern form of the culture-power fusion, usually unequal, hierarchical, and ascriptive, and construct an equal and at least formally homogeneous one. The demand of nationalism here, is for equal spread of power over culture as the transition to nation. Historically, this internal aspect of the nationalist struggle has been formulated as the right of self-determination for individuals. The nationalist process of politicization in modernity takes hold of culture in its totality, empowering all its members with equal rights and responsibilities, and sets them apart from cultures and individuals outside it. The mobilization of the nation's masses in nationalism takes place not merely on the basis of a certain primordial affinity in culture, as in ancient times, but on the basis of commonality of political purpose and destiny as the emergence of a socio-political community. The mass of men and women who were hitherto excluded from the arena of public power through ascriptive hierarchical structures of privileges/liabilities in society and dynastic rule in polity, now emerge politically in nationalism to constitute the new politico-civil society of equal rights and liabilities. Such is the specific form of congruence between culture and power in modern nationalism. The modern national congruence between culture and power thus consists of two simultaneous movements—one, a movement away from the other culture i.e. appropriation of power from without, and two, a movement away from the past or pre-modern form of unequal or differential power-realization in one's own culture, i.e., homogenization of power within. The meaning of the phrase 'homogenization of power' is specific: the even distribution of power and recognition of equality of socio-political status among members, at least in principle. Together, this double movement of power over culture constitutes the social change or transition to nation, demanded and affirmed by nationalism as an ideology. Here, another congruence between the two movements of power in relation to culture is implicit. Any attempt to explain nationalism solely in terms of either one of the movements to the exclusion of the other, will be partial not only in theory but will also be an incomplete representation of history. Nationalism as self-determination for the cultural collectivity is inextricably tied to nationalism as self-determination of the individuals within that collectivity. The two are but phases of a single move towards modernity and nationalism (A.D. Smith 1983: 67).

While the movement of power between cultures has been amply documented as the ideology and movement of nationalism by political theorists and historians, it is the movement of power within culture as the transition to nation, that sociologists have concentrated on. This becoming of the nation has been deconstructed by Gellner as the universalization of literacy, functional diversification, social mobility, formal equality and anonymity of membership. Gellner himself speaks of this process as the creation of a meta-local homogenous culture. But it is better viewed as homogenization of power/access to power or at least as the creation of the cultural conditions for a new and formally equal form of power distribution within culture (E. Gellner 1983: ch. 3-4). Anderson expresses the same ideas, when he says that nations are imagined communities constructed through the emergence of print capitalism on the basis of a 'new found deep, horizontal comradeship' (B. Anderson 1983: Introduction; L.L. Snyder 1954: 40). That a political process such as nationalism takes place within a relatively homogenous cultural entity described problematically as ethnicity, seems to be the implication of most of the important writers—Gellner, Anderson, Connor, Smith and others.

State-formation as such, does not figure prominently in this enterprise; consolidation of a national polity is nothing but a contractual formalization in politico-juridical terms of the changes that have been set in motion and the most important of such categories are territorialization and citizenship. While the concept of territorialization refers to the boundary between cultures for the purposes of exclusion of aliens and alien cultures from structural power, citizenship is the affirmation of inclusion via membership, in the share of the same power.

The foregoing discussion of nationalism as the congruence between culture and power largely centres around the problematic of power, its movements, transformations and transpositions. If culture is treated as a given, it is because culture emerged as a major problematic within nationalism since the late sixties of the present century. The 'persistent cultural core' of nations as ethnicity, is the concern of the contemporary ethnic nationalisms, challenging the poly-ethnic constitution of the liberal-democratic idea of the nation-state. Questions such as whether meta-local cultural homogeneity as ethnicity is a modern or pre-modern phenomenon; are not ethnicity, identity and homogenity, all products themselves of modern politics; is not 'cultural/national tradition, invented or imagined', form the substance of current discussions on nationalism.

However, our tentative theoretical forays are limited in intent. A theoretical elaboration of nationalism is beyond our scope and ability. The intention here, in the light of recent sociological discussions on the subject, is to highlight those aspects of nationalism which became the central concerns of different forms of politics during the colonial period of the subcontinent's history. While problems of culture, ethnicity, identity, etc., did form a strong undercurrent during this period, they emerged as a major challenge to state power only in the post-colonial era. The marginal contestation that did take place, could be seen as a fall-out of debates on the sharing of power within. This research thus deals only with the movement and transposition of power within culture as the overwhelming agenda of the colonial period, while holding the culture itself as somewhat constant. Needless to state, this is a limitation dictated by constraints of space and the complexity of the subject. A more complete sociological interpretation of Indian nationalism would follow both the cultural as well as political discourses during the entire period of modern Indian history.

Value Orientations. The main value orientations and pre-suppositions of this study are as follows:

The cleavages within the hierarchical, pre-modern Indian society which became enlarged, distorted and polarized, to some extent at the intervention of the British, are at least as important a contradiction (if not more) as the cleavage without, i.e. between the Indian and the British, in determining the origin, development and direction of Indian nationalism. This is in accordance with the double reference points—one external and the other, internal—that theory has suggested for the study of nationalism.

The study seeks to locate itself within the broad streams of the critical traditions of the social sciences. This means that the data or the facts are not taken as normative. A tension is sought to be maintained between what 'is' and what 'ought to be', not certainly in the sense of imperatives but in the sense of tracing the disjunctions between the professed and the real. Through efforts at separating appearance from reality and professed motives from unintended consequences, it proposes to challenge and criticize the given radically and probe for alternatives from within. To borrow the words of Ranajit Guha, this is a study of the 'historic failure of the nation, to come to its own' (R. Guha 1982: 6-7).[21]

This study also attempts to seriously and consistently take the point of view of the submerged masses, on the different aspects of the problematic, without at the same time sacrificing historical truth or mutilating conventions of evidence. The underdog's point of view is a value in itself, besides being the superior one in representing the majority's view for a praxis-oriented sociology. The study then, is to be seen as a dialogue with the masses and as a part of the process of their overall emancipation.

Structure of Study.   The insights and observations from both the new critique of modern Indian historiography and the sociology of nationalism which have been pooled together in the preceding pages will be brought to bear on the colonial period in the subsequent chapters.

Chapter II will analyse the net result of the interaction between traditional Indian society and colonial rule, particularly from the point of view of the restructuring of power relations within. The analysis will address the following questions: What was the impact

---

[21] However it should be made clear that in substance, this study moves away from the general approach of those who have come to be known as Subaltern historians.

of the British on the segmented and traditional Indian society? Were the changes brought about during colonial rule conducive to the becoming of a society based on social mobility and anonymity of membership? Finally, what kind of infrastructural foundation was laid for the rise of political consciousness and articulation of nationalist thoughts and sentiments?

Chapter III is concerned with one category of political awakening in the country with a definite notion of nation and nationalism. It will delineate the arena, the issues and the methods of contestation of power of the different groups involved in this political process. Secondly, the theoretical insights of Gellner which have been highlighted in the first chapter, will be used to examine their presuppositions and implications to nationalism. Concretely, this Chapter will survey and analyse those struggles—anti-caste, anti-feudal and pro-autonomy—which claimed to create a national society which is homogeneous with respect to power.

The nationalist movement as the movement to eject the alien culture from power is examined in two parts in Chapters IV and V. A short survey of different schools of thought would be followed by a contextualization of the birth and growth of the anti-imperialist movement. This laying bare of the historical conjuncture of the movement, it is hoped, will throw more light on its real nature and its ideological and political trajectory. The dichotomous nature of Indian political response to colonial rule and the mutual relationship between what are traditionally but non-problematically labelled as the national and communal movements will be emphasized.

Chapter V traces the development of the ideologies of nationalism—cultural and political—within the conflicting socio-political situation. The nationalist ideology was not monolithic and did not go without contestation. Nationalism as an intellectual-cultural construct, too, was diversified within the subcontinent. Construction of the past was differential, the contestation at present was polarized and the visions of the future were divergent.

The latter phase of the nationalist movement, known as the Gandhian era, will be seen as an attempt to bring together the two streams of national and nationalist (or national and communal as per established historiography) awakenings. The nature of this attempt, its outcome, as well as fall-out would form the substance of Chapter VI. In the context of the new situation currently developing in the country, this Gandhian legacy has assumed a new significance, at least among the ruling circles and the established academia. Hence a critical review of the same is in order.

Nationalist mobilization is a combination of both vertical and horizontal political mobilizations within society. It is both integrative as well as disruptive. One of the astute attempts to grasp the nature of this mobilization at the theoretical level, is that of Antonio Gramsci. Our last chapter, then, is again a semi-theoretical one, which proposes to situate the Indian national synthesis within the Gramscian notion of the 'National-popular' and 'Hegemony', and examine whether nationalism has indeed invented the nation or not.

II

Colonial Rule and the Old Order

The colonial period of Indian history is not merely a period of shame and servitude but also a period during which, in its own peculiar way, India stepped into modernity. For our purpose, it is a period of great social and political upheaval in which we shall seek the emergence or non-emergence of a new national community. It is also the period in which the ideology of nationalism was articulated through the nationalist movement and brought to a successful conclusion, with the formation of India as a modern nation-state. In short, it is the period of transition to nation and nationalism in India. In terms of our theoretical framework, this is the period during which the double congruence between culture and power needs to be examined. Power during this period was relocated with respect to two referral points—the British and the country's past—to the present nation-state. In this chapter, then, we are analysing the material and non-material changes that took place under colonial rule. We are also examining their role in the political awakening of different sections of the people which inspired them to wrest power from both the British as well as the past socio-political order.

Sociological studies of social change in India are largely variations within the predominant structural-functionalist paradigm. They attempt to capture the changes in society within the polar categories of tradition and modernity. While lacking a theoretical dimension, these studies are mainly ahistorical and tend to avoid the rather troublesome area of the change of power with respect to social structure. They are better described as studies of cultural change.[1] Within the Marxist tradition, these changes were seen rather mechanically as the transition from feudalism to capitalism by the early Marxists, and as peculiar combinations of several modes of productions by later generations.[2] What most Indian Marxists share, however, is an economic-reductionist approach in which power and politics are functions of economic change. This, in spite of the fact, that elsewhere within Marxism, recent scholarship has moved away from reductionism and is now paying serious attention to cultural and political theory.[3] In India where economic- and class-reductionism has collapsed, instead of developing more sensitive historical-materialist analyses, Marxists seem to be content with presenting a variation of the nationalist historiography.[4] The study of change within economic history has largely confined itself to debating whether India gained or lost economically during foreign rule.[5] Political modernization studies concentrate on the working of modern political institutions within the country (R. Kothari 1970). Finally, political histories study the change during the colonial period descriptively, as a backdrop to the all-important political movement interpreted rather narrowly as the nationalist movement for freedom (S.R. Mehrotra 1971).

These different approaches to the study of change in colonial India are useful in throwing light on the period, and we shall draw on them continuously for material. However, our search is for a particular kind of change not highlighted by these approaches—changes that were commensurate with the development of nationalist ideology. We are looking for material and non-material (ideological) changes

[1] For different approaches to the study of social change in India, see the ICSSR Trend Report on Social Change and Stratification by Yogendra Singh (1977). His own 'integrated approach' (1986) to the problem is hardly an improvement on others.

[2] Examples of early Marxist approaches are M.N. Roy (1971), R.P. Dutt (1948) and A.R. Desai (1948). For later views, see 'mode of production' debates and particularly H. Alavi (1980). Not that there were no honourable exceptions. For example, though S.K. Ghosh (1985) speaks of feudalism, it includes a definite cultural component, too (see n. 20).

[3] The best example for our purpose, of course, is that of Gramsci, (1968, see Chapter VII).

[4] The obvious example is Bipin Chandra; note the change of approach between his earlier and later works. A less obvious shift informs the works of S. Sarkar; too compare his work on Bengal (1973) with 'Modern India' (1983).

[5] The 'drain theory' of Naoroji, elaborated in the 'de-industrialisation' theory of R.C. Dutt was challenged by M.D. Morris. See Morris et al. eds (1969). While D. Naoroji's (1901) thesis would be true in the main, what became politically determinative was the cleavage that had developed within society rather than the overall 'drain'.

specifically as they bear upon power-realization within and without socio-cultural structures. In other words, the focus is on economic and social changes as well as changes in political structure that took place during the colonial period, and the extent to which they helped or hindered the formation of the new national community. The questions this chapter seeks to answer in this context are two: firstly, what were the general and particular contours of pre-modern India in terms of power distribution within social relations? And secondly, whether or not the material and ideological changes during the colonial period prepared the ground for the transformation of the pre-modern forms of social power? If so, to what extent, and in what direction? Discussions of these two themes will provide the starting point to the understanding of subsequent political awakenings, especially the nationalist movement, from the perspective of social change, or, the modern form of congruence between culture and power as the formation of a new national political community.

Power: A Perspective. The view, that social power is not limited to its formal political manifestations and needs to be viewed from a non-reductionist perspective, has been noted often enough.[6] Recent developments have emphasized the multiplicity of forms that power assumes within society, as well as its ubiquitous presence (S. Lukes 1986:1-18; M. Foucault 1990: 92-7). Incorporating these insights and extending them further, power is seen here, first of all, as located primarily within social and group relations in the context of the political economy of a society.[7] Secondly, despite its ubiquitous presence and diverse forms, power tends to organize itself around a single nodal point or principle, settling into a harmonious unity in the form of a cultural specificity over a period of time.[8] This means social power in a society has two facets: one, common to all societies and the other, unique to a society. Thirdly, power expressed as aspirations of individuals, groups and collectivities is always contested, and as contestation is always

[6] See M. Weber's note on Marx's idea of class (1985) pp.180; F. Frankel and M.S.A. Rao (1989) Vol.1, argue for a distinction between social.dominance and state power, p. 2.

[7] While economic reductionism is to be avoided, the other extreme of considering power as primordial, atavistic or irrational and unrelated to political economy is rejected here. Power is a contestation for resources—economic, cultural and intellectual.

[8] Within the Marxist tradition, this was considered the primary contradiction among several others; see A. Touraine (1985).

between forces unequally positioned or equipped, power manifests itself either as dominance or as resistance. To resist, is as much an expression of power as to dominate.[9] And fourthly, while power can be analysed in terms of this bipolarity, several moments of ambiguity between the polarities mark concrete social relations.

PRE-COLONIAL INDIA

Complex and advanced agricultural societies were broadly marked by an unequal, hierarchical distribution of power among diverse groups, following somewhat rigid, hereditary occupations. This ascriptive inequality permeated all spheres of social relations and tended to divide the entire society into relatively isolated segments such as orders, status-groups, castes etc. This inequitable power distribution system was legitimized by generalized cultural and religious concepts.

Such a system of privileges for some and disabilities for many on the basis of birth, was the pre-modern expression of power as dominance. However, this dominance had to be achieved and maintained in the face of continuous opposition from power as resistance. Pre-modern forms of resistance to ascriptive and hierarchical power distribution took several forms: subversion, sabotage, flight, revolt or the creation of a counter-culture/ideology. These have been studied as primitive revolts, social banditry, messianic or chiliastic movements, formation of heterodox cults and sects or simply as peasant movements. While only a few conscious and organized struggles to create an egalitarian system of power distribution could be identified, all these attempts by disadvantaged groups intended to a greater or lesser degree to change the current form of power distribution either by escaping the disabilities or by appropriating more powers (R. Bendix 1961).

The concrete configuration of power distribution in pre-modern societies was, in general, an articulation between ascriptive inequality —hierarchy as dominance and primitive utopianism as resistance. This articulation between opposing social forces as a form of societal equilibrium was dynamic and differential over space and time. More specifically, the constraints that operated were the availability of means of production and communications. The struggle, negotiation and

---

[9] See M. Foucault (1990) p.95; 'Each mode of production will give rise to at least two significantly separate ideologies corresponding to the class position of subordinate and superordinate classes', B.S. Turner (1983) p. 78.

accommodation between the social forces ranged on either side was intense where agricultural productivity was high and food security stable over a period, such as in river-valleys and other fertile areas. The generally dry, non-agricultural areas and commercial centres represented the periphery, where the rule of ascription was very much attenuated and even at times, unheard of. However, the terrain of struggle in pre-modern times was clear enough: ascription was the principle of social power distribution. This was true of Europe as well as India.[10]

The specific form of ascriptive hierarchy and unequal distribution of power in India is known as the caste system. The hierarchical structure of ascriptively segmented occupational and endogamous castes, endowed with differential distribution of privileges/disabilities and sanctified by the dominant religious categories of Karma and Dharma was certainly a pan-Indian phenomenon, though spread unevenly. Despite intra-regional differences, the pattern of hierarchy was remarkably uniform over different regions and has been so, for more than a millennium—with the Brahmins at the top, other literary, propertied and clean castes following and *shudra, ati-shudra*, labouring and polluted castes at the bottom. The hierarchies of different spheres of social relations tended to coincide—the religious hierarchy of purity and pollution, which was a rough reproduction of production relations and ownership patterns, also expressed itself in an unequal privilege/disability structure in public life. The foundation of the entire edifice was status determined by birth, legitimized and sanctified by the dominant Brahminic religio-cultural symbol and belief traditions.

M.N. Srinivas's summation of the scenario runs thus:

> Caste is undoubtedly an all-India phenomenon in the sense that there are everywhere hereditary, endogamous groups which form a hierarchy. ... Everywhere there are Brahmins, untouchables and peasant, artisan, trading and service castes. Relations between castes are invariably expressed in terms of pollution and purity. Certain Hindu theological ideas such as *samskara, karma* and *dharma* are woven into the caste system ... the ordering of different varnas is clearly intended to support the theory of Brahminical supremacy.[11]
> (1966: 3ff.).

---

[10] See J. Blum (1974, 1978), G. Duby (1980), A. de Tocqueville (1970) and C. Bougle (1971).

[11] See also A. Béteille (1980) pp.110 ff. and H. Gould (1987) chapter 1. For a particularly

The Chaturvarna ideology of the Brahmanas and other Dharmashastras is the single most powerful ideological formulation of
this ascriptive hierarchy. While the classical varna system was a Brahminic aspiration as well as the ideological codification of the dominant
groups, which nowhere and at no point of time was exactly replicated
in society, it was none the less not very far from reality.[12] The
uneven process of evolution of the subcontinent as a caste-society
took more than a millennium. Once evolved, the importance and
intensity of the caste system fluctuated from period to period, depending on the overall structural circumstances. However, it would be
correct to argue that the caste system and caste ideology—the Brahminic
version of social order—pervaded the entire region to a greater or
lesser degree through religio-cultural symbolism in the form of
mythologies, ubiquitous temples as social institutions, Sanskrit as the
sacred language, codification of laws and .customs, and most of all
through the actual socio-economic dominance of Brahminic and
other collaborating upper castes, and imbued society with a sense
of cultural unity.[13] This situation, as generalized custom and tradition
of the land, was normally upheld by the scattered and changing
forms of political power.[14] The cultural unity of the subcontinent,

---

sharp formulation of the pre-modern social order as religiously legitimated inegalitarianism see M. Weber (1958) and L. Dumont (1970). M. Weber (1958) calls
India 'a land... of the most inviolable organisation by birth' p. 3. Nationalist and
early Marxist historians in general describe pre-modern Indian society in terms of
the political order (dynastic politics) and the economic order (feudalism) respectively
and consider the British take-over as the transition point to the new order. See
A.R. Desai (1948). That the key to the understanding of power in India lay within
society was realized early enough by minority historians and a good number of
sociologists and is increasingly being accepted by others as well; see R. Thapar
(1975), A. Rudra (1981), G. Omvedt (1982) and J. Brown (1984).

[12] For example W.H. Wiser (1958) investigated the Jajmani system in an U.P.
village and found remarkable correspondence between the actual and the ideal as
expressed in. the *Manusmriti*. Whether hierarchy in India derives its inspiration from
any model other than the Varna/Brahminic one has exercised the minds of many.
Historically, in all probability it did, as all advanced agrarian societies had some kind
of hierarchy. The varna model itself is a framework developed out of the inchoate
hierarchies already found here but the relevant point is that no other hierarchy is
as elaborated as this one and most socio-politically relevant hierarchies eventually,
had come to articulate through this Varna model to a greater or lesser degree.

[13] See D. Shulman (1985) and A.T. Embree (1989), 'The use of the adjective
'Brahminical' is not meant to imply an ideology that is confined to one group but
rather a set of values, ideas, concepts, practices and myths that are identifiable in
the literary tradition and social institutions'. p.10.

[14] The question, whether the secular-temporal power as represented by the kingship

then, is mostly derived from the ascriptive and hierarchical elements of power as dominance.

It needs to be emphasized that the caste system of India is only a particularly tenacious and rigid form of the general ascriptive hierarchy found in varying forms in many other pre-modern societies (C. Bougle 1971: 7; L. Dumont 1970: 24-5; J. Blum 1978). Here, separation among the communities took an extremely all-inclusive form, creating a multiplicity of social worlds. Hereditary occupations were so rigidly ascribed that even when social mobility did take place, the entire group ascended or descended the scale of hierarchy or changed occupations. All apparently extraneous counter-influences were absorbed over time. The system survived, adjusting itself and adapting to new influences, and its spirit continued to shape the minds of individuals and the world-view of groups and communities. The extraordinary tenacity and astonishing longevity of ascriptive dominance as both a system and an ideology in India is linked to two inter-connected factors. Firstly, unlike in many other societies, ascription here enjoyed relative autonomy from the fluctuations in the polity and in politics. Several observers have noted this discontinuity between society and polity in the subcontinent. (E. Stokes 1978: 19-23). Despite the frequent rise and fall of dynasties and expansion and shrinkage of political boundaries, the social order as a universalized norm of custom and tradition was stable, absorbing the marginal and minimal changes. Kingship as an agent of change in South Asia has become controversial recently and the view of the oriental despot is sought to be re-established through micro-studies, in reaction to what is considered an obsession with uppercasteism/Brahminism or even 'sociologism' (N. Dirks 1987: 3-5, 126-9; A. Appadurai 1981: pp. 6ff.). However, it has been established through studies in different disciplines, that the king's role was, in general, limited and his rights were contained in several specific ways (A. Wink 1986: 19, 67, 214, 220, 377, etc.; R. Thapar 1966: 19; C. Drekmeier

---

was subsumed under the sacred-spiritual power as represented by the Brahmins or the other way round, in pre-modern India, has become a much exercised one, especially through the writings of N.Dirks (1987), R. Inden (1986,1990), A. Appadurai (1981) and others. Our point is that such a polarity of sacred/secular itself is misconceived. The Brahmins as a force were not limited to the sacred realm. They wielded enormous power within the secular realm of society. Political institutions of kingship most often included Brahmins as the main and important functionaries. The king himself upheld the Dharma of the caste system, as much in deference to the shastric injunction, as to ground realities within society.

1962: 245-62). Therefore, without arguing for an eternal and non-problematic fixity of social relations at all levels, one could conclude that the macro-structure of society was characterized more by continuity than by change. The second factor is, that the old order in India was symbiotically and hence inextricably intertwined with the dominant Brahminic religious traditions through the core ideas, concepts and beliefs evolved in the historical-mythical context of race relations between groups identified as Aryan and Dravidian. While in the case of monotheistic religions, social inequality was largely a result of the divergence between belief and behaviour, here, it was the fruit of the convergence between the two; hence, the relative strength of the Brahminically legitimated ascriptive hierarchy in India.[15] The disjunction between belief in equality and practice of inequality in the former, allows a space for criticality and signifies potentialities for change. This space is absent within the latter Brahminic Hinduism, which believed, preached and practised an elaborate and a universalized form of social inequality. Since the ideology and practice of actual, dominance, differentiated into land owning, clerical, merchant and ruling sections, centred around the sacred authority of Brahminism, religion and culture worked as the major media of socialization and social control. The almost pervasive hold that religion enjoyed over society had two serious consequences. One, it obviated, very often, the need for brutal physical force to wrest compliance from the masses, through the lie of their willing subservience.[16] Second, it made change doubly difficult as all change in power relations would necessarily appear as a revolt against culture and tradition. Thus, autonomy from polity, on the one hand, and 'syntonomy' (if one could coin a term)with religion on the other, is what is specific to ascriptive dominance in pre-modern India that accounts for its seeming invincibility.

If the Brahminical social order as an ideal-type was power in the form of dominance, contra-Brahminism/casteism, in the multiplicity and diversity of its manifestations was the ideal-type of power

[15] The Church's upholding of medieval social hierarchy, the theological justification of the system of orders, etc., are to be seen within the overarching belief and preaching of 'Christian agape' and the fatherhood of God.

[16] For the unique role of ideology in the maintenance of dominance in general, see L. Althusser (1971) and G. Therbon (1980); and in India, A. Rudra (1981) and F. Franco & S.V.S. Chand (1989).

as resistance.[17] Varna ideology was contested at all times and in all places though in an uneven and imperfect manner *ab initio*, over the entire region. Since the main anchor of the hierarchical principle in India was religion in its dominant Brahminic tradition, challenges to hierarchy largely came from within the same religious framework. Beginning with the Ajivikas and Sramanas, nearly 2500 years ago, the subcontinent's history is replete with inadequately researched, anti-hierarchical socio-religious and cultural manifestations. Pan-Indian heterodoxies such as Buddhism, Jainism and the Bhakti movement; regional sects, such as Vira-Shaivism, Sikhism and Kabirpanth, and numerous other local movements, to a greater or lesser degree, were expressions of anti-hierarchical aspirations and values.[18] The emergence and development of modern Indian languages could also be viewed as an aspect of the generalized resistance to the uniformizing and dominating tendencies of the Sanskritic idiom. Parallel to this rise of the vernaculars is the burgeoning of regionalized and non-Brahminic popular religious forms, festivals, pilgrimages etc. More tumultuous and localized forms of resistance such as social banditry, caste boycotts and peasant-tribal movements against the impositions and excesses of caste-feudalism in pre-modern times still await serious study. These multiple and disparate forms of resistance against ascriptive hierarchy in its specific Indian form along the course of their long history, did not develop into a conscious, unified and pan-Indian socio-cultural agenda or counter-ideology. However, the fact that such an ideology and agenda is implicit in all of them in varying levels of consciousness, cannot be denied. This relative absence of a formulated, pan-Indian counter-consciousness is both the strength as well as the weakness of these forms of resistance, for diversity in the subcontinent draws its inspiration from power as resistance.

Caste, permeating the entire gamut of economic, social, cultural, political and religious relations of society as a complex matrix of contestation between the unifying and centralizing Brahminical social

---

[17] While within the micro-studies, the anti-hierarchical nature of the heterodoxies and sects was recognized, this was scarcely integrated within macro-level, generalized and theoretical studies on Indian culture and society. In this sense, the Weber-Dumont tradition of viewing Indian society as caste society is only a partial one. If Indian society was casteist it was also anti-casteist.

[18] See R. Thapar (1966: pp.67-9, 214-16, 260-5, 308-313). However, the extent of the egalitarian thrust of the different movements is a subject of controversy; see, for example, U. Chakravarti (1987: pp.94-122); see also B.S. Turner's discussion on Engel's views on religion (1983: pp: 63-86).

order as dominance on the one hand, and contra-tendencies in differential and diverse forms of egalitarianism as resistance on the other, together constituted the specific form of power-realization in pre-modern Indian society. This ideal-typical bipolarity of dominance versus resistance has been concretized as an uneven process of articulation in the form of confrontations, concessions, compromises, accommodations, and at times, though rarely and temporarily, as role reversals. The several ecologically bounded and unevenly developed ethnic regional communities are but moments of negotiated settlements between dominance and resistance within the terrain of caste relations and caste ideology. In this sense we do have multiple concrete configurations of the caste system (L. Dumont 1970: 33).

The society and history of pre-modern India cannot be reduced to the dialectics of castes; several other contradictions such as gender, class, ethnic-region etc., were operational throughout its long history. However, the overarching form of contradiction, providing a scaffold for all others, suffusing both base and superstructure of society was caste. Within this framework the different contradictions aligned and jostled for primacy. Gender oppression appeared as a function of caste–patriarchy; class relations expressed themselves as Jajmani relations and patterns of land ownership and cultivation rights; and relations between regional and ethnic communities at both micro and macro levels were expressed in caste terms. Conversely, attempts to rescue these different contradictions—gender, class and ethnic-region—were invariably part and parcel of most anti-caste movements.

Finally, this pervasive contestation of power anchored in caste dialectics was extended to and elaborated in the realms of culture and ideology, creating a vast collage of ideas, concepts and discourses. Hierarchy and egalitarianism, collectivism and individualism, idealism and materialism, spiritualism and pragmatism, religiosity and rationalism, theism and atheism, conformism and confrontationism, authoritarianism and democracy are found in the contesting aspirations and ideologies of individuals, groups and other social formations, in differential degrees of emphasis and articulation, in different periods of the subcontinent's history (D.P. Chattopadhyaya 1959). If most of the egalitarian, pragmatic, rationalist discourses and dispositions emanating from power as resistance lie buried within the baffling diversity of local/regional and dialect/vernacular idiom, codified and set against the easily identifiable hierarchical, spiritual, traditionalist discourses and narratives, it is certainly not the fault of history, but of historiography.

To this ideal-typical sociological picture of the power-configuration within pre-modern Indian society, a historical note needs to be added. Generally, the pre-modern ecological and communication constraints, mentioned above, to the spread of the rule of ascriptivity is crucial. Despite more than a thousand years of its growth, the varna ideology could not penetrate vast areas of dry zones, and hill-forest regions and failed to dominate territories far removed from its strongholds. Owing to low levels of technology (production as well as communication), combined with linguistic-cultural differences resulting from racial diversity, large sections of the population had managed to remain independent. Some of these, the tribals for example, had not taken to complex agrarian organizations. Others, as in the south, due to the racial notions undercurrent in varna ideology, resisted it and in course, had developed their own versions of stratification, which although hierarchical, were very dissimilar in operation to that of varna and more importantly, lacked its powerful religious legitimation. Yet others, by appropriating egalitarian religious ideologies such as Buddhism, Christianity, Islam, had developed tensions between the actual and the ideal. Varna ideology in pre-modern India was certainly powerful in those numerous river-valley settlements from the Gangetic plain to Cauvery and Narmada to Brahmaputra, through their political organizations, cultural values and religious forms; but it could not be termed monolithic nor considered to be universally accepted. Other traditions, cultures and value systems, with equal spread kept it in check. Particularly, the century immediately preceding the British take over, in the period between 1650 and 1750, was marked by important changes within both society and polity that had the effect of furthering the interests of those resisting the varna ideology. This period, till recently, was viewed pejoratively as one of political fragmentation and social anarchy. However, recent scholarship has begun to interpret the facts differently. It is increasingly being seen as the period in which regional states emerged, economy diversified, commerce and industry expanded, feudal-agrarian relations loosened and, in general, the structures of the *ancien régime* weakened.

The combined effect of non-agricultural activities—wars, manufacture of arms, clothes, etc., increased spatial mobility of men and materials, expansion of trade and commerce—on the social structure, was to release the generally lower and labouring groups from several kinds of bondage. Working largely within the south Indian context, Burton Stein, David Ludden, Sanjay Subramanian and others have pointed out that the general balance of power during this period tipped against the river-valley based agrarian social structure and its ideological buttress, the varna principle.[19] Washbrook in an important article notes:

> For those groups who had been at the very bottom of the *ancien régime's* social order the epoch offered a number of rare opportunities... and... as many contemporaries claimed, the world appeared to be turning on its head: with Pariahs and never-do-wells owning land and wealth and developing social pretentions while Brahmins and respectable people were murdered in their beds and chased by marauding armies.... (D. Washbrook 1993: 79).

Even if many fail to see the golden age for the Pariahs in the eighteenth century, it could easily be argued that the period was one in which the hierarchical uniforming forces, i.e. power as dominance, were losing their edge over those of egalitarianism and diversity, i.e. power as resistance.

Pan-Indian generalizations on culture, power, society and history of the pre-modern subcontinent are necessarily hazardous and such attempts could be faulted on numerous scores, especially at a time when regional diversity is gaining recognition, both in contemporary politics and historical study. However, the political unification of India and the subsequent emergence of several forms of social conflict specifically *vis-à-vis* this unified and centralized form of polity, have made such generalizations imperative, as a method of historical explanation. The above delineation of social power in pre-modern India is accordingly, functionally minimal and limited to stating the general conclusions of established scholarship on South Asia. It has a diachronic perspective in indicating the long and continuous trends within history. For it is within these streams of pre-modern history that British rule, its impact, and the transition to nation and nationalism need to be situated and studied.

Our next query could be formulated thus: what was the impact of British rule on this form of power-realization in the subcontinent? We must seek to identify the material and non-material changes that took place during the colonial period and their effect on the

---

[19] See I. Habib (1995) pp. 180-258, T. Raychaudhuri (1983) and S.K. Ghosh (1985).

pre-modern forms of dominance and resistance in India. In other words, how could the colonial change be viewed as the prelude to the emergence of nation and nationalism, a new form of congruence between culture and power?

MODES OF CULTURAL INTERACTION

The interaction between the British and Indian cultures was not monolithic in form on either side: on the side of the British, there were several streams of influence not always acting in unison—the official, the missionary and the civilian; the Indian side, multi-cellular and hierarchical, also responded differentially to the different aspects of external influence. In terms of time and space too, the interaction was uneven—the coastal presidencies displaying deeper impact than other regions and provinces. Sectionally, the interaction varied from one group of communities to the other. From the point of view of the British in general, the impact itself was determined by their pragmatic self-interest which was trade and revenue (A. Maddison 1971: 35).[20] Except for a very brief period between 1820 and 1855 when some social reform legislations were pushed through and several territories were annexed, resulting in the abortive Mutiny of 1857, the British on the whole were very reluctant to intervene in the status quo. Whatever changes that had occurred then, were necessitated from their side by political considerations or in fact were unintended consequences of their actions. The Indian side did not passively accept these changes but was an active partner, now appropriating and demanding more, now opposing and accommodating. While official intervention was characterized by ad hocism and pragmatism, the zeal of the missionaries knew no such inhibitions once they were allowed entry in 1813. Although their contribution to actual changes within society was rather marginal, they helped transform the ideological climate of the country by provoking several controversies in the realm of cultural and religious practices.

Karl Marx's early journalistic pieces on India's revolutionary social changes under British Imperialism, characterizing them as painful

---

[20] See S.K. Ghosh (1985) p.153 ff. The author's argument that there was no real antagonism between the local emerging bourgeoisie and the imperial rulers has been recast in the context of development of nationalism by both the Subaltern as well as Cambridge schools of historians, as solidarity of interests against the masses.

yet inevitable, crude but progressive, has largely provided the lead
for the Imperialist, Nationalist and Marxist historiographers studying
colonial transformations in India (S. Avineri 1968: 83-9). That Marx
himself later modified many of his views on colonialism's capacity
for effecting progressive change, does not appear to have been useful
for the ideological purposes of these historiographers (S.K. Ghosh
1985: ch. 5). Reacting largely to these writers' eagerness to see
radical change anywhere and everywhere, the new social and economic
historians, such as those from the Cambridge and Subaltern Schools
went after the non-European foundations of European imperialism,
especially through detailed analyses of practices under the various
land settlements (R. Robinson 1972). They found that the all-powerful
'Raj' was as much an illusion as a reality; that, under the shining
'white umbrella' of the centralizing authority, the tiny little 'white
ants' of local influence were corroding the political structures silently
but effectively (J. Brown 1984: ch. 11; R.E. Frykenberg 1965: 230-
44). The meaning and import of these well-documented studies
is quite clear: the British did not and could not affect any serious
change within Indian society, the old order won in the end. Also,
the British period was characterized more by its continuity with
the past than by a revolutionary break with it. While these recent
studies are definitely an advance over the previous ones in terms
of their detailed research, as well as in the light of later developments
in the country—and this study will be relying, to a great extent,
on their findings and conclusions—they do not provide us with a
holistic picture, especially of the consequences of the seeming continuity of the social structure as a whole. For the purposes of our
study we shall first, state those changes (both material and non-material)
which are considered important, and which occurred during the
British Raj. Second, we shall try to highlight their impact on the
old socio-political structure of the society. The aim is to draw certain
conclusions that would link these changes and their structural consequences to the subsequent political awakenings in different sections
of the populace.

Changes: Material and Non-material

Colonial changes as uneven and incomplete processes comprising
interactions of multiple groups both Indian and British, can be ten-
tatively grouped under the following heads: structural unification,

economic transformation, expansion of civil society and introduction of liberal, secular ideas and reforms. Marx's enumeration of colonial changes in India largely coincides with the above, except for the inclusion here of ideological changes (E. Stokes 1978: 24-5). In the Marxian agenda, change in the superstructure was not as important as it is for our purpose here. Nationalism is a politico-cultural theory and requires explanation, in its own terms, of changes within the ideological superstructure.

Effective structural unification under the British was a new phenomenon in Indian history. The process was incomplete, with nearly one third of the area of the subcontinent being retained by the Princely States, and uneven with the regions being brought under the central authority at different times and under different circumstances, terms and conditions. The most important implication of this unification is that it caused a transition from competitive and wasteful warlord aristocracy to effective and diversified bureaucracy (A. Maddison 1971: 37). It was thus a process of bureaucratization which had its own political implications. The nature of power over society and the method of wielding it also came to be transformed. To rule, now, is to administer. This change is significant, for in the new set-up men with qualities and skills different from those of warriors are called forth. Literary skills in general, and modern education in particular, came to be viewed as providing access to this new realm of power. Politico-administrative unification was aided by the physical linking of the entire country by various communication networks—railways, roads and telecommunications. Although their development was skewed as they were primarily intended to serve the purposes of imperialism, they laid the foundations for spatial mobility as a possible prelude to social mobility.

Economic transformation refers to changes in agrarian relations and the expansion of business and industry. Land revenue was the topmost priority of the British and accordingly land settlements benefitted those who were likely to offer maximum revenue without much social or political disturbance. The different forms—zamindari, ryotwari and mahalwari—that the settlements took, were dictated more by local realities of land control and power relations than by any ideological considerations (E. Stokes 1978: 31-2). Here too, bureaucratic intervention and expansion could be noted; measuring every piece of land, affixing it to individuals, estimating the revenue to be paid and the like involved tremendous amounts of paperwork for which trained personnel were required. Once trained, these men wielded enormous power over the illiterate rural majority. Commodification of land and commercialization of crops are the other developments pertinent to agrarian relations. The striking fact about the non-agricultural changes—expansion of business and industry (especially the latter)—is their limited nature (J. Brown 1984: 103). Industrialization of the country was not and could not be part of the imperialist agenda. Whatever developments took place were unevenly spread, both region- and population-wise, determined largely by the needs of the mother-country and its war efforts. However, within this framework some native industries, especially textile, steel, and jute came up, not so much inspite of imperialism or in antagonism to it, but as collaborative efforts with the British.

Enlargement and diversification of civil society is intimately linked to the introduction of the new education and the growth of professions—lawyers, doctors, teachers, journalists, judges and officers. Intended to create a class which may become the interpreter between the British and the people, English education spread unevenly, concentrated mainly in the metropolitan cities of the coastal presidencies, and created an elite that wielded power and influence disproportionate to their small number, by filling out the already proliferating professions in the cities (A. Maddison 1971: 43). The direction and nature of education was determined not only by the imperialist need for collaborators but also by the structural constraints of Indian society. Eventually, the subcontinent came to be dotted with several islands of English-educated people in the professions and bureaucracy, and these islands were to play a determining role in the country's future.

Modern liberal-secular ideas percolated the Indian thought-world through several sources, the more important of which have been identified as the official, evangelical and the free traders. Each of them had its own compulsions and trajectory. Under this three-pronged attack, with varying degrees of legitimacy derived from state-power and accompanying structural changes, the socio-cultural and religious world of the dominant Hindu castes went through serious changes: old values, some of them at least, had to be discarded, while others were rejuvenated; traditional legitimacies had to be revamped; new sanctions had to be dovetailed into a pattern; a new ideology had to be articulated to serve old ends; new interests had to be pursued with the old rationale; new challenges had to be neutralized or co-opted. In short, the Hindu conceptual world, especially at its top levels of Brahminic ideology, went through a trauma of instability, change and finally, reincarnation.

What was the bearing of these changes upon the hierarchically-stratified, religiously-legitimated endogamous groups? Revolutionary change or simple continuity are theories better described as ideological positions and do not as such take into consideration the number of insights offered by recent scholarship. With regard to each of these changes, we could start examining which levels of the old social order appropriated the new opportunities, how they did it, and which levels lost out in the process. More significantly, was there a change in the ordering itself? If so, to what extent?

Land Relations   Following a somewhat different approach, changes in agrarian relations and their impact on social structure have been the subject of intense research in recent times. Detailed district level researches have repeatedly revealed that the earlier euphoria over the presumed revolutionary changes in landholding was definitely not warranted. The British needed, because of their scarcity of finance and personnel, strong, mainly political, local buttresses, if they were to continue ruling. Their search for allies led them to groups and communities that were already dominant and influential in the different localities. For these groups too, the imperial connection was not without its rewards, mainly by way of conferring a new secular and enlarged legitimacy to strengthen their position of dominance. So, far from upsetting the existing order of superordination and subordination, British rule tended to act as a freezer on the social structure by sharing the new legal and moral authority (with the locally dominant). Needless to say, these dominant communities were largely the upper castes—Brahmins, Rajputs, Kayasthas, Vaidyas or Sat-Shudras. Whatever be their local nomenclature, they had a stake in the existing social hierarchy and the Brahminic ideology of legitimation. There were some honourable exceptions. These exceptions themselves subscribed to the same ideology of legitimation, and so do not vitiate the general picture. Whatever relations took shape within the realm of agrarian changes, will have to be understood within this basic limitation.[21]

---

[21] For a general discussion on the new orientation to the study of colonial land relations see E. Stokes (1978) and N. Bhattacharya (1986). For particular area researches, See R.E. Frykenberg (1965, 1969), A. Yang (1989), L. Brennan (1970), B. Cohn (1987); see also A. Maddison (1971).

The most important change that affected the entire rural social structure was the acquisition of absolute property rights by those upper caste groups that had hitherto only the right to surplus produce (revenue) of the land. This was the result of the operations of the different kinds of land settlements.[22] Land in pre-colonial India was the context in which the hierarchical interdependent interests and rights of different rural communities converged in mutuality. While the purer castes had the right to surplus, the polluted ones had the right to work within a Jajmani framework. But this arrangement gave way to the consolidation of private property rights for the superior tenure-holders (of revenue rights), thus making the lower tenure-holders, of whom there were several rungs, landless (A.T. Embree 1969: 47; R. Suntharalingam 1974: pp. 14ff.). True, the effect of land becoming a saleable commodity in the hands of the revenue-holders was to be felt only gradually, but the process had been set in motion. More than half a century had elapsed (in the case of Bengal, more than a century) before some legislative attempts to secure the rights of the occupancy ryots were made, but by then enough damage had already been done and the legal remedies themselves were largely nullified by the manipulation of the working procedures of the courts and tribunals, by the very same communities which held land.[23]

The second important change was that more and more people who were traditionally neither rural nor connected with the land came to acquire interests in land. Moneylenders, traders and petty bureaucrats, who could muster up capital, invested in land, the owner-ship of which aided the acquisition of high social status. These new land owners, of course, stayed where they were and continued to collect their share of the surplus. In such cases, what in effect took place was the addition of yet another layer of parasitic ownership, increasing the burden on the lower level tenants. Needless to say, many of those who lost land through the machinations of the moneylenders-bureaucracy nexus were economically weak or/and ritually low on the scale of hierarchy.[24]

[22] A. Maddison (1971: p.47), A. Yang (1989), p.228, E. Stokes (1978) p.32. and A. Seal (1968) p.79. R. Suntharalingam (1974) notes the rise of Brahmin power in ryotwari areas, p.14.

[23] The earliest attempts to protect the land rights of the ryot were in 1859 (Bengal), 1873 (North West), 1868, 1886 (Oudh), 1885 (Bengal), 1900 (Punjab), etc. See B.B. Misra (1976), p.72.

[24] Of the Benares region, B.Cohn (1987) notes how the transfers of lands were

The third impact was the emergence of tax-farming as an accepted and prevalent practice. Taking the cue from the British, landlords released the land to the highest bidder, changing the tenants as often as it suited their convenience. Traditional tillers of the soil thus became the tenants-at-will, indentured labour or bonded labour.

The numerous land transfers, foreclosures, distress sales and auctions that were earlier advanced as evidence of land reform, at closer inspection reveal circulation of property among individuals of the same community or among a small number of communities within the Brahmin dominated upper caste cluster which had developed in different localities (A. Yang 1989: pp 227 ff.). This was the extent of mobility initiated by the land settlements. Huge holdings were broken up, but the fragments remained within kinship, clan or caste groups. When Rajputs lost, the Brahmins gained; when the zamindars became bankrupt, the money-lenders became landlords. But the entire rotation took place within a tiny circle of dominant communities whose dominance was traditionally legitimized by a religious ideology. So what appeared to be the new class from above, was not a new class at all when viewed from the bottom, and those who had this view had no reason to turn euphoric over the changes.

The imperial connection meant different things to different sections of people. In the context of the new agrarian relations, the existing cleavages were considerably widened. At the lower end of the scale, the labouring castes lost their lien of right to work on land. They could be, and indeed were, evicted fairly often. Land had been parcelled out in the names of different people and the government, and common property resources were all but dried up. Thus, there was a serious rupture between land and labour. Inadequate commercialization of agriculture and lack of industrialization pre-empted a large scale detachment of labour from land. The new arrangement, therefore, meant severe losses to those who were socially, economically and ritually, the downtrodden. While the British could take credit for the legal abolition of agrestic slavery, their land-settlement policies and practices brought into existence several new forms of agrarian bondage.

The acquisition of standardized property rights on land by several near-equal castes on the one hand and the simultaneous loss of the

---

largely to the 'writer castes'. 'They knew how the courts worked because they worked in them', p.337.

stable right of the masses to labour on the other, had two consequences.
One, was the horizontal widening of the gulf between the small
number of owning groups and the labouring masses, and two, the
coming together of different endogamous groups, at least, in a limited
way, now united in their interest in private property rights and
the material and immaterial structural arrangements to protect the
same. Limited social mobility among these groups, access to a vision
beyond one's caste group towards a larger community, and a certain
relaxation of ritual rigidity with regard to the newly acquired opportunities were initiated. Even within this upper caste block of
communities the walls did not breakdown in any significant manner.
They all remained separate, conscious of their ritual and social differences. But they were now united in property, in interests and
in the new arrangement of the secular-political realm.[25] Economic
and political expediency demanded that they recast their old notions
of legitimacy. A parallel mobilizational process could be noticed lower
down the social scale too, of course for opposite reasons. There
seemed now to be no *raison d'être* for the communities to have
a hierarchical ordering, at least when confronted by an 'ownership
syndicate of several castes'. With important differences with regard
to pace, pattern and combination in different parts of the country,
this, in general, has been the process initiated by land settlements
within the graded society: the beginnings of polarization and parallel
horizontal processes of mobility.

Education and Civil Society   The pattern of colonial impact on the
old order of the Indian society in the context of land relations was
repeated and reaffirmed in other contexts too, such as the introduction
of English education and the consequent expansion and diversification
of civil society into professions. The determining influence of the
old order upon the birth, growth and direction of this new education
has not been as intensely researched as that in the realm of land-
relations. However, sufficient insights and observations have been

[25] A. Yang (1989) concludes his study of the Saran district thus: 'Anchorage of the
colonial regime at the local level was therefore attained by setting up a system that
tacitly, if not explicitly was geared towards the maintainance and enhancement of
the prevailing indigenous system of superordination and subordination', p.229. R.E.
Frykenberg's (1965) conclusion of his study on Guntur is more forthright: 'The elite
groups of the district were those light varnas or castes who dominated the high
positions in the local hierarchy...The elite groups wielded the religious, social and
economic sanctions by which they maintained the status quo...' p.232.

generated in the context of the study of nationalism, to safely affirm, that here too, the old dominant sections of society managed to monopolize the new opportunity structure generated by the introduction of English education.[26] It has been noted consistently by nearly all writers on Indian nationalism that the groups and communities who reaped the maximum benefit of this new education during the whole of the nineteenth century and a good part of the first quarter of the twentieth were upper caste, and more particularly the Brahmins, in all the important centres. This observation hardly requires documentation. The most unambiguous formulation of this fact has been the one by Anil Seal. Noting that English education was concentrated in the three coastal presidencies, and here too mainly in the metropolitan centres, Seal describes, how in Bengal, 'it was the Brahmins, Kayasthas and Baidyas, in Bombay, the Brahmins in solitary, perilous pre-eminence and so too, in Madras held the near monopoly of education and that they were not any new class but just the same old wine in new bottles' for 'yesterday's scholars of Persian, now became enthusiasts for English' (A. Seal 1968: 11, 38-97; J. Brown 1984: 77).

If, in the establishment of zamindari the British were looking for native political buttresses, the creation according to Macaulay of a 'class who may be interpreters between us and the millions whom we govern' was also intended for the same purpose in the administrative arena (A. Maddison 1971: 41). Starting off as allies and partners of the colonial regime, these two groups very soon came together (if ever they were separate in terms of caste affiliations) by virtue of common interests to be preserved and strengthened, and to this extent their endogamous isolation gave way to a limited horizontal mobility among themselves on the one hand and on the erection of a new secular boundary (Bhadralok, for example) against the rest of the population on the other.[27]

The top-heavy structure of Indian education, its lopsided emphasis on literary and classical aspects to the exclusion of technical and

---

[26] The relations between the new education, the expansion of civil society and the rise of nationalism has been rightly focussed upon by nationalist historiographers. Therefore it is really crucial to understand and evaluate critically the context out of which the new professions turned nationalist; for discussions see next chapter.

[27] This coming together of landed groups and the new literary groups in terms of secular interests as well as ritual-caste ideology has been noted by J. Brown (1984), p.72; B.B. Misra (1961), p.106; and A. Rudra (1989).

vocational knowledge, the relative absence of interest in the spread of mass primary education, etc, have been duly noted. This view is only partially accurate and needs to be supplemented with the observation that the situation suited the groups and communities that were appropriating the new education, and since these groups were dominant, there was no need for, nor any pressure on, the government to change policy or practice.[28] In fact attempts to vernacularize education at the instance of some orientalists met with resistance from the beneficiaries of English education.[29] The new education was increasingly becoming a powerful politico-administrative weapon of dominance within society, and the strategic limitation of this tool was very much in the interests of the traditionally dominant communities. The net result was that the English education and the professions based on it, during the first century of British rule, was not very distinct from the pre-colonial monopoly of literary knowledge by ritually high-ranking castes, of course, suitably modified by co-options.

The introduction of modern education did not bring about social revolution or change to any significant extent in the Brahminic ideology of the old order, nor indeed give birth to any new class. On the other hand, it was used to turn a tiny elite into 'imitation Englishmen' and a somewhat bigger group into government clerks filled with the same old notions of ascription and hierarchy (A. Maddison 1971: 43). This is forcefully brought out by the fierce and ubiquitous resistance this elite offered to the entry of polluted castes into state run educational institutions. For the depressed classes and groups the right to entry into educational institutions, was no less bitterly contested and wrested than the right to entry into the temples. It suffices here to quote from the census report of 1901, reproduced in B.B. Misra:

> Cases are by no means rare, the report said, where the attempts made to enforce an equality of treatment for the depressed castes have led to large schools remaining closed for years and to dis-

---

[28] Wood's despatch of 1854 recommending mass vernacular education for all practical purposes remained in the files for a long time.

[29] S.R. Mehrotra (1971), p.218; agitation against change of policy was 'unprecedented in intensity and magnitude'; also note that one of the administrative responses to the 1857 revolt was the setting up of three universities, a step calculated to pacify and pander to the interests of the dominant sections of the society.

turbances of peace and the destruction by fire of the crops and huts of the people belonging to these castes (1961: 322).[30]

Modern education in nineteenth-century India, with the marginal and minimal exception of the missionary efforts to educate the lower castes (see next chapter), by and large widened and strengthened the already existing differences in society by setting in motion limited, parallel and horizontal mobilities at both ends of the hierarchy. The different communities at the apex of the traditional ritual hierarchy tended to come together, breaking, to a limited extent, the taboos among themselves.[31] They thus created a wider circle which included a handful of upper castes and excluded the rest of the population whose reality and perception of their relative deprivation of the new opportunities increased enormously and in its turn, too, set off a similar process of horizontal stretch.[32]

One need not belabour the same point in the context of the expansion of civil society which was contained largely within the traditional ideological framework. However, the traditional and hierarchical power-vortex out of which Indian civil society was elaborated into bureaucracy, business and profession is vital to our understanding of subsequent political awakenings. Profession after profession repeats the same story of drawing its personnel from a tiny group of dominant communities already suffused with common ideological values and cultural ideas.[33] Thus the new diversification took place without rupturing the old order and infact empowered it along polarized lines. The modern was dovetailed into tradition with minimum pain of transition:

[30] See J. Brown (1984), p.77; D. Keer (1964), 'Brahmin opposition to the education of the lower castes was a prominent feature of the India of his day', p.52; see also B.R. Ambedkar (1990) Vol. V pp. 27–61.

[31] It is in this context that many of the social reform activities of the upper castes are to be explained. Several traditional caste constraints that stood in the way of appropriating the new opportunities and of consolidating new alignment of forces were done away with, making the elite critical of the traditions. This also marks the limit of such activities.

[32] J. Brown (1984), p.77 ff.; Also B.B. Misra (1961) p.106 and 307.

[33] 'The Indian Public Service Commission reported in 1887 that of 1866 Hindu members of the judicial and executive services as many as 904 or nearly half were Brahmins and 454 or nearly quarter were Kayasthas who were called Pralilus in Bombay. The number of Kshatriyas or Rajputs was 147, of Vaisyas 113, of Shudras 146 and of others 102' B.B. Misra (1961), p.322.

In fact, from the peculiar circumstances of their growth, the professional classes in India continued to comprise those who also ranked high in the hierarchy of caste.... Though composed of different castes they developed a common interest and outlook, a common language and behaviour pattern.... (B.B. Misra 1961: 307).[34]

Industry and Trade   Industry and trade developed in opposite directions: there was significant expansion of trade and severely limited growth of industries. The stunted nature of Indian industry today is no doubt in part attributable to the contradictory colonial structure. Whatever growth there was, on the one hand, did not proceed out of the advanced handicraft industry, and on the other hand, did not grow in antagonism to imperialism (S.K. Ghosh 1985: ch. 7). Our modern industry is again an outgrowth of landed and trading capital in collaboration with the British, as their junior partners. While the extent of de-industrialization under British rule continues to be debated among economic historians, the large scale pauperization of communities earlier involved in handicraft, particularly in the textile sector, people invariably belonging to the lower rungs of ritual hierarchy, is accepted by all.[35] Instead of handicraft transforming itself into manufacture, we have, thanks to the British, brokers, dalals, shroffs, money-lenders and others becoming industrialists. Again, these men preserved their values, cultures and habits; for their expansion took place as communities and not as individuals (J. Brown 1984: 109). The most obvious example of this spread would be that of the Marwaris who followed the establishment of Pax Brittanica from Rajasthan to Assam via Calcutta (S.K. Ghosh 1985: 133). The growth of Parsis, Banias, Chettiars and others was similar. Their collusive relationship with the imperialists and their accommodation with landlords and money lenders made them virtually insignificant as agents of change in the social structure (J. Brown 1984: 116).

Structural Unification and Cultural Uniformization   It has been generally observed that pre-modern Indian society was characterized by a disjunction between society and polity; the socio-economic and cultural realm was autonomous of politics, and changes in the latter

---

[34] 'The brown bureaucracy of British India remained largely Brahminical and definitely dominated by the members of a few upper castes', ibid. p.323.

[35] S.K. Ghosh (1985), pp.120 ff.; B.B. Misra (1961), p.36.

were not reflections of changes in the former. Marx spoke of the timeless self-sufficiency of the village societies, independent of the unstable and ever changing political structures (E. Stokes 1978: 19-23). E. Stokes calls this the discontinuity between the social base and the political superstructure.[36] In fact this discontinuity has given birth to the dilemma of locating feudal power, or the older power realization, within society or in politics. Our own choice had been the former, equating it with the caste system and Brahminic ideology as the nodal point of order in society. Structural unification had been effected by the British through a process of bureaucratization of the extended and enlarged polity replacing the multiple warlord aristocracy. In view of this we propose that structural unification simply meant the removal of the discontinuity between the social and political. The social base and the political superstructure became continuous, albeit under the aegis of colonial regime. By transforming the dominant castes within society, who had hitherto maintained their hereditary hierarchical dominance through religio-cultural ideology in the scattered polities, into a unified bureaucracy for administration with effective power, the British abridged the gulf between social dominance and state power and also provided the former with a new secular legitimating ideology. Of course this process was effectively completed with India becoming independent. Bureaucratization is the process by which social dominance acquired state-power in India.

Unification at the level of political structure had also triggered off a process of uniformization of culture. Brahmins were scattered all over the subcontinent while retaining a strong similarity of culture and interests, and their dominance was the significant source of order in pre-modern society. Thus, since they were the most consistently empowered group during colonial times, cultural uniformization was also based on the Brahminic ways of living and thinking. Administrative unification of the country, as a whole, subsequent division of it into smaller units of provinces and districts, and the appointment of more or less exclusively Brahmin-upper caste personnel to decision-making and value-enforcing positions in these, were the stages through which the entire country was brought within the uniform sway of the ascriptive ideology of the old order (B. Stein 1969: 175-216). In the absence of any serious challenge posed by newly empowered and antagonistic class or classes, religious traditional legitimation of

---

[36] Ibid, p.20. See also n.10.

the old order gradually fused with the secular modern legitimation
of the new, expressing itself in terms of religious nationalism.[37] But
before we go into this, we shall review the ideological changes
that took place during the colonial rule.

Ideology   British colonialism was first and foremost pragmatic,
intended to serve the Empire; and to this end it was willing to
go to any length to accommodate local forces, however antagonistic
the latter were to their own socio-cultural value system. The most
significant aspect of the British policy towards the Indian social system
and its values was its non-interference. What this non-interference
meant *vis-à-vis* the *ancien régime* in India, has become the subject
of research only recently. In Marc Galanter's view, 'Non-interference
implied doing what the rulers in India had always done, actively
up-holding and supporting the caste order' (M. Galanter 1984: 19).
There was however a crucial difference between the earlier rulers
and the colonial ones. As the harbingers of modernity to a pre-modern
society and as the first to bring the entire subcontinent under one
political framework, the British rulers, by upholding the status quo,
were in fact conferring a modern, secular legitimacy to the sacral
order. By upholding caste segregation in the public domain, maintaining Hindu temples, doling out 'dakshinas' to the Brahmins, making
state visits to temples on occasions by implementing the shastraic laws
as the 'Gentoo Code' and through other such activities' the colonial
rulers earned the epithet of 'wet nurse to Vishnu' from the wrathful
missionaries (J. Brown 1984: pp 68 ff.). The situation was compounded
by the work of orientalists who set the foundation for the revival
and glorification of ancient eastern wisdom, Sanskritic learning, and
to top it all, the Aryan theory of race. The notion that the Brahmins
of today are the progeny of the Aryans of yore, and along with
the British form one racial stock, became prevalent during the
nineteenth century. This did not augur well for the liquidation of
the hereditary sacral hierarchy or its ideology. The educated upper

---

[37] F.R. Frankel and M.S.A. Rao Vol. I (1989: 23) notes 'The Brahmanical tradition though
it is said to have preserved the cultural unity of India, constructed formidable obstacles
to the creation of a powerful centralised state'. With regard to the pre-colonial society of
which they are speaking, they are definitely right. But during the colonial times, having
acquired the modrn means and weapons of control, it was the Brahminical tradition that
constituted the bulwark of the newly emerging unified state.

caste Hindus responded to this theory of race in a contradictory manner. While on the one hand, they had recourse to this theory to claim equality with the rulers, the same theory on the other hand, was used to distance themselves by invoking pollution rules, from their countrymen.[38] It has to be remembered that this ideological rejuvenation of the old took place on the solid foundation of material prosperity and empowerment of the Brahmins and other upper castes. The codification of Hindu law from the Brahminic texts during the colonial times, made sure that even those areas and sections of people who had hitherto successfully resisted Brahmin ideological domination, were brought within the ambit of Hindu law by glossing over the crucial difference between the two terms—Hinduism and Brahminism.[39] Census operations which used the varna model of Hindu society in fact revived the then anaemic Brahminic ideology.[40] Relinquishing government control of the temples in favour of committees in 1863, too meant Brahminic empowerment, for many of these hithertofore had little or nothing to do with Brahminism (P.C. Pillai 1933: ch. ciii, ix; G.A. Oddie 1991: 64-82).Indeed, Professor M.N. Srinivas is right when he says, 'it is my hunch, that the varna model became more popular during the British period as a result of a variety of forces....' (M.N. Srinivas 1966: 6).[41]

This is not to deny that the introduction of modern civil and criminal laws based on the principle of rule of law and egalitarianism in general in the 1860s, and the specific acts of removal of caste-disabilities, 'opened some possibilities for advancement and change to the lowest castes, as it did to others. But it did not provide any special leverage for untouchables to use these opportunities so that their use tended to correspond to the existing distribution of power' (M. Galanter 1972: 236-7). The evangelical agents were however ferocious in their attack on the inegalitarian nature of social Hinduism, albeit due to mixed motives. Consequently, a handful of the elite started rethinking the dominant value system, and the

[38] For the differential use made of the Aryan theory of race by men in public life see J. Leopold (1970) and also chapter V.

[39] See, Swami Dharma Theertha (1946), pp.164-78; U. Baxi (1986), pp. 11-45; D.R. Banaji (1933), pp. 217 & 219-25.

[40] See, L. Caroll (1978); also H. Tuinman (1984), p.42.

[41] On the question of how British rule renewed Brahminism see Swami Dharma Theertha (1946), pp. 176-7. See also F.R. Frankel and M.S.A. Rao (1989), Vol.II, p.483, and J.D. Derrett (1968).

aspiring among the lower castes, had some opening to initiate several movements for equality. As time elapsed, liberal western ideas began to percolate through multiple channels and the intellectual and moral atmosphere in the country itself became more liberal and differentiated, albeit to a limited extent, as the spread of literacy was insignificant.[42]

THE IMPACT OF COLONIAL RULE

Tying together the different strands of our discussion, the major thrust and consensus within recent scholarship is then to suggest that colonial rule neither intended, nor was equipped to bring about any revolutionary change. The changes that did come about were the result of self-perpetuating activities of imperialism and most of them were unintended consequences. Within these limits, however, it affected changes serious enough to transform the traditional forms of dominance and resistance into modern ones; the transformation being more in form than in substance.

The most pervasive effect of imperialism on the old order was the rupture of the traditional bond that held the segmented groups and hierarchy together. Prior to this, custom and tradition had developed several attenuating and mitigating factors to blend together the antagonistic forces of dominance and resistance, particularly within the all-important sphere of land relations. Under the new order, the checks, limits and obligations of dominance snapped; and this rupture in land-relations spilled over to the socio-cultural sphere too, disrupting the image of harmony that traditional society had presented. This rupture again was followed by the accentuation of the deep and wide horizontal cleavage between the Brahmin and other regionally dominant and ritually pure castes on the one hand, and the generally deprived Shudra, Ati-Shudra, tribal, marginalized and polluted groups on the other. The general pattern of colonial impact was to empower the already powerful and further deprive

---

[42] The Attribution of egalitarianism to British efforts requires to be contextualized. Both imperialist and nationalist historiographers would have us believe that egalitarianism is a gift of the West. But nothing could be further from the truth. The egalitarian ideal perhaps is totally foreign to the dominant communities in India. The masses had a millennia-old tradition of struggle against oppressive inequality, though this largely found expression only in the realm of religion. With the erection of the modern political structure the lower castes' aspiration for equality got naturally extended to civil society. Thus, egalitarianism as the effect of colonial changes is correct only in a limited sense.

the depressed. The policy of non-interference in practice meant upholding the status quo, and in the period of transition, this resulted in the excessive aggrandizement of the uppercastes into the new civic sphere at the cost of the excluded masses. Near monopolization of the new opportunity structure by the traditionally dominant minority created its own counterpart—the mass of the deprived majority. The skewed developments in agriculture, commerce and industry only tended to strengthen this process. There were exceptions, but these were too few, scattered and weak, to make any definitive impression on the general pattern. Rupture and cleavage lead to the polarization of communities, a movement towards a shrinkage of the socio-political space between near-equal communities in the emerging new political economy, both at the top and bottom of the social ladder. Horizontal mobilities were initiated at both ends of the hierarchy, opening up, though in a limited way, the endogamous groups to equal and near equal groups, the one set getting united in the new empowerment and the other in deprivation. In the process, a certain relaxation of inconvenient ritual rigidities took place without loosening group demarcations. Slowly but surely the terrain was being prepared for a bipolar social formation in which the cleavage induced by the political economy would play a significant role.

For Bengal Anil Seal deserves to be quoted:

> Between Brahmins, Kayastha and Baidyas on the one hand, and the rest of the Hindu society on the other, there was a considerable gulf in social status and ritual ranking ... for all their squabbles among themselves they still had a common interest in preventing these arrivistes from arriving. (A. Seal 1968: 39)

Popular awareness of such contemporary polarization found expression in common speech all over the country: *dwija/ekaja, bhadralok/chotelok, dikku/adivasi, ujjalalok/kaliparaj,* brahman/shudra, *badajat/chotejat, melchati/kizhchati* etc.

Rupture, cleavage and polarization were the first faltering steps towards class-formation and polarization. This thumbnail picture of colonial impact on pre-colonial India requires three qualifications. The first relates to the uneven, incomplete and limited nature of the transition. While vertical mobility in any significant sense was rare, the parallel and horizontal mobilities at both ends of the social hierarchy were uneven over regions, riddled with ethnic and linguistic diversities and differential historical development. Secondly, the rupture, cleavage and polarization were a continuity as well as break within history. They constituted a break in the sense that a new dimension of economy and politics had become part of the terrain of struggle between groups. These changes were also a continuity in the sense that the alignment of social forces remained the same and occupied the same old power positions. The process of polarization merely modernized the earlier caste-power dichotomy: the traditionally dominant became modern in a modified form while the submerged of earlier days became the oppressed.[43] The sacred thread symbolically binding together the ritually pure also became, in the new context, the chord to unite more or less the same groups in terms of economy and politics. The third qualification is the ideological importance of the small and scattered cases of exceptions to this general pattern of polarization within society. While they were too insignificant to intervene effectively in political economy they did pose a serious ideological challenge to the fusion of legitimacies traditional/religious with modern/secular within the new political structure.

Changes in ideological environment were no less ambiguous. On the one hand, the erection of a new political structure, minimal state action, and missionary educational efforts heightened the sense of deprivation among the lower caste masses; egalitarianism now appeared to be an ideal within reach. Ascriptive superiority and inegalitarianism were now increasingly under attack and on the defensive. On the other hand, with the economic and political elevation of Brahmins and other allied upper castes, and the conferment of secular legitimacy on their sacred practices by the British virtually upholding Brahminism, the ideology of sacred ascriptivity had gained a new lease of life, though in a modified form.

It has been suggested that colonial rule strengthened the traditional social structure and simultaneously weakened its sacral ideology.[44]

---

[43] In the words of D. Ludden (1985) 'Villages neither transformed nor stagnated under the imperial impact but slowly changing through the colonial era on lines consistent with developments that predate the founding of British rule' p. 7.

[44] See F. Frankel and M.S.A. Rao (1989), Vol.I pp.8 ff; and Vol.II p.483; Tuinman (1984), p.40; A. Béteille (1980), p.119. Frankel and Rao for example say 'the very fact that they interjected the power of the state into India's religious society and made it the proximate source of local dominance, helped to undermine the sacral ideology...' Vol. II p.483. However, what is being ignored is that the new construction of the State itself was composed of those very elements constituting social dominance. The State power in colonial India largely rested on local social dominance till it was taken over by these very forces. Since this is a fusion of power there is the

But this is an insufficient observation. It is true that religion and religious legitimacy in general had lost some of its poignancy in the overarching process of secularization. The ritual and pollution aspects of the ideology had to some extent disappeared, yielding ground to the ascending importance of political economy. Besides, Brahminic ideology as found in the sacred texts could not be revived (if ever it was practised in that way at all). However, the fact of the enormous empowerment of the ritually higher castes as caste groups and clusters within the modern context, the virtual absence of effective challenge from lower strata, social dominance becoming political power, and the cumulative effect of non-interference by the British, prepared the ground merely for a change in the form of expressing the sacral ideology in secular terms and categories. Viewed in the context of the slow erosion of the pre-colonial social structure that had been taking place, the impact of colonialism was to arrest the social progress, economic diversification and emergence of culture-based polities, and revert to an environment and climate of pan-Indian Brahminical, feudal consolidation, although within the colonial framework. 'A highly mobile and economically differentiated society rendered stationary and 'traditional' is how Washbrook describes the transition (D. Washbrook 1993: 68). In other words, colonialism diverted the flow of events in the history of the subcontinent and boosted power as dominance through collaboration and ambiguously worked to control and contain power as resistance. M.N. Srinivas has only touched the tip of the iceberg when he observes that: 'The establishment of Pax Britannica has set the caste free from the territorial limitation inherent in the pre-British political system' (M.N. Srinivas 1962: 16).[45] The articulation of caste and anti-caste ideologies now took several forms and the study of these leads us to the political awakening during colonial rule.

---

corresponding fusion of sacred and secular ideologies also. Note, A. Béteille (1980) is also aware of this fusion when he speaks of the role of hierarchical values of the past 'being taken over by the coercive state apparatus', p.120. In fact, the fusion of local dominance with the political structure is one of the themes of the Cambridge historians. See Washbrook (1976) and C.J. Baker (1976).

[45] See also B.B. Misra (1970) p. 4ff; S. Bandyopadhyaya (1990) p 2; That an adjusted hierarchy along with a modified Brahminical ideology have survived colonial rule, has been confirmed in a number of micro-level village studies from different parts of the country; see N. Patnaik (1969), C. Parvathamma (1971) and K. Ishwaran (1968).

III

Nation: Homogenization of Power within Culture

The transformation of the subcontinent through radical change—social or economic—was not part of the British agenda. Whatever changes came about in the realms of society and polity were largely by-products of the pursuance of the main objective of the British—exploitation of the land and its people. The net result of these changes on traditional, segmented and hierarchical Indian society was earlier seen as setting in motion parallel horizontal mobilities both at the top and bottom of the social ladder, thus widening and deepening the already existing cleavages within society. On the one hand, the British rule empowered, enlarged, elevated and even nationalized the upper strata of society consisting of Brahmins and other allied *dwija* castes. The lower strata, on the other hand, consisting of Shudras, Ati-Shudras, tribals and others lost the security and complacency of the old order; they however, did gain a certain consciousness of their deprived and degraded status and the scope to change it. The structural unification brought about by the British thus contained within it deep fissures. The disjunction in the social and economic worlds naturally found its expression in and through the political awakening which was of a dichotomous nature during the colonial period.

RISE OF POLITICAL CONSCIOUSNESS

The rise of political consciousness in colonial India has largely been traced to the associations of uppercaste, urban segments of the population and the subsequent emergence of the Indian National Congress.[1] This understanding is based on a very narrow view of politics and is rooted in a certain ideology. The identification of the rise of political consciousness with the emergence of the Indian National Congress, serves the purpose of legitimizing the Congress movement in national-political terms *vis-à-vis* other forms of consciousness and struggle that are termed social-communal. Broomfield points out:

> One of the most prevalent distortions in historical writing on modern India is the equation of nationalism with politics and it bears repeating that in the early twentieth century there was much politics to which nationalism was irrelevant or only marginally important. (J.H. Broomfield 1975: 135)[2]

According a place of privilege to the political over the social and the national over the communal is more often than not used as a weapon in ideological struggles; these are labels that identify those labelling as well as the labelled. However, in a work that seeks to critically review nation and nationalism, a more inclusive understanding of political consciousness is in order. Political consciousness can be seen as the perception of power relations within society and of one's own (individual or group) position in that frame. It also refers to an urgency to take collective action to strengthen or alter that position. For Weber, 'Striving to share power or striving to influence the distribution of power, either among states or among groups within a state, is the core of politics' (M. Weber 1985: 78). In this essentially sociological notion of political consciousness, the attempt to capture power within the formal political apparatus is but one form of politics, and not necessarily, the most significant within the overall context of socio-political change.

Nineteenth century India witnessed scores of concrete political awakenings and organizations, characterized by unevenness, among several segments of the populance, spread all over the subcontinent. The awareness of signs of change in the old socio-political order and of the emergence of a new opportunity structure was reflected

---

[1] See, C.Y. Chintamani (1937), S.R. Mehrotra (1971), B.B. Misra (1976), and R. Suntharalingam (1974).

[2] The author cites, as an example, the Muslim efforts at removing educational backwardness.

in the aspirations and ambitions of peoples and groups differentially located in society. Numerous expressions of such socio-political aspirations emerged in the form of incipient organizations, activities and struggles, varying from place to place, community to community, issue to issue, both in intensity and spread. However, being responses to and reflections of, the infrastructural changes in society and polity, they were basically dichotomized. This dichotomy of modern political awakening was a carry-over of the double form of power as dominance of, and resistance to, the religious ascriptive hierarchy of pre-modernity. Within our theoretical paradigm, of nationalism as the congruence of power and culture, this means that while one kind of awakening spoke the language of homogenization of power within culture, the other demanded the transference of power to culture. The fact, that these two sets of political movements are related to each other and in fact provide the context for each other, will be analysed later. This chapter examines the attempts to homogenize power (in the sense of even distribution) within culture, in order to bring about the nation as the new form of congruence between power and culture. The pre-modern form of the culture-power fusion was unequal, hierarchical, and legitimized by Brahminic tradition as well as, the present collusive, colonial power-structure. This movement away from pre-modernity and colonial modernity towards an egalitarian and homogenous spread of power constituted the emergence of the national-political community. This urge towards the nation was indeed a continuity, albeit in a modernized form, of the pre-modern manifestations of power as resistance.

Awareness of the changing power relations seems to have dawned first upon the lower rungs of the hierarchy. These were communities who at one time, had been the most exploited, and hence were sensitized to possible escape routes. These communities, all of them below the pollution line, largely engaged in supplementary services in semi-rural and urban areas, had improved their economic position to a certain extent. Finding themselves out of step with the age old congruence of secular and sacred hierarchies, they were the first to make the most out of the situation and challenged the old order and its religious sanction. These attempts to shake off the yoke of ascriptive bondage, under the emerging modern political structure, took varied forms, depending on the concrete circumstances of the struggling groups. Although they were all interlinked and holistic, they have been classified broadly under three heads, for the purposes of our review.

Against the Ideology of Ascriptive Hierarchy

At the turn of the nineteenth century the Izhavas, an untouchable, agricultural caste of the state of Travancore, rose in a collective attempt to challenge the monopoly of the Brahmins in ritual matters. In the first recorded attempt of the modern era to overcome civil and religious liabilities several lives were lost:

> ... in about 1800 an attempt was made by some Izhavas to enter the temple at Vaikom but they were butchered and their bodies buried in a tank at the north-eastern corner of the temple. The tank is known as dalvi kulam.[3]

Not much later, the Shanars—untouchables of Madras Presidency and the state of Travancore initiated their century-long struggle against the degrading custom of partial nakedness of women in deference to the Savarna castes. Known as the 'breast-cloth controversy', the struggles of this toddy-tapping community during the first quarter of the nineteenth century, demonstrated the emerging political consciousness of the changing order. The series of collective efforts to clothe their women decently like any other human being, much against the will of the dominant castes of Nayars and Nambudiris, attempted to confirm and carry forward the changes that had come to stay.[4]

These two communities though subsequently excluded from the scheduled lists of castes, were originally untouchables and unapproachables. The Izhavas (Malayalam speaking) and Shanars (Tamil speaking) were engaged in the polluting occupations of toddy-tapping, jaggery-making and selling etc. Both had profited marginally from the new order; the Izhavas through the breaking-up of the Nayar Tarwad (matrilineal joint-family system), and the Shanars through the expansion of trade and business (the latter also gained through

---

[3] M.S.A. Rao (1978) p. 59 quotes a Malayalam source. This was nearly a quarter of a century before the Congress was hesitantly dragged into the temple-entry controversy and that too, regarding the same temple at Vaikom.

[4] Ibid. p. 29; as early as 1814 the Shanars had wrested from the government the right for their women to wear jackets 'not similar to that worn by the caste women'. For the Shanar struggles see R.L. Hardgrave (1968 & 1969).

education provided by missionaries). The newfound, economic well-being of several caste members formed the basis for challenging the social structure in its aspects of social hierachy and Brahminic legitimacy. It is significant, that the earliest struggles of the oppressed in the modern era, attack the religio-ritual and cultural spheres of the old order, indicating the most damaging aspects of the system. In fact, in classical Marxist terminology feudalism in India is 'caste-feudalism and Brahminic ideology'.[5]

The century that followed the abortive mutiny of 1857 is replete with conscious, systematic and collective public action to intervene in the existing and changing power-relations, and to challenge the emerging oligarchy of Brahminic and other twice-born castes across the subcontinent. The issues were different from place to place. The forces that initiated them were situated differentially within the social and economic hierarchy. The intensity and spread of the movements too, varied from struggle to struggle, and their political import was unevenly felt. Yet there was a clear pattern and trajectory emerging from these varied attempts. They originated from communities below the pollution line, their themes were all similar, aspirations the same, and the methods used were constant.

The early nineteenth century Shanar struggles for equality expanded quickly to cover more and more areas of civil society including the right to education, which in turn lead to diversification of occupations. They appear to have sparked off something akin to a civil war in the emerging industrial subtowns of Sivakasi, Kalugumalai etc. by their demand for temple-entry. The colonial regime, true to its nature, finally came down on such agitations in the form of the Privy Council judgement in favour of retaining custom and tradition. Parallel to their efforts to enter temples which were increasingly coming under the control of Brahminism, the Shanars also developed a non-Brahminic religion around the person of Muthu-Kutty Swamy. The religion known as Ayya Vazhy—the path of the elder—required its followers among other things to wear headgear, traditionally forbidden for the lower castes, as a sign of emancipation.[6] While the Shanar movement gained additional strength through mass conversions to Christianity in their war against civil liabilities, their counterparts, the Izhavas of Travancore made headway by developing

[5] See G. Omvedt (1982), A. Rudra (1981), B.Patankar and G. Omvedt (1979).
[6] See M.S.S. Pandian (1991), and C. Rajamani (1991).

a non-Brahminical Hindu religion under the leadership of an Izhava, Sri Narayana Guru. The guru's message of monotheism and equality of all men, and his establishment of vedic schools for all castes, particularly the most despised Pulayas, and non-Brahminic temples wherein he installed Izhava Shiva, made the temple-entry struggles and conversion to another religion redundant. The triumvirate that emerged among the Izhavas: Sri Narayana Guru (1855-1928), Dr Palpu and Kumaran Asan (1873-1924), effectively laid the first foundation stones for the new civil society in Kerala through promotion of education both literary and technical, diversification of occupations and vertical social mobility.[7] These state-wide social processes were a formidable challenge to the old order of social and ritual hierarchy. The Shanar-Izhava movements were well advanced at the turn of the century. The Pulaya caste, the 'lowest of the lowly', erstwhile agrestic slaves, took the cue from these movements. Ayyankali (1863-1941) the fondly remembered leader of Kerala, himself an uneducated Pulaya, went about setting up schools for Pulaya girls in the face of resistance by the Savarnas and advocated education and occupational diversification through technical training for all. The first ever agricultural workers' strike in the country (around 1914), credited to Ayyankali, was not for any economic demand but for the right of Pulaya girls to enter educational institutions. The right to walk on main roads, of entry to the market place, to the removal of the imposition of wearing Kallumali (garland of stones), and the right to own land were the other issues raised in the Pulaya struggles.[8] The converted Pariahs of what is now Kerala set up a separate brethern church for the lower castes under the leadership of Poykayil Jchanan during the first decade of the present century, when they discovered that existing church structures would not accord them equal treatment (S. Fuchs 1965: pp. 281 ff.). With the Izhava-Pulaya struggles for social and political democracy well under way, there was a further expansion of horizontal mobilization through the Izhava-Pulaya-Christian-Muslim alliance under what is known as the Abstentation movement. They formed the Civil Rights League in 1919, demanding universal franchise and equality of citizenship for

[7] For information on the Izhava struggles in Travancore see M.S.A. Rao (1978), A. Aiyappan (1965), T.K. Ravindran (1972), and R. Jeffrey (1976).

[8] For information on the Pulaya struggles see K. Saradamoni (1980) and J. Mathew (1986).

all, especially in the context of public employment.[9] These struggles were made possible by the existence of a native ruler in Travancore; here, instead of being obsessed with foreign rule, the movements could pay valuable attention to the demolition of caste-feudalism within, paving the way for a relatively more homogenous spread of secular and sacred power.

While the Shanar-Nadar struggles for social emergence were spreading across the southern districts of the Presidency, the Pariahs, another large untouchable community, opened up several fronts for negotiating the power structure in the northern districts—Madras, South and North Arcot etc. These and other inchoate lower caste groups, through recruitment in the army, migration to mining and urban centres both internal and external, and employment with the British in diverse menial positions, had bettered their economic condition. By adapting their indigenous and autonomous Tamil literary traditions, they evolved a strategy to face the new reality. During the third quarter of the previous century several Tamil journals sprang up. As socio-political organs, they informed the people of the need to give up the old and appropriate the new through the spread of education. They ridiculed Brahminic exclusivity and interpretation of history and contested the monopoly of the upper castes in civic-public life. In and through the columns of these early journals and parallel organizations such as the Dravidar Kazhagam of 1882, questions of non/anti-Brahminism, Dravidianism and the like were raised and debated, laying the foundation for the future work of Periyar and others. Among the stalwarts of the movement—R. Srinivasan, John Ratnam, M.C. Rajah, Madurai Pillai and others, the name of Iyothee Dass stands out in clear relief. The ideas and activities of Iyothee Dass from 1880 until his death in 1914, were far ahead of his time and appear strikingly modern even today. Realizing the emancipatory potential of the Buddhist tradition and drawing on the earlier Tamil-Buddhist connection, this scholar tried to interpret the history, religion and literature of the Tamils from the point of view of Buddhism which was once popular and prevalent in the South, half a century before Dr Ambedkar. He established the South Indian Buddhist

---

[9] The name 'Abstention' was given to the movement in order to differentiate it from the Non-Cooperation Movement of the Congress. Public employment was not open to these communities in Travancore, because, temple administration was part of the Revenue Department and hence polluted castes could not be employed in it; see K.K. Kusuman (1976).

Association which by 1910 had several branches both in India and abroad. Educational centres sprang up in lower caste enclaves in the urban centres of the Presidency. Though his activities concentrated on the lower caste groups, Iyothee Dass' concern was the new political identity of Tamils in general, and to this end he succeeded in bringing together individuals and groups from the whole range of the Tamil social hierarchy. The journal 'The Tamilian' and scores of pamphlets published by the core group around Iyothee Dass, were circulated widely among Tamils everywhere and carried the message of social emancipation, Buddhism, rationalism, anti-Brahminism, and the emergence of the new egalitarian Tamil-Dravidian identity.[10] In Telugu country before the mass exodus of the lower castes towards Christianity, Yogi Pottuluri Veerabrahman and his disciple Siddappa were organizing the Madigas into Rajayogis to oppose social slavery and Brahminism.[11]

These socio-cultural and intellectual efforts came to the political surface with the announcement of the Montagu-Chelmsford reforms during the second decade of this century. The non-Brahmin movement that began in Madras swept the entire presidency, opening out new social and political avenues for hitherto excluded castes and Muslims. The movement contested the monopoly of power exercised by traditional Brahmin castes. The focus was urban: appropriation of education was not only a means for the capture of new emerging power–structures but also for emancipation from the rigidity of ascribed, occupational status—the basis of caste-feudal relations; a share in the political power of administration and legislation was the other issue. They set up hostels for students to reside in cities and towns, published journals condemning Brahminic nationalism, pressed for communal representation and elaborated an ideology of nationalism and patriotism different from that of the Congress movement. The Justice Party standing in direct opposition to the Congress, which it branded as Brahminical, came to power in the Provincial Assembly in the 1920 election and passed several legislations pertaining to civil

[10] Research on the late 19th and early 20th century Pariah emancipatory effforts are meagre, leading to the false conclusion that Dalit movements are a post-Independence phenomenon. For Tamil Buddhism see I. Loganathan (1993), V. Geetha and S.V. Rajadorai (1993), W.R. Vijaya Kumar (1974) T.P. Kamalanathan (1985).

[11] S. Fuchs (1965) pp. 260 ff.; for reference to another egalitarian sect called Narsaiah sect, see R.K. Kshirsagar (1994) p. 42.

marriages, franchise for women, Hindu Religious endowment, the communal G.O., reduction of educational fees for Muslims etc. The sum and substance of these legislations was to enlarge the role of the non-Brahminic castes and ensure their appropriate representation in public life. However, the elite orientation of party leaders prevented them from mobilizing the masses, particularly the untouchables and the Muslims.[12]

If the leaders of the non-Brahmin movement busied themselves in altering the legislative and administrative machinery at least marginally to serve the aspirations of the new arrivals to the political community, E.V. Ramaswamy Naicker, also known as Periyar, who had quarrelled with the Congress leadership on its Brahminic bias and left the party, blazed through rural towns and the contryside with his self-respect movement. He debunked Brahminism from the standpoint of rationalistic atheism and social criticism. His cultural-ideological onslaught on the traditional social structure did go a long way to delegitimize it and to expose it as nothing but greed for exclusive power.

As early as 1921 the non-Brahmin movement in the princely state of Mysore wrested concessions from the traditional power oligarchy through Miller's committee—a prototype of today's Mandal commission. This was followed by fierce Hindu-Muslim riots.[13] By establishing the principle of reservation as protective discrimination the movement established a space, albeit a narrow one, for non-Brahminic castes in the emerging civil society dominated more or less exclusively by the Brahmins. The movement was remarkable for its effort to include at least in its initial stages the aspirations of the Muslim community.[14] Other lower caste struggles for entry into political society have been noted in the area today known as Karnataka; those of the Waddars and the Holeyas, both of them untouchable castes. They tried to adopt the ways of clean castes—to

[12] For non-Brahmin and Justice movements in Madras, see E.F. Irschick (1969) and I. Rajagopal (1985). The speeches of Justice leaders have been compiled in V.T. Naidu (1932).

[13] Throughout the colonial period there are more than coincidental connections between the lower caste anti-Brahminical struggles and the incidence of Hindu-Muslim riots in several parts of the country (Note Mandal–Mandir connection of our own times). This area requires further research.

[14] 'Non Brahmin Movement in the princely state of Mysore' is the subject of L. Dushkin's unpublished Ph.D. thesis (1974) in the University of Pennsylvania; see also B. Hettne (1978) and J. Manor (1977).

educate and clothe themselves in a decent manner and refuse to carry out traditional menial services for upper castes. The work of the Waddar lady Srimati Yellamma of Kolar and Sri Manjari Hanumanthappa of Chitradurg has been remarkable during the nineteen thirties and forties, both in spreading education among the Waddar boys and girls, and in organizing caste-associations. The Holeyas demanded to be treated better than the Brahmins on account of their better observance of pollution rules and thus challenged the existing social hierarchy.[15]

The pattern of political awakening that took place in the south among those who had lost the most in material terms due to British intervention, got replicated in Bombay Presidency and its surrounding native states with certain modifications. As early as 1852, Jotiba Phule (1827-90) was given public recognition for his services to the cause of female education. The radical nature of his educational campaign among the Mali and other Maratha lower castes provoked virulent opposition from the dominant Chitpavan Brahmins. Phuley practised what he preached, unlike most uppercaste social reformers, by allowing access to his well for all castes, defying opposition from his own caste members. Phuley challenged the Brahminic caste ideology *in toto*, set up a Bali Rajya of equality of all men in opposition to Ram Rajya based on Varnashrama Dharma, and elaborated the ideology of Dravidian origin to counter the prevalent Aryan theory of race among the Brahmins. The Satya Shodak Samaj founded in 1873 spread his ideas and activities throughout Maharashtra and laid the foundation for the transformation of the social identity of lower castes into a common Maratha one. The issues of the struggles were the same as those of similar samajams among lower castes elsewhere: widest possible horizontal mobilization of all deprived castes, spread of education as a means of emancipation, share in the political and administrative power, pressurizing the administration to pay attention to the problems of cultivators and diversification of occupations into trade and technical fields to break the rigidity of the caste system. The democratization of civil society to enable the maximum number of people to enter the new political community was the basic thrust of the work of Jotiba Phule and the Satya Shodak movement.[16]

---

[15] The Waddar movement has been studied by C. Bhat (1984); for Holerus see E.B. Harper (1968).

[16] Of late, Phuley and the activities of his followers have been well documented.

Shri Sahu Maharaj continued and extended Phuley's vision in Kolhapur and other native states though in a less radical form. In retaliation to a conspiracy of his own Brahmin officials against him, he ridiculed their pollution preoccupations by hosting ceremonial dinners for people of all castes (K.K. Kavlekar 1979; A.B. Latthe 1924). The ensuing country-wide popularity and efficacy of the work of Dr Ambedkar' was based partially on the groundwork of these earlier stalwarts in the cause of the homogenization of socio-political power.[17]

The Mahar movement lead by Shiva Ram Jamba Kamble focussed on the issue of reinstatement of the Mahars in the army.[18] Kamble also organized the Indian National Anti-Revolutionary Party committed to the complete removal of untouchability and the overthrow of the Chaturvarna school (E. Zelliot 1969: ch. 2). With the emerging presence of Dr Ambedkar during the twenties, the movement acquired a holistic nature in the sense that it struggled for the emancipation of the Mahars from agricultural bondage in the Watan system, championed the cause of education among those freed from slavery, challenged the Brahminic monopoly of ritual power by conducting temple entry and common water-source movements. These efforts rallied against uppercaste resistance, and carried forward the struggle within the power arena newly acquired by Brahminism—nationalist politics. The consistent support extended to these struggles by the Muslims is significant (ibid: ch. 3). Dr Ambedkar was not merely a Mahar leader but a national leader of all disadvantaged classes, with an articulate and alternative vision of society, nation and politics. Depressed classes of the subcontinent expected him to wrest for them an honourable space within the new polity. The following statement of Ambedkar captures the very core of the issues at stake:

> The depressed classes were not anxious for the transfer of power under the present circumstances but if the government wanted to transfer power it should be accompanied by such conditions

---

See G. Omvedt (1976), D. Keer (1964), J.R. Shinde (1985) and R.O'Hanlon (1985). However, the writings of Phuley himself are not easily available in English.

[17] For Dr Ambedkar and his movement see D. Keer (1962) and E. Zelliot (1969, 1970).

[18] The East India company officials had formerly utilized the services of the depressed classes in the army to establish their rule; but once established, recruitment to the army became regular, many of the clean castes became 'sepoys' in deference to whom the depressed classes were not taken in the army any more. See S. Natarajan (1959), p. 17 and S.P. Cohn (1987).

and by such provisions that the power should not find itself into the hands of a clique... it should be shared by all communities (D. Keer 1962: 178).

Orissa, despite being a stronghold of orthodoxy was not free of its share of anti-Brahminism. The small and scattered native kingdoms of eastern India were a hotbed of small and large anti-caste rebellions during the colonial period. But specific mention must be made of the attempts of the Bauri community in and around the seat of Brahminical power—Puri. This excluded community revived an earlier Mahima or Alekha Dharma as a socio-political weapon under the leadership of Bhima Boi and stormed the gates of the forbidden Jaganath temple on 1 March 1881 demanding entry into the temple, and equality in religion. Needless to say blood was shed that day, furthering the cause of egalitarianism, though the attempted temple-entry itself failed (B.S. Das 1987; R.K. Barik 1987).

That the whole of Bengal presidency supported the Bhadralok sponsored renaissance and the subsequent phenomenon of Swadeshi nationalism is a myth perpetrated by most writers. The separation of the eastern part of Bengal from the west strengthened this notion and did much harm to historiographical writing on this part of the country. The impression continues to this day along with the false claim that caste and caste consciousness does not exist in Bengal (S. Bandopadhyay 1990: 2). What is true however, is that uppercaste consciousness is so dominant among the intellegentsia that little research has been done on the egalitarian aspirations emanating from the traditionally depressed communities. Bengal is no exception to the general pattern of political awakening that took place all over the subcontinent. The much touted renaissance and the nationalist movement emerged within a conflict-ridden conjuncture along with several other antagonistic and more popular political awakenings among the Rajbansi, Kaibarta, Namashudra and Muslim communities—all broadly and loosely unified with respect to secular and concrete socio-economic interests. Nothing much is known of the Kshatriya movement among the Rajbansis of North Bengal, the Bhurmalis self-help movement in East Bengal, and the educational activities of the Mahisyas, except for the fact that they all organized themselves for education, cooperation and respectable status. When the nationalist movement arose they perceived it as a Bhadralok affair, antagonistic to their own interests, and stood apart from it (Bandyopadhyay, 1990: pp. 152 ff.).

As early as 1872, the Chandals, an untouchable caste constituting the largest single caste group as well as the majority of the Hindu agricultural population in Eastern Bengal, started a protest movement in Faridpur and Bakarganj districts against the social ostracism practised by the upper castes. They refused to perform traditional services for the dwijas and demanded equality of treatment in jails. However, their economically deprived position forced them to surrender and most of them had to return to the land owners. The movement thus petered out within a few months till it was revived some years later.

During the 1880s as elsewhere among the depressed castes, the Chandals developed the Matua cult, a de-Brahminized form of Vaishnavism, to develop widest possible caste cohesion, renamed themselves Nama Shudras and claimed Brahminic origin. Hari temples sprang up everywhere. The cult chief Guru Chand set the agenda: 'educate yourself, earn money and be respectable' (S. Bandopadhyay 1985: 324).[19] In the teeth of resistance the Nama Shudras pushed ahead, established 'pathasalas' and student residences, first with the help of missionaries then with the support of the colonial government, for which the community as a whole remained grateful.

At the turn of the century in 1902 the objectives and organization of the community became clearer. The newly founded Nama Shudra Hitaishini Samiti gave the call to awake to the new day and to take advantage of the widening horizon of opportunities thrown open to everyone irrespective of caste and status. It outlined the need of education both for boys and girls, the evils of early marriage, the plaint and plea of the widows, the new ideal of the fatherhood of God and the brotherhood of men (ibid: 331). The Nama Shudras resisted all attempts of the missionaries to convert them and 'imbibed just so much of Christian spirit as would enable them to forge ahead to a place of independence and respectability' (ibid: 340).

The partition of Bengal in 1905 brought the Nama Shudras into a head-on collision with the nationalist movement. Believing that the Swadeshi movement and the anti-partition struggles were meant to restore the pre-colonial slavery of the caste system, they stood

---

[19] On the Nama Shudras, significant research has been done. See S. Bandopadhyay (1985, 1989, 1990).

away from it and resisted all coercion by the nationalist Zamindars. They organized several anti-boycott campaigns in alliance with the Muslims, another dominant agricultural community, together with whom they perceived themselves as equally despised and exploited by the high caste Hindu gentry. The consistent alliance between the Muslims and the Nama Shudras against what they considered Hindu and Bhadralok politics was significant; this alliance continued inspite of the intermittent quarrels between themselves as near-equal communities competing for the same set of opportunities. These Nama Shudra-Muslims quarrels were exaggerated beyond proportion in the uppercaste media which tried unsuccessfully to convert these into Hindu-Muslim riots, at least till the Khilafat Movement.

The same pattern of political awakening reproduced itself in the Brahmaputra and Surma valleys of Assam. The Vaishnava revival among the Moamarias elaborated itself into a significant anti-Brahmin and-British movement. The numerous lower and relegated castes— Doms, Keots, Brittyal-banias, Sonar-banias and others, opted for different names and identities, organized themselves into associations to promote education and diversification of occupation, and claimed reservation and other provisions in order to be able to catch up with other castes. The All Assam Depressed People's Conference in 1929 under the leadership of Sonadhar Das Senapathy, cast its lot with Ambedkar and refused to agree to a joint electorate, 'which would mean perpetuation of disgraceful treatment from the caste Hindus'.[20]

Elsewhere, in Bihar and U.P., the Mahatos and Yadavas started caste associations at the turn of the century to organize themselves to challenge the old hierarchical order.[21] They struggled for their right to wear the sacred thread, refused to perform free traditional labour for the Bhumihars and the Brahmins, promoted education and internal social reforms etc. All these activities were struggles, for they had to suffer many atrocities at the hands of the dwija castes who realized that monopoly power was slipping out of their hands. Not much is known about the activities of the Tribeni Sangh, a federation of local Koeri, Kurmi and Yadav castes, and the Raghav Samaj, an association between the Kurmis and Koeris, except that these Shudra castes, in the wake of rising political consciousness,

[20] B.J. Dev and D.K. Lahiri (1994); also S. Fuchs (1965) pp. 134 ff.
[21] See M.S.A. Rao (1978), K.K. Verma (1976) and H. Jha (1977).

organized themselves to challenge the Brahminical order and came forward to join the new political community.[22] The entrenched castes far from welcoming the new arrivals did everything in their power to stop the latter from achieving political status.

In Madhya Pradesh, Uttar Pradesh and Bihar, the Shudra caste of Noniyas claimed the status of the Chauhan Rajputs subsequent to their improved economic position as contractors for public works. In 1898 Lalla Mathura Prasad Singh founded the Rajput Advancement Society and donned the sacred thread. It is interesting to note that in 1936, after a defiant, collective symbol-appropriation ceremony, the Noniyas were beaten up by the Kshatriya landlords. Their sacred threads were ripped off and collective fines were imposed on them. Later when these Savarna elements turned a blind eye to the Noniyas donning the sacred thread, the latter lost interest in this form of protest (W.L. Rowe 1968).

The Chamar caste of North India is perhaps the biggest yet the most despised of all the untouchable castes. They made heroic attempts in several scattered locations to break the chains of social and cultural slavery, and to appropriate a share in the emerging power structure. In Chattisgarh, where they were immigrants, they could overcome their ritual barrier to land ownership and managed to improve their economic status. Consequently, they transformed themselves into Satnamis, a sect founded by Ghasi Das (1756–1836) who preached unity of God and equality of all men. This, by yet another de-Brahminized Hindu religious sect, was essentially a social uprising challenging the authority of the higher castes. Balak Das, son of Guru Ghasi Das was brutally murdered in 1860 for daring to don the sacred thread. Well before the end of the previous century they had mustered enough strength to overcome their traditional civil disabilities of prohibition against footwear and the use of horses or palanquins. In 1917, they brought down the wrath of the Savarnas for publically organizing a thread-wearing ceremony. The Savarnas punished the rebels by beating them up, beheading several of them and branding sacred threads on their chests and backs with red hot iron. In 1925 a political drama was enacted in which the Satnamis were decorated with sacred threads in the presence of Gandhi, and immediately after this, once back in the village, several of them

---

[22] For casual reference, see F.Frankel and M.S.A. Rao (1989). See also W.R. Pinch (1990).

were beheaded. Soon after this disaster a Satnami Mahasabha was founded which demanded changes in identity, political representation and their share in educational and job opportunities. Several self-help activities too, were initiated such as hostels for students, associations for maintaining social equality among themselves and for basic human rights.[23]

Further north in Agra, the leather-working Chamars known as the Jatavs, also improved their economy by expanding their leather business and supplying shoes to the army. In this field they had to confront very few competitors, the occupation being a polluted one. This new economic plank enabled the Jatavs to obtain education by setting up schools, some on their own and later a few aided by the Christian missionaries, the Arya Samaj or the government. In the 1920s their attempts at diversification of occupation were resisted by caste Hindus and a Jatav selling sweets was murdered for his audacity. During the political imbroglio that followed in the 1930s the Jatavs aligned themselves with Ambedkar against Gandhi, burned the effigy of the Poona Pact as the Brahmin Wolf and conducted an anti-Congress Mass Movement during which more than three thousand Jatavs were jailed (O.M. Lynch 1969).

In Rajasthan, Ramdeo Panth among the Dheds, and Naval Dharam among the Bhangis preached against Varnashrama Dharma during the early nineteenth century. They also made efforts to rise above their ascribed status through education, diversification of occupation etc. (R.K. Kshirsagar 1994).

The Chamar brethren of the northwest Punjab province gave a clarion call to all the depressed classes, during the second decade of the present century, through a newly founded (1925) religion called Adi Dharm:

> We are the original people of this country and our religion is Adi Dharm. The Hindu quam came from outside and enslaved us. When the original sound from the conch was sounded all the brothers came together—Chamar, Chuhra, Sainsi, Bhanjre, Bhil all the untouchables—to make their problems known. Brothers there are seventy millions of us listed as Hindus, separate us and make us free (M. Juergensmeyer 1982: 46).

The first agenda of Mangoo Ram, the founder of Adi Dharm,

---

[23] See A. Kumar (1985), L.A. Babb (1972) and S. Dube (1992).

was to get the changed identity of the Adi Dharm Community officially accepted; in the 1931 census more than 400,000 untouchables were listed as Adi Dharmis. Armed with the might of numbers, a crucial factor in any democracy, the Adi Dharmis jumped into the political fray in direct confrontation with the Congress and Gandhi. Like most of the new lower caste organizations, the Adi Dharmis too 'wanted no part of independence if independence meant government by uppercaste Hindus'. Bitter hostility ensued between the Adi Dharmis and the Congress; the former obstructed the salt-Satyagrahis in 1930, and stood with Ambedkar against Gandhi, on the question of separate electorates.

It seemed to the Adi Dharmists that there was no possibility of achieving general social equality without first securing a measure of power and respect for those sectors of society currently being denied such equality, namely the lower castes (M. Juergensmeyer 1982: 130).

Through a semblance of a modern bureaucracy, a newspaper (Adi Danka) and a host of upadishaks and pracharaks and an elementary form of democratic functioning, the Adi Dharmis announced the dawn of the new era. They propagated egalitarianism and called upon the upper castes to accept the change with grace and play a fair role in society.

Movements like Adi Dharm have been separatist only to the extent that they have insisted on separating their followers from old ideas of social integration. They have tried to provide new visions of society in which the upper castes are also invited to play a role, albeit a more humble one than at present (ibid: 275).

If the urban centres of Western India were made restless by the ideologies of Phuley and Ambedkar and those of Southern India by the non-Brahminism and Dravidianism of Justices, Periyar and others, those of the Gangetic belt reverberated with the fiery speeches of Swami Achchutanand and were rocked by the generalized Adi-Hindu movement. The Swami attempted to make Hinduism stand on its feet, as it were, by repudiating Brahminism and its ideals. Anchored deeply in the pre-modern popular Bhakti traditions, Swami Achchutanand was for a period under the influence of the Arya Samaj. But soon he came to the conclusion that the 'Samaj aimed to make all Hindus slaves of the Vedas and the Brahmins'. He subsequently established units of Adi-Hindu Sabhas in all the important towns of the United Province. The Adi-Hindu ideology rejected caste inequality and claimed a different origin and development for the mass of Hindus and sought to alter the position of the untouchables from within the framework of Hinduism (N. Gooptu 1993).

These several streams of pro-equality social forces from different parts of the land, during the 1920s, made concerted efforts to hold conferences and consultations among themselves, in order to project a minimum acceptable programme of power homogenization within culture through the formation of a number of federations. They were sponsored by Ambedkar, Srinivasan, Mangooram, Swami Achchutanand and others who became not merely spokespersons of their respective caste-clusters, but leaders with an alternate vision of the future national society (R.K. Kshirsagar 1994: pp. 144ff.).

Fleeing the Stranglehold of Caste Slavery

Those communities, who through gain of land, trade expansion or army service, had raised their economic position at least to a certain extent, managed to organize themselves through associations and sabhas and discovered new forms of de-Brahminized religion and myths of more dignified origins, to challenge the traditional hierarchical Brahminical social order in all the newly emerging arenas of civil society. Others who were less fortunate found other means of escaping their millenia old despised status. An important escape route was conversion to another religion. Mass conversions of the lower orders of society taking refuge in an alien religion was not unknown during pre-British times. However the second half of the nineteenth and the first half of the twentieth century saw mass movements of conversions, especially to various forms of Christianity, in widely separated parts of the country.[24] It was observed in the 1930s that: 'one half of the Roman Catholics in India are descendants of mass movement converts and...not less than 80% of the 1,800,000 Protestants are the product of mass movement (J.W. Pickett 1933: foreword).[25]

---

[24] For material on conversions to Christianity in the larger context of the struggle against inequality, see J.W. Pickett (1933), M.M. Ali (1965), G.A. Oddie (1969, 1975, 1979), D.B. Forrester (1980, 1991), D.Kooiman (1989), S. Manickam (1977) and J.C.B. Webster (1994).

[25] Not only successful conversions but unsuccessful attempts too, are of relevance to our purpose; for eg. when the Megs, an untouchable group inhabiting the foothills

Group conversions took place all over India—among the outcastes of Gujarat; the Mangs and Mahars of Bombay; the Chuhras and Mazhahabis of Punjab; the Doms of Benares, Kumaon and Garhwal hills; the Dhusiya Chamars of Shahabad (Bihar) and Ballia (U.P.), the hill tribes of the North-East; the Karta Bhojas of Bengal; the Mundas, the Oraons and the Santhals of Bihar and Bengal; the Bhils of Central India; the Mallas and Madigas of Andhra; the Sambavars, the Shanars and the Pariahs of Madras; the Panchamas of the Kanarese districts of Madras and Orissa etc. However the movement from the traditional religious fold into Christianity took on mass proportions among the Chuhras of Punjab. By 1915 all but a few hundred members of the caste got converted. The converted tribals of Chotanagpur, who in 1857 were 900, were 400,000 in number by 1931. Christian Mallas-Madigas of Andhra Pradesh were only a few hundred in 1869, but swelled to 1,225,000 in 1928, and within a short span of three years, several thousand Shanars became Christians.

That these mass conversions were all spiritually motivated and that the converts were moved by a 'deep conviction of sin and a strong desire to be saved' was not anybody's argument, neither of the membership conscious missionaries nor the converts themselves. However to call them all 'rice' Christians or assume them to be dumb like cows, blackmailed into Christianity by the conniving missionaries is an insult to the humanity and the rationality of the converts.[26]

The colonial times were times of restlessness, anxiety and tumult for all sections of society. The widening cleavages between the different segments of population brought about an acute sense of deprivation and resentment on the part of the Shudras and untouchables, the victims of the old order. While those who had become economically capable raised the banner of revolt against the Brahminic monopoly of social power, others sought to flee from it to other patrons and benefactors.

The prospective converts to Christianity—the lower castes—acted

---

of Jammu mountains en masse declared their faith in Christianity in 1859, large-scale violence was let loose by the landlords who managed to kill the movement altogether, see Fredrick and Stock (1975) pp. 33-56.

[26] M.K. Gandhi (1954) pp. 131-135, 137-139. Gandhi also thought that it is lowering the standard of religion itself to preach it to 'Harijans'. He said "to approach the Pulayas and Paraiah with their palsied hands and palsied intelligence is no Christianity", quoted in D.B. Forrester (1980) p. 179 and p. 190.

in a conscious and concerted manner. Rationally weighing the pros and cons of the situation, they chose to be converted only on those occasions when they felt that such a course of action would result in the much sought after freedom from socio-cultural slavery, enhance their human dignity and respect, liberate them from the fixity of ascriptive occupation, and possibly open out new avenues for material advancement. When such a possiblity was not present the masses refused to move no matter what the inducement. Acceptance of equality, in direct opposition to the unequal treatment meted out to them within the traditional order was the touchstone for the decision regarding conversion.

Pickett narrates an interesting anecdote:

A less prominent Hindu leader of the North who said that he objects to conversions, told that the sweepers had become Christians for three entirely unworthy motives:

1. They want to be treated like respectable people and only the missionaries and a few foolish Indian Christians will treat them that way.
2. They want to quit doing sweeper's work or at least to find other work for children.
3. They want the help of the missionary when their landlords or the police complain against them and Christian officials have to decide their cases (J. W. Pickett 1933: 159).

Most of the converts themselves would have readily agreed to this view of conversions by the Hindu leader. When these 'unworthy motives' were not present, conversions did not take place. The Izhavas of Kerala contemplated converting to Islam, Buddhism or even Judaism but not to Christianity, for due to a situation peculiar to Kerala they would not have had equal treatment within Christianity either. The Nadars of Nagercoil sensing that caste discriminations were being practised within the church itself, promptly left the community to start a 'Hindu Church'. The Nama Shudras inspite of many attempts by the missionaries did not take to Christianity; on the other hand 'they imbibed just so much of the Christian spirit as would enable them to forge ahead to a place of independence and respectability' (S. Bandopadhyay 1985: 340). Conversions to the different denominations were roughly proportionate to the practice of equality and brotherhood within the Churches—the Roman Catholics had the lowest, as they had accommodated the caste system within Christianity.

The rate of conversion took off only after 1850 when all the Protestant missionaries jointly decided not to give quarter to caste inequalities and discriminations within the Christian communities. The need for brotherhood, human dignity and fellow feeling among the depressed castes was powerful and they yearned for liberty and freedom at any cost.[27] Conversion to Christianity thus, 'like the earlier conversions to Islam, symbolised attempts on their part to break away from the strangulating hold of the caste system' (S. Bandopadhyay 1990: 98).[28]

Flight from the oppressive caste system and ideology also took the literal form of 'running away from the field'—migration, both internal and external. While this form of escape from an oppressive situation was always availed of by the labouring castes in the premodern days, it assumed gigantic proportions during the colonial period. The British in most instances promoted migration of labour for their own ends such as ensuring a supply of labour for different projects and in order to increase land revenue. Large scale migration occurred from several areas of settled agriculture to urban and mining centres, arid areas and to overseas colonies; needless to say most of these migrants were lower caste agricultural labourers. The established view on colonial migration, in general, is that it was somewhat forced by the rulers and that the new situation in fact did not bring about any change in the migrants' economic conditions. While there could be some truth in the above view point, the possibility of freedom from religiously legitimized agricultural bondage, that of occupational diversification and anonymity within a larger society, and the chance of radical self-determination appear to have been the main motivations on the part of migrants in most cases. Although migration-studies conducted from this point of view are rare, the spokespersons from among the lower caste communities held this opinion. Leaders particularly from the South, have indicated that the problem of migration from rural areas is certainly linked to the practice of caste and of Varna ideology, and that the problem

[27] The new converts often had to face the wrath of the upper caste Hindus and the landlords in particular; for conversions were followed by the refusal to do the traditional free labour, refusal to contribute to the village festival, and by attempts to educate themselves; see M.M. Ali (1965) pp. 161 ff.

[28] The most publicized and politicized mass conversion of Dalits in modern history to Buddhism in 1956., with the self-conscious objective of fleeing Brahminism, took place under Dr Ambedkar's leadership.

itself could be solved if caste were abolished both in theory and practice. Again, both within and without the country the areas of new settlements by the lower castes often became hotbeds of anti-Brahminical and egalitarian movements and ideologies. The most telling examples are the Kolar Gold Fields in the South, Chattisgarh in the central area and the Delta Region (coastal districts of Eastern Bengal) in the East of the country.[29]

Against Caste-Feudal Land Relations

While the Brahminic ideology of hierarchy and ascriptive division of labour was challenged in the towns and cities and was being boycotted in the semi-rural and suburban areas, what was happening in the very 'lion's den' of feudalism ie. land relations?

Is there a peasantry in India? Was there a widespread peasant revolt in British India? If so where was it? If not, why? Can we construct a typology of peasant movements in colonial India? These and other questions are yet to be answered satisfactorily and have been exercising greater minds for sometime now; the recent apotheosis of the peasant in Subaltern historiography has only served to mystify the situation further.[30] Here we are concerned only with the indentured or bonded labourers of rural areas, the agricultural labourers, share croppers, tenants-at-will, nominal cultivators owning insufficient or useless lands and forced into one of the several forms of agricultural bondage prevalent then. This segment of the rural populace invariably belonged to communities below the pollution line—either Shudra or untouchable. Here again we refer to the battles waged by these 'peasants', if that appellation is appropriate, against all forms of customary bondage and servitude known as 'Abwab, Corvee, Begar, Salami, Bhusavan, Motorovan, Hathyavan, Pakawan', and the practice of free labour, rent-farming, arbitrary evictions, cheating, juggling of accounts, and all forms of physical maltreatment including not too rarely, murder.

As has been noted in the previous chapter economic disparity increased enormously between the 'haves' and 'have nots' in colonial

---

[29] For example, M.C. Rajah in J.S. Pillai (1930) p. 70. See also S. Manikam (1993) pp. 77-84 and N.K. Arooran (1985) pp. 18-37.

[30] For discussions on these and connected issues see D.N. Dhanagre (1983), G. Shah (1990), R. Guha (1983), and A. Béteille (1980), pp. 113-15.

India, subsequent to the vesting of ownership of land in uppercaste revenue collectors. A significant invasion of non-rural interests—moneylenders and urban officialdom—took place in land-holding with the commodification of land and its products. This, combined with the minimal expansion of trade and business and the negligible industrial development, worked to strengthen rural bondage further. Caught in the vice-like grip of the new form of commercialized Brahminic feudalism, it is no wonder that the rural masses failed to stage any widespread popular uprising. However the picture was not altogether dismal.

Franz Fannon has made a pertinent observation:

> In the colonial countries peasants above all are revolutionary for they have nothing to lose and everything to gain. The starving peasant outside the class system is the first among the exploited to discover that only violence pays, for him there is no compromise, no possible coming to terms; colonisation and decolonisation are simply a question of relative strength (D.N. Dhanagre 1983: 3).

Firstly, refer to the great peasant revolts of the nineteenth century—the Deccan grain riots, the Pabna agrarian league, the earlier Mappilla revolts etc. on the one hand, and the tribal revolts of the Santhals, the Mundas, the Hillmen of Gudem-Rampa and the like.[31] These revolts were against arbitrary evictions, moneylenders' juggling of accounts, land alienation, compulsory collection of revenues, hoarding during famines, or forced labour etc. While it is true that many of these revolts had several characteristics of a transitory type—transition from pre-modern to modern, in their harking back to Ram Rajya or Birsa Raj etc. they also had an inkling of the future to come. These movements, more than any other, systematically exposed the collusive and collaborative nature of colonialism—a product of complicity between the imperial and indigenous elite against the lower castes and tribes who constituted the majority.

---

[31] See I.J. Catanah (1966), K.K. Sengupta (1970) and K.N. Panikkar (1989); for tribal revolts see V. Ragavaiah (1971) and K.S. Singh (1982). Most of the tribal revolts were set against imperialism—propped up native, caste—feudalism. The British invariably supported the local, dominant non-tribal interests, see S. Fuchs (1965). R. Guha's (1983) clubbing together of peasant and tribal movements appears to distort the specificity of tribal consciousness which had nearly always a territory-based identity component.

Secondly, most of the great and small social movements of the nineteenth and twentieth centuries too had their rural component of the struggle against customary land relations. As Arnold and others have pointed out:

> Even if a caste association had no more than a dozen members who were concerned with their own and not their community's advancement, it might nonetheless express the embryonic ideas and aspirations of a far larger group (D. Arnold et al. 1976).

The great movements of the Shanars, Parayar, Izhavas, Mahars, Mahalis, Chuhras, Chamars, Mahtos, Yadavs, Nama Shudras and others, far from being associations of a dozen members or so, in unbridled pursuit of selfish and group interests, were mighty organizations spreading their tentacles and new message far into the rural areas. The dawn of new politics was not lost on the rural lower caste masses; they had a symbiotic relationship with their more enlightened castemen who were raising the banner of revolt in towns and cities. The refusal to perform Abwab, Corvee, Begar or forced/free labour in whatever name, was part of one gigantic, anti-Brahminic thrust, embracing the Pulayas in the deep south, the Chuhras in the northwest, the Mahars of the west, and the Nama Shudras in the east. Unfortunately the rural component of these urban movements have not been explored by historians who are by and large prejudiced against these anti-Brahminic attempts.[32]

Third, the ensuing tribal movements of the twentieth century reveal two distinct types of political awakening. Wherever the tribals were a minority, mixed up with non-tribal peasants and to greater or lesser extent feudalized, they tended to follow the general pattern set by the lower caste peasants of the area of effectively sabotaging the nationalist movement that had prodded them to action by setting up their own consciousness and trajectory.[33] The other type was visible wherever the tribals were in majority, occupying a contiguous territory and had more or less successfully resisted feudalization; these tended to become conscious of their territory-related identity and

[32] For a brief reference to the rural base of Yadavas' anti-Brahminic movement see A.N. Das (1983 : 70–2). See below for comments on the treatment of anti-caste movements by social scientists.

[33] A typical example is D. Hardiman (1987).

demanded autonomy. The most significant case was the rise of Adivasi consciousness among the different tribal groups of Jharkhand.[34]

Fourthly, political expediency had led to the attempts by the participants of the nationalist movement to mobilize the peasants from the 1920s onwards. Several groups of peasants did respond to the proddings of the nationalist leadership. However, this does not obviate the fact that the peasants did wake up but to a different set of realities with more or less autonomous consciousness and their own political trajectory which was consistently anti-feudal as well as anti-imperialist, much to the embarrassment and discomfiture of the leadership. The disjuncted consciousness of the so-called peasant movements under the nationalist leadership has been the focal point of Subaltern historiography.[35]

The thrust of these varied peasant and rural uprisings has not been sufficiently studied. They are either labelled as primitive revolts or simply termed anti-feudal in a generalized way. These movements were neither Utopian nor socialist, and within their own existential context they sought to defeat the economic base of the Indian caste-feudal structure by denying those services and liabilities which custom had imposed upon them on account of their ascriptive status. In this project they played the role of the rural and economic counterpart in the struggle against Brahminic ideology and feudal production-relations.

A Pattern in the Battles

In a rather elaborate manner in the foregoing pages, we have tried to describe and categorize one stream of the new political consciousness that rose in colonial India specifically against the traditional order of hierarchical caste ideology and infrastructure. They were seen in the form of a spectrum of three types—revolt against Brahminic ideology, attempts to flee from the Brahminic stranglehold, and struggle

---

[34] See K.L. Sharma (1976), K.S. Singh (1977) and J.C. Jha (1987).

[35] See in particular D. Arnold (1982), and G. Pandey (1978). For a discussion on the way the nationalist leadership sought to contain and control the peasant movements see chapter-VI. This is not to deny that in isolated places the fringe elements of the nationalist movement (particularly progressive and communist) did mobilize the rural masses against landlords etc; however these were few in number and scattered, so the mainstream leadership did not have much difficulty in effectively neutralizing them. See for example the work of Swami Sahajhanand in A.N. Das (1983).

against caste-based land relations. The exercise is intended to highlight three important aspects of this new political consciousness. The first is the ubiquitous nature of this awakening during the entire colonial period consprising the nineteenth and twentieth centuries. The map of the subcontinent was dotted with the rise and spread of such consciousness, leaving no region or locality free from its effect. Waves of protest and struggle against the old order, of course varying in intensity and spread, appear to have flooded through the length and breadth of this land under different forms and incarnations. So much so, that Professor M.N. Srinivas who is normally not very sensitive to power-relations within social structure was constrained to note: 'It was as though they suddenly woke up to the fact that they were no longer inhabiting a prison' (M.N. Srinivas 1966: 91).

The second is the almost identical pattern in all these movements. There were attempts to capture a new identity, group as well as individual, through a change in nomenclature, the ostensible discovery of usually superior, mythical origin followed by concerted action to get the new identity officially recognised.[36] Also important was a search for a non-hierarchical religio-cultural framework either through a rediscovery of the different forms of non-Brahminical Hinduism, or by forsaking the whole of Hinduism itself or rarely, by taking to atheistic, rationalist ideologies.[37] Group efforts were on to reform themselves and become respectable human beings according to the dominant models available to them.[38] A new found solidarity expressed itself in associations and sabhas whose membership extended to the broadest possible understanding and definition of caste (maximum horizontal stretch) as opposed to the pre-modern endogamous exclusivism. There was a universal emphasis on literacy

---

[36] See S. Bandyopadhyay (1990), pp. 100-1; I. Ahmed (1971) writes of the 1931 census in the provinces of North India, 'there were 148 castes whose members wanted to be returned under new names or high varna titles. In all there were 30 claims to Brahmin status, 83 go to Kshatriya, and 15 to Vaishya rank making a total of 128 claims to dwija rank'. From the point of view of these castes it was not important as to which model of choice—Brahminic, Kshatriya or Vaisya had been sought as has been claimed by Prof. M.N. Srinivas (1966), but the possibility of escape from the despised Shudra and Acchuth models and the ability to cross the pollution line.

[37] Examples of non-Brahminic Hinduism are Adi Dharm (Punjab), Satnami (M.P.) Matua cult (Bengal), SNDP (Kerala); the rationalist streak was articulated prominently by E.V. Ramaswamy Naicker (Madras).

[38] See below for a discussion on Sanskritization.

and education as a means of appropriating the emerging forms of power structures. The struggle to escape the hereditary and ascriptive fixity of occupations was conducted usually through possible avenues of upward social mobility; indeed occupational diversification was specifically intended, against the old form of division of labour. Also, there was a refusal to accept the view that the new politics could continue to be the monopoly of a particular group or caste, however high-born that segment might be, and the antagonism of interests between the native and foreign elite was used as an opportunity tool to push through demands for political share and representation.

The third aspect of this new political consciousness that must be highlighted is the ideological and philosophical scaffolding upon which the multifarious collective activities of these lower caste groups were erected. One finds within these movements varying degrees of expression of their view of the new vision of society and socio-political relationships. The range of clarity of vision and articulation was indeed large and varied. On the one hand we have the vocal and contesting articulations of Phuley, Narayana Guru, E.V. Ramaswamy Naicker, Mangoo Ram, Guruchand, Ghasi Das and finally of Ambedkar. On the other hand, there was the implicit vision of the new society in the mass movements of the peasants and agrestic slaves. A case in point is that of the Holerus of Karnataka, the most humble of castes, who challenged the ascriptive basis of Brahminic superiority through the achievement of observance of pollution rules themselves!

THE NATION'S STRUGGLE TO BE BORN

What is the 'national' import of this stream of new political consciousness? Movements against ascriptive inequality during colonial times are generally devalued within the social sciences. Political historians of yesteryears, from both imperialist and nationalist schools hardly show any awareness of their incidence, while the latter-day progressive ones, non-problematically consider them as movements of caste/communal consciousness and a result of the divide-and-rule policy of the British.[39] In sociology however, they were all considered

---

[39] See S. Sarkar (1983) pp.55 ff. However the author more than once describes himself as a writer of a 'history from below', see p.11 and p.43; for his recent self-criticism see (1990). E.V. Ramaswamy Naicker comments: 'A minority community has been from time immemorial acting on the basic assumption that it is a privileged

till recently as processes of Sanskritization, attempts at positional change within the hierarchy (M.N. Srinivas 1966). But of late the progressive nature of these egalitarian movements is increasingly being realized largely due to the new approach to the study of social movements in the West.[40] Within India itself the more recent writings of Professor M.S.A. Rao represent such a positive evaluation of the anti-caste movements. Rao's point of departure is a critique of the Sanskritization thesis: these attempts are rather challenges to ritual exclusivism, in order to overcome civil and religious disabilities by crossing the pollution line and doing away with differentiating and distancing religious and secular symbols. These processes are basically social protests and challenges to ascriptive hierarchy, and they were understood as such by the upper castes whose wrath was kindled so as lead them to brand or even behead the men who publicly wore the sacred thread as an act of defiance. A number of studies analysing concrete individual egalitarian movements have similarly responded to the Sanskritization thesis.[41]

Professor Rao makes two important distinctions in the study of movements: one, between the pre-modern egalitarian movements and those in modern times where he notes the political dimensions of the latter whereas; earlier ones like the Bhakti movement were predominantly religious (M.S.A. Rao 1977). The second distinction is that between reform movements among the upper castes which were merely adjustive in nature, designed to strengthen the existing power relations, and the transformative movements among the lower castes which challenged the 'established social order, the value system and the patterns of superordination and subordination relationships'...'they affected adversely in different degrees the existing pattern of dominance, distribution of political power, and access to scarce economic and educational resources'.[42]

---

and exclusive caste, superior to all other castes and distinct from that of 97% of the people. If the latter become alive to their rights and realise the absurdity of the claims of the so-called superior caste and that is called 'communalism', I wish we may always have that communalism as the cardinal principle of our life' quoted in K.N. Arooran (1980), Chapter VIII; see also, K.K. Kusuman (1976), p. 77.

[40] See R. Heberle and J.R. Gusfield (1968), H. Blumer (1969) and R. Bendix (1961).

[41] See M.S.A. Rao (1984), p. 197, L. Rudolph and S. Rudolph (1967), p. 36, S. Bandyopadhyay (1990), p. 129, G. Omvedt (1976), p. 154 and D. Hardiman (1987), p. 163.

[42] See M.S.A. Rao (1986) p. 301; and also K. Sardamoni (1980), p. 121. Raja Ram Mohan Roy: 'The ground which I took in all my controversies was not that of

Our argument however, is that the anti-Brahminic, egalitarian, and anti-caste-feudal movements of the colonial era are national in the primary sense of the word; their thrust, in all their unevenness and inspite of their partial nature, was towards the creation of a national socio-political community as distinct from the colonial society on the one hand, and from the society based on ascriptive status on the other. Their discourse is homogenization or equitable distribution of social power within culture; the main component elements of this discourse are political democracy or citizenship, mass or universal literacy, social mobility and on the agrarian front, denial of ascription, in determing social roles.

The modernity of the modern nation or nation-state consists specifically in the notion of citizenship within a definite territory or acceptance of minimal power homogeneity within culture as the organizing principle of the new society.[43] Political life in a nation is different from that in the traditional order, in that under the latter, participation in civic-public life and leadership questions are determined by the ascriptive status of individuals and communities. In the former on the other hand, it is in the hands of citizens, who as members of a territorially defined nation-state are equal among themselves with uniform political rights (R. Bendix 1961). The social movements are oriented towards the actualization and expansion of this notion of political democracy, in other words to translate the notional into the real.

'The existence of the citizen presupposes a certain decline in the dominance of hierarchical social structures and the emergence of egalitarian horizontal relationships' (B. Turner 1986: 18-19). The anti-Brahminical movements in so far as they refused to accept the secular hierarchy duly sacralized through Brahminism, and staked their claims for their share in the new power as the emerging citizens of the new polity, were in fact, struggling for and supporting the process of the birth of a nation. Thus the very notion of national self-determination is erected on a radical understanding of it as individual self-determination. Again, to quote B. Turner:

Citizenship involves essentially the question of access to scarce

---

opposition to Brahminism but to a perversion of it' quoted in S.R. Mehrotra, 1971, p. 2.

[43] The basic readings for the modern and broadened view of citizenship are B. Turner (1986, 1986a and 1988) and D. Held (1984), Chapter 7.

resources in society and participation in the distribution and enjoyment of such resources. Whereas political theory typically considers citizenship in terms of civil and political rights of access to decision-making and the selection of government, a broader notion of citizenship involves the question of social membership and participation in society as a whole (Turner 1986: 85).

This was precisely what the Shudras and Ati-Shudras, hitherto languishing beyond the social and political horizons under the old order, now as the 'nouveau arrive' were struggling to achieve. The Rudolphs have argued the point sharply. Speaking of the new caste associations of the lower castes they say:

> By initiating, managing and encouraging the efforts of the lower castes to become twice born, to don the sacred thread symbolizing high ritual rank and culture it, in effect if not in intention drains the caste hierarchy of meaning by homogenizing and democratizing it (L. Rudolph and S. Rudolph 1967: 36).

Egalitarianism as a social principle and citizenship rights as the basis of all political life are the twin themes of these anti-hierarchy (sacred and secular) movements expressed in their various struggles for a share in religious, educational, administrative, and property-power realms.

The second main component of these movements is the near universal emphasis on literacy and education. Within the Brahminic order, literacy was the monopoly of the clerical castes. But with the coalescence of 'vertically segmented and laterally insulated agrarian communities' into one large polity coinciding with culture (i.e. the nation-formation), the 'clerisy gets universalised' as Gellner puts it. For him mass literacy and education is at the heart of the transition from pre-national to the national form of society.

> What happens when a social order is accidentally brought about in which clerisy does become at long last, universal, when literacy is not a specialism but a pre-condition of all other specialisms and when virtually all occupations cease to be hereditary?
> ...In an age of universal clerisy and mamlukdom, the relationship of culture and polity changes radically. A high culture pervades the whole society, defines it and needs to be sustained by polity. That is the secret of nationalism (E. Gellner 1983: 18).

For Gellner therefore, mass literacy is one of the foundations upon which the modern nation is erected. From this point of view one has fresh insight into the insistent emphasis placed on literacy and education by almost all the leaders of anti-caste and egalitarian movements. The significance of the battles fought all over the length and breadth of this country during colonial times by the Shudras and untouchables to gain entry into schools and other educational institutions, much against the resistance, atrocities and oppressions of the powerful high castes, could be better grasped if they are seen as the birth pangs of a modern nation.

As early as 1889 when the Prince of Wales visited Poona, Jotiba Phule had one message to convey to the Queen—the need for education of the lower castes. He made the first generation school children of the Mahar and Mali castes recite: 'Tell Grandma we are a happy nation, but 19 crores are without education' (D. Keer 1964: 111). Before the turn of the century, Sri Narayana Guru advised his followers: Educate that you may be free and organise that you may be strong' (M.S.A. Rao 1978: 43). A couple of decades later, Dr Ambedkar thundered, 'Educate, Organise and Agitate' (D. Keer 1962: 197).

Social mobility is the third theme of the social movements against the hierarchical social structure. Hereditary fixity of occupation had been the hallmark of the old order in India; the lower castes were born to serve the higher castes who were ritually prohibited from engaging in any manual work. With the dawn of modernity and the formation of the nation, communities held down through brute ideological force realized that this principle no longer obtained. Refusal to perform the customary slave labour, aspirations and attempts to diversify occupation and particularly to escape the ascriptive status became endemic among the lower castes, signalling the advent of the new era. Here again it is Gellner who speaks of the nation as a society in which a profound change has taken place, a change about the principles of social anonymity and mobility.[44] A society with hereditary and fixed division of labour is not a nation. The economic changes during the British times were indeed limited and opened up only marginal avenues for vertical social mobility. However, with the development of means of communication and transport, spatial mobility had increased significantly, leading to social anonymity

---

[44] E. Gellner (1983), see chapter I.

and the undermining of feudal land relations. These limited changes were grasped at by the notionally freed lower castes, to make maximum possible headway in the direction of occupational diversification, as an important means of bringing about a more egalitarian society.

On the agrarian front, the struggles were concentrated on the question of customary services based on the ascriptive and caste status of the agricultural labourers and marginal land owners. In the changing context, the customary and free services traditionally extracted from the labourer, who were invariably also the lower castes, by the land owning upper castes had begun to appear arbitrary and unreasonable. The bonded labourers, agrestic slaves and attached menial workers by refusing to abide by custom and tradition, were indeed demonstrating their understanding that times were changing, a society based on principles other than ascription was emerging, and that they were part and parcel of this epochal transformation. The underlying weltanschauung of these anti-caste-feudal struggles though mostly not articulated in words was clear enough: no more differential duties but uniform social rights.

The political awakening of the lower caste groups of the Indian subcontinent under the colonial rule was premised by an implicit (often also made explicit in the sayings and writings of the prominent leaders) vision of a new nation, of a new form of congruence between culture and power, and a new way of relating the self with the other. This vision itself was deconstructed above, into three component parts, actualization of the concept of citizenship, mass literacy as the basis of new civic life, and social and spatial mobility as a new principle of social life. This three-pronged struggle, the aspirants hoped, would lead to transformed interpersonal relationships suffused with fellow-feeling and grounded in egalitarianism, a relationship engendering a commonality of purpose in public life as the core of the nation.[45]

The puritans among the social scientists would still not be convinced. They would point out the fact that in several of these so-called anti-inequality movements the aspirants tried hard to become equal with those above them while rejecting similar attempts from those below them. Puritanism appears more as a criterion to judge the polluted and it is rarely used as a yardstick to measure oneself. However,

[45] E. Gellner (1983), p.6; also L. Rudolph and S. Rudolph (1967), p.132; B. Anderson (1983) Introduction.

this objection needs to be met. We want to suggest that these movements often stopped short of escalating into a full-fledged war against the hierarchical principle in totality, primarily because there was no corresponding egalitarian sense emanating from the other side of the fence. Those who were labelling these struggles as caste, sectarian or communal, far from advocating any form of egalitarianism, mustered all their newly acquired political power and secular ideologies to thwart and abort the incipient struggles for equality. Under the circumstances it is but natural that these movements could not realize their potential and stopped short. As a leading group of communities, the dominant castes, instead of meeting these struggles midway and carrying them forward, tended by and large to sabotage them, over and above finding them below their standard of perfect revolution. Castes lower down the scale of Brahminical hierarchy were, locality- and region-bound and highly differentiated among themselves in terms of language, culture, and ecology. It was not within the reach of such amorphous groups and clusters of scattered communities to launch a pan-Indian united struggle. Such a possibility existed only among those higher up in the ladder. To what use they put their traditional and newly acquired vantage positions in the advancement of culture-power dialectics is the theme of the next chapter.

MUSLIM POLITICAL AWAKENING

Despite their precise and egalitarian set of religious beliefs, Indian Muslims for historical reasons, are not a monolithic or homogenous community (M. Hasan 1991: ch. 1). Hierarchy and differentiation are as pronounced within Muslim society as in that of Hindu society and the bonds linking the two, several and strong, have developed in the course of the long pre-modern period.[46] Internal differentiation followed more or less the same pattern as among non-Muslims: beginning with the difference in origin between a small minority from outside the subcontinent and the vast majority of locals, the community as a whole was characterized by more or less segmented, endogamous, and occupational groups. Entrenched within regional cultures, they spoke different languages and followed different traditions—cultural as well as religious. There were also relatively stable

---

[46] For details of caste-like systems among the Muslims see G. Ansari (1960), I. Ahmed (1978) and L. Dumont (1970).

regional hierarchies among the groups in spite of the strong Islamic belief in egalitarianism and the injunction against ascriptive inequality. Their multi-tiered relationship with non-Muslims has a complex history nearly as old as Islam itself: the mass of Muslims, are converts from among the lower castes and a minority came from the upper castes.[47] If conversion had helped the majority to escape some severe forms of caste oppression and disabilities, it apparently did not result in significant vertical mobility. Hence most of them remained agricultural labourers, marginal farmers or tenants, artisans (weavers in particular) and petty traders, bound to the upper castes, and a small number of Muslim landlords and moneylenders. In the United Provinces and to a lesser extent in Punjab there were Muslim landlords, the remnant of earlier ruling and warrior groups, exercising dominance over their dependents, Muslim or otherwise, much in the same manner as other landed gentry of the area. The horizontal solidarity of interests between these differentially positioned Muslim groups and their counterparts among the non-Muslims was as much, perhaps more substantial, than the vertical unity of fellowship among themselves, at least in the day to day concerns of social life; for links between the religious communities spilled over to the realm of culture too. While Urdu, the language of ruling groups united the upper echelons of society, particularly in judicial administrative centres, religion and culture among the lowly were rarely distinguishable (A. Hamid 1967: 40).

Class-like cleavages, therefore, characterized the Muslims no less than the others indicating the possible bifurcation of their political awakening. However, the picture was made complex by the presence of disparities between the Muslims as a whole and caste Hindus: in the high concentration areas of Bengal, Malabar (Madras) and to a lesser extent in Punjab, the religious division had a high degree of coincidence with the division of labour. Secondly, in the view of caste Hindus, all Muslims, high and low, along with the lower castes, were polluted and held inferior status in the socio-religious hierarchy.[48]

[47] P. Hardy (1972) Chapter 1; S.F. Dale (1980) Chapter 1; and J. Sircar (1973) pp.227-8.

[48] 'The feeling was mixed concern and contempt for the Muslim peasant whom we saw in the same light as we saw our lower caste Hindu tenants or in other words as our live stock', N. Chaudhuri quoted in S. Sarkar (1973) p.412. However, this attitude must have become more prevalent during colonial times.

The colonial impact on this diversified world of the Indian Muslims was understandably not simple. First of all, the vast majority of them— the agricultural labourers, tenants, share-croppers and artisans—along with the lower caste masses, lost a great deal of their earlier traditional role and security under the new dispensation of power and this increased the already existing cleavage between the dominant and the dominated in general. The minority of the landlords and hitherto ruling groups also lost, either morally or materially or both, unlike their caste-counterparts.[49] The rapid spread of education and sub-sequent enlargement of a middle-class among them, furthered the estrangement of the two sets of elites. This created a new division between the religiously bifurcated, dominant section, particularly in the United provinces. This double-edged, colonial impact on the Muslims, resulted in three more or less simultaneous movements: one was the movement away from the dominant communities belong-ing to the upper Hindu castes who were moving closer among themselves within the new opportunity structure. This movement manifested itself among both the majority of the erstwhile suppressed as well as the totality of Muslim community including the hitherto dominant minority. The second was the movement towards other groups within the Muslim community itself; while cleavages within were not done away with to any significant extent, as losers in the new scheme, their sense of solidarity already existing as believers in Islam, increased. The third movement was towards other similarly losing communities outside the Muslim fold, such as the lower caste masses and tribals. While political consciousness is not merely an epiphenomenon of economics and the latter itself becomes salient in consciousness the different positional changes, both within and without the Muslim community, with regard to the generalized social structure became the context in which the community faced the orientational choice: either a totality or a part of the mass of the deprived. The possibility of waking up to a political consciousness antagonistic to that of the dominant upper caste Hindus clamouring strictly for the transfer of power from the British, while taking all precautions against its spread within (see Chapter IV), was high and in the event it was actualized (P. Hardy 1972: 131). Apart from this fair certainty, the Muslim political awakening had a dilemma

---

[49] P. Hardy (1972) Chapter 1; W.W. Hunter (1969) pp. 138-206 and N.G. Barrier (1968).

from the beginning. On the one hand the all-round strong similarity of interests with the generally deprived mass indicated the possibility of the development of a common political nation, through the struggle for the homogenization of power within. On the other hand, the new perceived commonality of deprivation within meant another possibility of development into a distinct Muslim-nationalism in parallel to the then emerging Hindu-nationalism. During its actual historical unfolding, the Muslim political awakening was indeed a combination of these two streams till the very end of the colonial period, the latter phase being marked by the ascendancy of a distinct religio-cultural nationalism. The similarity of the early Muslim political awakening with that of the generalized mass of the lower castes, both in their common priorities of education, diversification of occupation, reforms within and reservation in employment etc., and in their antagonistic posture towards the dominant communities' sectarian-nationalist thrust has been noted by many historians. Several parts of the country witnessed the united and common struggle of the Muslims with the anti-Brahminic groups, constituting the generalized political movement for homogeniza-tion of power within culture as the becoming of the nation.[50] All these different groups, together forming the majority of the population, perceived the nationalist movement as Hindu, upper-casteist, Brahminic; the latter, in its turn, branded all of them indiscriminately as minorities and communalist or pro-imperialist. The early decision of Sir Syed Ahmed Khan to concentrate on the spread of power within through appropriation of modern education, was certainly in continuity with the efforts of Phuley in the west, the Nama Shudras in the east and the Izhavas in the south. The general imperial policy of limiting the official educational effort only to the dominant had goaded all these excluded communities towards tremendous self-effort and a common struggle.[51] The partition of Bengal in 1905 saw all these disparate groups coming together in their struggle against the anti-partition move-ment of the nationalists. Indeed in Bengal the Nama Shudras consistently displayed a unity of interest with the pre-dominantly lower class Muslims in wresting concessions from the dominant groups and the government, despite occasional quarrels among themselves as near-equal groups.[52]

[50] B.B. Majumdar (1965) p. 259; J. Brown (1984) p. 152; B.R. Ambedkar (1990) vol 8, pp. 359-60.

[51] S.A. Husain (1965) p. 36; P. Hardy (1972) pp. 53-8.

[52] S. Bandyopadhyay (1985) pp. 348, 414, 422; R. Thapar (1989) pp. 223 ff.

The non-Brahmin movement of the south both in Madras and in Mysore in its earlier phase, was indeed a corporate effort between the different non-Brahmin groups and Muslims.[53] In Bombay the Muslims consistently extended support and cooperation to the anti-Brahminic struggles of Dr Ambedkar.[54] Militant Muslim-led pre-1920 agrarian movements both in Malabar (Madras) and Bengal were far from indiscriminate in their attacks on non-Muslims; while the polluted castes were spared as a rule, murderous attacks were mostly limited (despite lapses) to oppressive upper castes.[55] As late as 1939 the call to celebrate the Day of Deliverance from Congress rule by Jinnah was enthusiastically responded to by Dr Ambedkar in the Bombay and E.V. Ramaswamy Naicker in the Madras presidencies (S. Wolpert 1984: 177-8). This political process of combined and concerted efforts aimed at homogenization of power within, to bring about a modern, politically equal nation, in substance represented the emergence of class-like formations and interest based politics. This however, posed an increasing threat to the stability of the Raj, as well as a challenge to the microscopic minority's claim to nationalism. Interactional politics of competition and conflict occasioned the emergence and subsequent dominance of an alternate course of political development among the Muslims at the conscious intervention of both imperialist and nationalist powers. The objective ambiguity and multiple possibility of the Muslim situation has been pointed out: issues such as cow-slaughter could easily become an excuse for a purely religious polarization, the religious division of labour in Bengal, Malabar (Madras), and to a much lesser extent in Punjab, was becoming volatile; the ruling remnant among the Muslims too were restless. However, all these were yet to be synchronized in order to become politically salient; they were all local issues that could be contained and their trend made reversible. If the colonial administration's policy of viewing people primarily as religious entities, regionalized these religious issues, the later day nationalists, not to be left behind, went

[53] E. Irschick (1969) speaks of the earlier cooperation of the Muslims with the Non-Brahmins and post-Khilafat disillusionment pp. 258-9; however the Justice party, and Periyar in general supported the Muslims and their struggles pp. 346 ff. and B. Homne (1978), pp. 131-57.

[54] E. Zelliot (1969), chapter III, note no. 20.

[55] S.F. Dale (1980) p. 31; K.N. Panikkar (1989) notes a serious difference between pre- and post-Khilafat movements p. 31.

ahead and nationalized them.[56] The most unfortunate and disastrous result of this politics of religionization was the arresting of the process of horizontal and class-like polarization, and the replacement of the same with a counter process of vertical polarization in politico-religious terms. The imperialist-nationalist imperative for such an intervention is readily understandable within the competitive nature of contemporary politics. The divide-and-rule policy was well within the logic of imperialism itself, but this policy also found its echo in the sectarian and class needs of the minority nationalists.[57] The perception of threat at the growing horizontal polarization and their own isolation, and the anxiety of the nationalists to arrest and reverse it was expressed by no less a person than Gandhi himself with brutal clarity when he said at the declaration of the Communal Award in 1931, 'Untouchable hooligans will make common cause with Muslim hooligans and kill caste Hindus' (M. Desai 1953: 301).

With Khilafat and cow-slaughter occupying the centre stage of nationalist politics under the leadership of Gandhi in 1920s, a distinct Muslim-nationalism in preference to the political nation along with the non-Muslim masses, had certainly started its career.[58]

MASS EMERGENCE AS ANTI-COLONIALISM

It is important to understand what this socio-political mass emergence in its multiplicity of forms focussing on the vital issues of education, diversification of occupations, respectability of social status, appropriation of positions in administration and political decision-making, meant *vis-à-vis* colonialism, i.e. the separateness of power from culture and the aspiration towards the unification of the two as nationalism. Did all these big and small, intense and weak, offensive and defensive efforts of the generally excluded communities represent, as we have pointed out above, a thrust towards a democratization process strictly within and not have any anti-imperial/colonial implications? Was anti-colonialism the monopoly of those who raised the slogan that the British must go because the culture, the native value system or the religion was in danger? Within our theoretical paradigm, the question to be posed is: what, if any, are the implications of

---

[56] F. Robinson (1975) p. 348; P. Hardy (1972) p. 116.

[57] See Chapters IV and VI.

[58] See Chapter VI.

the process of homogenization of power within culture for the concomitant process of transfer of power from without? What is nationalist
about the emergence of the nation.

The nationalists thought that these democratizing attempts were
inspired and abetted by the colonial rulers and therefore pro-imperialist.
As these were also rooted within the traditions of the subcontinent's
cultural diversities and not pan-Indian in form, they were considered,
at least by implication, anti-national i.e. communal, casteist, regional,
chauvinist and the like.

Historiography and the social sciences in general have faithfully
continued to maintain this position in the study of nationalism in
the subcontinent. In the bargain, the real bearing of the internal
democratization process on colonialism in the South Asian context
is hardly paid attention to. First of all, the attempts of the lower
classes to appropriate socio-political power cannot but have the same
implication as those of the attempts of the upper castes, for instance,
the aspiration to become civil servants under the Raj. In this sense,
the attitude of those who chose to call themselves nationalists towards
the 'nationists' was nothing but hypocritical. One of the non-Brahmin
leaders of the South pointed this out: 'If we ask for a ministry
it is job-hunting, and if congressmen ask for it, it is patriotism'
(C.J. Baker 1976: 306).

Secondly, within the specific context of the traditional social power
configuration in the subcontinent the struggles of the hitherto excluded
communities bear the special significance of signalling democratic
revolution, however uneven and irregular, against the vested interests
of the dominant, both native as well as foreign. The pact between
the native and foreign dominant groups on which colonialism itself
was founded, was indeed based on the premise that the status-quo
of power, resource and leadership distribution within the colonized
country was to be maintained and that rule itself was to be indirect,
through the medium of local dominance. The British–imperialist
policy of non-interference was not based on any good will or appreciation of Indian culture, but on compulsion, and they had no
choice in the matter. In this situation, the lower class/caste struggles
did have the unfortunate effect of upsetting the precariously balanced
applecart of colonial power structure and ideology. The British were
certainly aware of this: the colonial educational policy, for example,
was dictated by the realization that if education descended from
the higher to the inferior classes, it 'would lead to a general convulsion

of which foreigners would be the first victim.'[59] Again, in practically all of the tribal and peasant struggles, the British solidly supported those groups and interests which could guarantee the safety and continuance of the Raj. In religio-cultural struggles too, the administration broadly supported the upper and Brahminic castes and upheld custom and tradition. For instance in the Shanar temple-entry movement, the Privy Council clearly ruled against the mass (R.L. Hardgrave 1969: pp. 126 ff.). In this way the multi-directional lower caste struggles were in essence not only against the Brahminical and feudal social order but also against the colonial collusive power structure. If any objective contradiction between the mass-Indian interests and ruler-British interests is to be located it is here within the internal democratization process, and not in some pre-ordained, primordial antagonism between the Indian and British. Within our own theoretical paradigm then, power homogenization within culture, i.e. the nation is the origin and basis of transfer of power from without, i.e. nationalism.

Karl Deutsch has pointed out that the beginning of mass emergence in colonial countries is also the beginning of the end of colonialism (K. Deutsch 1969: 79).[60] In a true sense, it is only when the colonial ruler is compelled to extend his patronage and distribute the colonially extracted surplus to all sections of the colonized population that the specifically colonial pattern of dominance is rendered politico-economically profitless and colonialism itself becomes meaningless. If the colonizer is to heed the voice of all including those who until now were voiceless, and to guarantee the welfare of everybody within the colony, what good is that colonialism to him? Instead, colonial withdrawal now becomes a realistic option. Thus, the genuine anti-colonial thrust and the potentiality of internal democratization processes particularly in the context of the pragmatic imperialism of the British in South Asia, can hardly be exaggerated. The demand for state protection by the excluded communities and the reluctant and piecemeal acceptance of the same by the British, needs to be interpreted then, not as a sign of compact between the two, but as the initial steps towards the dismantling of the colonial order.

It is however a fact that the scattered struggles towards social democracy could not transform themselves into a pan-Indian form;

---

[59] See chapter IV, note 22.
[60] K. Deutsch (1969) p. 79.

and pan-Indianism had been identified as nationalism as a matching response to the pan-Indian colonial state. The reasons for this are crucial—economic, cultural and ideological, the inherent difficulties of a generally traditional, subaltern and colonially dispossessed social position, particularly in the absence of widespread economic change, was the first. Secondly, these struggles were well-rooted in the vernacular, regional cultures and were a continuity of the alternate subcontinental tradition not only of power as resistance but also power as diversity which the colonial compact did much to damage. In this sense, the diversified, vernacularized and hence the rootedness of these movements were indeed an asset that could have lead to a federal and de-centralized modern India. Thirdly, the antagonistic pan-Indianism of the nationalists towards this process of internal democratization articulated from a traditional as well as colonially empowered social position is the ideological reason why mass emergence as the nation could not but be stopped from formally and verbally articulating the anti-colonial nationalist ideology.

The difference between the meagrely articulated and politico-economic-interest based anti-colonialism of the nationists and the high rhetoric of religion- and culture-based anti-colonialism of the nationalists was not limited to mere form but also extended to substantial issues of power and its redistribution within the nation to be.

IV

Nationalism: The Movement for Transfer of Power

If congruence between culture and power is what nationalism is about within the overall context of social change, this congruence has two aspects: one, the movement towards a homogeneous spread of power over culture, leading to the becoming of a modern nation and the formal affirmation within a nation-state through the notions of citizenship and territoriality; two, the movement to wrest power from the alien culture and reinvest it in one's own. What is crucially national then, is, that there exists a congruence between these two aspects themselves. Nationalism is thus a complex of congruence between power and culture. The principle that power should be congruous with one's own culture itself can be viewed in two ways: either as resistance to the threat of existing congruence, or as a struggle to regain lost congruence, accompanied with the concomittant attempt to refit culture-power relations in a specifically modern way.[1]

The revolt of 1857 has been considered both as a simple Sepoy Mutiny as well as the First War of Independence.[2] Modern scholarship would reject both these extreme views. While 1857 cannot be easily dismissed as a revolt of a few disgruntled sepoys, for there was mass involvement in several places, it can neither be seen as the birth of the modern nationalist movement. This is because the movement

---

[1] See E. Gellner (1983), chapters 4 & 5; also our chapter 1.

[2] For a differential evaluation of the 1857 Revolt by various schools of historiography, see J. Chaturvedi (1990) chapter II; see also A.T. Embree (1968).

of 1857 lacked an all-India character, a commonality of purpose and a vision towards a different future of Indian society.[3] The struggles of 1857, as so many other similar ones, contained no vision of the future society as distinguished from their immediate past; they were, implicitly or explicitly, attempts to re-establish the old order and their antagonism with the British was largely based on race, colour, and religious differences. Though discourses on nationalism seldom manage to escape the long shadows of racism, the two are by no means identical (E. Balibar 1991: 37; R. William 1976: 178). Race antagonism cannot by itself be the foundation of modern nationalism, though the former does play a role in almost all manifestations of the latter. The birth and growth of the Indian nationalist movement during the course of the nineteenth century is tinged with racist sentiments and overtones. When our over-enthusiastic nationalist historians paint a picture of objective antagonism between what is Indian on the one hand, and what is British on the other, as two monoliths, tracing the core of the antagonism to the fact of being Indian or British, they are betting on the wrong horse, a racist one, in the race of nationalism. The Indian freedom struggle did claim to be a nationalist movement different from the earlier struggles in having precisely these characteristics of an all-India spread, a commonality of purpose and a vision for the future. That there existed a difference between the two movements has been generally recognized. But to what extent did the difference penetrate and manifest itself in the freedom movement? What is the specific context out of which the nationalist consciousness was born? What is the justification of the movement's claim being an all-India one? Was there a commonality of purpose among the contestants for power? What was the content of the nationalists' future vision of India? These are some of the questions with which this analysis of the earlier phase (upto World War I) of the nationalist movement is concerned.

The non-contextual study of the Indian nationalist movement and its excessive claims to universality and unanimity have been rightly decried by scholars of different schools.[4] The remedy to this

---

[3] On the reaction of the emerging educated groups in the coastal presidencies to the 1857 Revolt, A. Seal (1968) says 'not a dog barked' p.8.

[4] O.J. Baker and D.A. Washbrook (1976) p 2, S. Chandra (1975) pp. 44-5 and S. Sarkar (1983) p 43. Sarkar's method of contextualizing the nationalist movement has already been commented upon, see note 15 under chapter 1.

is not to drop the study of the ideology based movement itself, but to restore its contextuality in order to explore its real character. Radical location of the origin and growth of the nationalist consciousness within the historical conjuncture of the power contestation by different groups out of which it arose, and in constant interaction with which it grew, is the much needed corrective measure. It will be seen, in concrete terms, how the movement from its inception had been posturing itself *vis-à-vis* the multitude of aspirations towards the new political society depicted in the previous chapter. In other words, the struggle for homogenization of power will form the context for the struggle for transference of power—for it is the unity of these two, that makes up the story and history of nationalism.

On Historiographies

Modern Indian historiography dealing with the questions of origin, nature, growth and fulfilment of the Indian nationalist movement has been differentiated into several schools of thought: Imperialist, Nationalist, Marxist, Muslim, Hindu, Cambridge, Subaltern and of course neo-Nationalist, neo-Marxist etc. These are not to be thought of as clear-cut systems having coherent or consistent views on all substantial questions.[5] On several important questions two or more schools tend to have an identity of views or at the most differ only in emphasis; on several other equally important issues some of them do not have clearly articulated viewpoints at all. Individual writers too, do not fall into one of these slots easily and could be fitted into more than one with ease. Many, have over the years shown tendencies to pass from one school to the other in response to the changed circumstances or to the proddings of more aggressive view points. The schools therefore are, at best, abstracted models suited only for limited purposes. It is still useful, however, to consider the ever increasing mass of writings on Indian nationalism, the movement and its ideologies, as arising from one perspective or another, emphasizing, one set of facts in preference over others and evaluating the overall performance one way or another.

For the Imperialist School, the focus is on the activities of British rulers in the subcontinent and in the context of these narratives, the birth and growth of nationalism is seen as a side effect or a

[5] See J. Chaturvedi (1990) for an attempt to treat the different schools as such.

by-product of the main and all important process of the rise and fulfilment of the British Empire. The evaluation of the movement and its leaders ranges between patronizing condescension and overt contempt. The neo-Imperialist version or the Cambridge School is, in fact, an extension of the former. Here, although the central concern is the Indians, the point of view is unabashedly that of the outside superior—the imperialist—the research being the product of perusal of home department files. Nationalism or for that matter any ideology is considered merely tactical to cover up what is essentially individual or, at best, group pursuit of power, profit, and position. For the classical Marxist, politics and ideology—and hence nationalism—are not autonomous; they are a function of structural changes in economy. To understand Indian or for that matter any nationalism, one should search and find the capitalist or the bourgeoisie—who could be made to require the nation-state as a market for products. At its worst, Indian nationalism is false consciousness as far as the masses are concerned, and at its best it is a genuine bourgeois democratic revolution. The Hindu and Muslim schools of historiography, far from being elaborated views on Indian nationalism, were contesting strains of thought within the movement itself, having their own distinct ideas on the nation as constituting exclusively of either community, and as existing prior to the articulation of nationalism. Often enough it is difficult to distinguish them, especially the Hindu variety, from the dominant nationalist school.

By far the most dominant and influential school of thought on the Indian nationalist movement and its ideologies has been termed as the official, nationalist, neo-nationalist, and secular-liberal etc. Over the years, this school has been protean in its manifestations, although maintaining its core consistently: in several senses, it is a continuation and elaboration of the Imperialist version, not limited to Tara Chand's four volumes on the freedom movement, having strong links with Hindu communal views on national unity etc, and laterly accommodating, to a larger extent, mild Marxist versions also.[6] Sumit Sarkar's summary of its character runs thus:

> The basic pattern was of an English educated 'middle class' reared by British rule engaging in various renaissance activities and eventually turning against their masters and so giving birth to modern

---

[6] S. Chandra (1979) specifically mentions the slow change of earlier Marxist Bipin Chandra into a nationalist, p 45 (references).

nationalism—out of frustrated selfish ambitions, ideals of patriotism and democracy derived from western culture or natural revulsion against foreign rule, the imputed motive in each case depending on the viewpoint of scholars (S. Sarkar 1983: 5).

Understandably, the nationalist writing and history has been criticised for its non-contextuality, rarefication and obsession with consensus. The political success of, and the subsequent rule by, the party that led the nationalist movement, has not had a wholesome impact on nationalist historiography. Monopoly state sponsorship of research has almost robbed it of its autonomous character. As socio-political crises within the polity are deepening, historiography appears to become increasingly hysterical and defensive. The nationalist movement, its leaders, its ideologies and its achievements have become objects of uncritical veneration not to be questioned by disbelievers. The progress of the movement is seen as 'everwidening consensus of the masses of the subcontinent; any suggestion of conflict within would be labelled as imperialist conspiracy'.[7] It is to this form of rarefied historiography that the hard hitting Subaltern footnote is added. The Subaltern School is better understood as a critique of the dominant and elitist historiography, than as an elaboration of the view-point of the subaltern masses themselves. It unerringly indicts the dominant school of unadulterated elitism by pointing out to the almost unbridgeable cleavage that existed between the dominant (native and foreign) and the dominated. The project and trajectory are accurate enough; the performance however is exasperatingly deficient. 'Subaltern' is defined in too general a term to be of any analytical significance, and the nationalism of these subalterns is unwarrantedly restricted to the search for a programmatic disjunction within the so-called elite nationalist movement itself.

Our own agenda is more eclectic; it will take Indian nationalism—the movement and ideology—as the subject of analysis on its own merit, considering it as dialectically related to politcal economy, searching for widening consensus while camouflaging internal conflicts. The approach will seek to radicalize the subalternist perspective by a specific definition of 'subaltern' in the Indian context, and visualizing it as autonomously moving towards a nationalism of a different and

---

[7] See S. Chandra (1979) p 44-5. See also J. Brown (1984) p 161.

superior kind—the struggle against the traditional order and its imperialist ally in the subcontinent.

THE BIRTH OF THE NATIONAL

The colonial impact on the ascriptive and hierarchical socio-political
order had been to widen and deepen the cleavages between communities by bringing together the Brahmin and allied upper castes
in uneven combination in different parts of the country, and to
enable them to transform their scattered social dominance into increasingly unified power in the newly erected lower echelons of
the administrative structure and the expanding civil society. Although
these political buttresses of the Raj—paying (landlords) as well as
the paid (service men and professionals) collaborators—had mutual
squabbles and rivalries over the share of power and privileges, they
were all insulated against the mass of lower caste communities, Muslims
and tribals, by virtue of not only their pre-modern social origins,
but also their modern economic interest and political prospects.[8]
It is from this conjuncture of the transformation of social dominance
into unified state power, under the aegis of colonialism, that nationalist
consciousness and sentiments first emerged. In the context, this meant
that the erstwhile collaborators were changing their position into
one of confrontation. While in history this progression from scatterd
social dominance, through political economy-based unification, to
state power represents a continuity, within our theoretical paradigm
of nationalism, it stands for the movement of power from without
to within culture, traditionally known as the nationalist movement.
Explorations into the forces and circumstances in which such a transformation took place in the third quarter of the nineteenth century
is in fact the study of the origin and development of early Indian
nationalism.

While the material changes during the colonial rule did enlarge
and expand the power and control of the upper castes and heightened
their sense of distinction and superior status, a counter process was
set in motion within the larger society through the structural constraints
of modern politics. The delegitimization of Brahminism was a by-

---

[8] A. Seal (1968) p 10, 11; 'for all their squabbles among themselves they still had
a common interest in preventing these arrivistes from arriving', p.39. See also B.B.
Misra (1961) p 12, 322; (1976) p 75.

product of colonial rule at least in the view of those who hithertofore were subjected to it. Firstly, the compulsions and constraints of modern political structure were such that measures had to be initiated to bring society into congruence with polity and a minimum balance between competing forces had to be maintained if colonial dominance had to last (A. Seal 1968: 345; B.B. Misra 1976: 75). Secondly, the lower caste communities, with a millenia old tradition of attempts to flee or sabotage oppressive Brahminism, could not in fairness be restrained from availing themselves of the new- found opportunity to carve out, for the first time in history, a more dignified position within the new political community. Thirdly, as we have already noted, the western impact was not monolithic—if the rulers were anxious not to intervene, there were others, civilians and more so the missionaries, with their own axe to grind, who were. For the now politically powerful caste-groups in the process of coming together due to new vested interests within the colonial political economy, who were aggressively sensitized to their own imagined or real superior status. These counter movements constituted concerted attempts to challenge and destabilize the traditional and indigenous socio-political order and religio-cultural value system. Threats to social traditions, cultural values and intellectual legacies needed to be checked and the old order that assured them of their unrivalled dominance required to be re-fashioned and stabilized. For this, the British had to go and Indian nationalism was born. The two levels of national consciousness, cultural-ideological and material, although two sides of the same coin, could be traced distinctly to their respective origins and growth. The two streams developed alongside each other throughout their history till their successful fusion into an all-India political Hinduism or an all-India religious nationalism. Though it is useful to see them as a single process clarity requires them to be treated separately.

Within the overall policy of non-interference in religio-cultural matters, the British had to initiate certain changes, if only to bring the traditional society into minimal congruence with the requirements of modern political structure. Beginning with the abolition of cult-inspired thuggery and infanticide, the colonial government initiated several measures of socio-religious reform, prodded by reformist up-percaste Hindus and under pressure from the missionaries. These measures were seen by the majority of the Brahmins and allied upper castes as challenges to their ritual and sacred monopoly. Important for our purpose among these measures are the abolition of Sati (1829), removal of caste and religious disabilities known as Lex Loci Act (1850), administrative measures undertaken to control plagues (1897) and finally the Age of Consent Bill (1902). Each of these governmental steps were occasions for acrimony, bitter controversy, and finally rallying points in developing a pan-Indian, anti-British front.[9] The alien government was increasingly seen as interfering with national religion with intentions of destroying national cultural legacy, tradition and civilization.

With the legal entry of the missionaries in 1813, another front of attack on Brahmanical ideology and the inequitable socio-political order was opened. If the bureaucrats were wary of interference in the establishment, the missionaries went out of their way to challenge and even insult what they considered rank superstitions, obscurantist practices and oppressive social hierarchy. Here too, the upper castes reacted in a differential manner; some of them, at least initially, saw eye to eye with the missionaries on several matters and thus threatened the unity and cohesion of the socio-religious dominance. The stray cases of upper-caste conversions in Bombay, Madras and Calcutta, the attempt to introduce Bible studies in governmental institutions as part of English Education and the public debates on religious matters provoked by the missionaries played the role of catalysts for the anti-Christian, both rulers and proselytizers, political mobilization through the establishment of a number of *sabhas* and associations to protect what was increasingly seen as the national faith—Hinduism (S.R. Mehrotra 1971: pp 32ff.).

The mass conversions of the depressed and untouchable castes in several parts of the country in the second half of the nineteenth century, and their implications for rural power relations have already been noted. Agrestic slavery was abolished in the South in 1843,

---

[9] The Lex Loci Act of 1850 in particular appears to have triggered off a nationwide controversy and agitation; the early usage of the term national seems to have been connected specifically with this controversy, see S.R. Mehrotra (1971) chapter 1. 'A Brahmin addressed an open letter to Dalhousie in which he warned the Governor General that if Lex Loci Act was not repealed Hindus would refuse to cultivate the soil, to pay the revenue ....' And there was a more than adequate rejoinder from a Bengal writer, 'What if we all combine together the Hindus and Mohammedans of whole India and resolve up so doing...'. In the subcontinent 'the national' took birth within the context of tradition, religion or religio-social crisis; this was freely acknowledged and even proudly proclaimed by leaders, like B.C. Pal (1958) and others and has been confirmed and elaborated by later historians also, see A. Seal (1968), p.249.

solely through the insistence of the missionaries. Christianity's attitude towards the social hierarchy and the caste system, although ambiguous and rather accommodative in practice, at the ideological level was consistent condemnation of the system as being anachronistic and inhuman. Community after community in different parts of the country was using its missionary patronage—through conversion or association—to deny the upper castes their customary, traditional, and religion-ordained free or slave labour, to cast away degrading caste-symbols and to defy caste restrictions and disabilities.

Lower caste masses everywhere were becoming restless and utilized every opportunity to get out of the traditional order of dominance and subjugation. Their attempts at sanskritization, education, claim for employment at par with the other castes and their stake to be represented in various public forums were indications of the passing away of the old order. These efforts had engendered confrontation and conflict between the upper and lower castes. By not actually suppressing these subaltern attempts, at least in their initial manifestations to defy the Brahmanical order, the colonial rule appeared to condone or even encourage them. The missionaries however did encourage them on at least certain occasions. The response of those who had stakes within the realm of culture-ideology to this multi-pronged attack of the West on the East can be seen in three increasingly political phases; reform, revival and the construction of Hindu nationalism.

The story of socio-religious reform among the upper caste communities of the subcontinent has been told and retold many times, often with the false claim to monopoly, and need not detain us too long.[10] Suffice it to say that the entire phenomenon of accommodative or antagonistic response to the British rule's negative impact (or positive, for it depends on the side of socio-political interest from which one looks at the question) on the old order was limited to the handful of dominant communities scattered across the country having real or imagined stakes in the status quo and it ended there.[11] This is understandable, for it was their economic

---

[10] Historians in general have completely ignored sociological research on the theme and have written reform history without any reference to the enormous amount of work done outside the narrow circle of the upper castes.

[11] The radically limited nature of upper caste-initiated reform movements has been noted by several writers, both within sociology and history; see M.S.A. Rao (1986), K. Sardamoni (1980) p.121 and S. Chandra (1975), Chapter 2. However, the intention

and ideological interest that was being threatened and in response they were trying out several ways of handling or neutralizing the negative impact till they finally succeeded in turning the whole process to their own advantage by developing a pan-Indian conciousness that was political and at the same time religious.

It has been said with some justification (though often exaggerated) that struggle against a common enemy brings scattered peoples and their interests together and the dominant historiography claims to have discovered this process within the birth and development of the Indian nationalist movement. However, very little work has been done to discover the processes by which the scattered sects, cults and culturally and religiously insulated communities were brought together under an 'imagined religious community of modern Hinduism as a kind of cocoon out of which a politically imagined community of a nation developed'.[12]

The history of the nineteenth century is not only the history of Indian nationalism but also of the birth and development of modern Hinduism as the womb that later delivered the political progeny. Pan-Indian consciousness developed around the socio-religious issues of conversion, introduction of Bible study as a compulsory subject in the 1830s and 40s and the Lex Loci Act of 1850. While the non-participation of the English educated segment in the Mutiny has been pointed out often enough, the spearheading by the educated or the new class in this ideological battle has not been sufficiently noted. The English newspapers of those times—'The Brahminical Magazine', 'Bombay Courier', 'Madras Male Asylum', 'Herald', 'Bombay Guardian', 'Bengal Hurkaru' etc.—carried intense debates con-

---

here is not to write off all nineteenth century uppercaste reform movements (for example on the women's question some pioneering work was done) but to contextualize them within the overall attempts by the lower castes to redistribute power in society. Note also, that on the caste question both Brahmo Samaj and Arya Samaj broke up.

[12] The socio-political history of the birth and development of modern Hinduism through a process of selection from among the plethora of sects, practices and customs etc, as an embodiment of the Brahminical belief system exclusively, articulated by neo-Brahminic interest groups is an area hardly explored. S.R. Mehrotra (1971) chapter 1 does indicate a possible direction for such a study; see R. Tucker (1976), and B.C. Pal (1958). The point that is being made here is that parallel to the evolution of nationalism is the transformatory evolution of Brahminism as 'Hinduism' which in fact is a much larger concept enveloping both Brahminical and anti or non-Brahminical belief and practice. R. Thapar (1989) comments that Brahminism has 'nationalized' itself into Hinduism.

cerning these issues, indicating the far reaching collaborations among the uppercaste elite of the different metropolitan centres to defend the national religion. On the occasion of the passing of the Act of removal of caste and religious disabilities (Lex Loci) *Englishman* was obliged to point out 'the 11th of April 1850 as the first legisla·ive step towards the expulsion of the British from India'. Collaborated petitions and memorials on the issues of conversion, Bible study and Lex Loci by the residents of the presidential towns to Her Majesty's Government, in defence of the 'national' interest had become the order of ine day well before the revolt of 1857.

Organizational and associational response to the western impact on Brahminic ideology was manifested in the Brahmo Samaj, Arya Samaj and Theosophy movement. With organizational headquarters situated strategically in the three presidential towns of the subcontinent, the agenda of reforming or reviving Brahminism was carried on through scores of branches scattered all over the country. Towards the end of the nineteenth century they had developed a definite all–India character, and held annual congresses which were later imitated by the Indian National Congress.[13] Rediscovery of the Vedas, Shastras and of Brahminic practices were considered by these organizations to be processes of national renaissance and regeneration. Adding intellectual substance and scientific legitimacy to these uppercaste endeavours was the orientalist scholars' theory and research on Aryanism—the real and supposed glories of the Aryan race, their superiority over all peoples on earth, and particularly the identity of their origin with that of the colonial rulers.[14] To this is to be added the colonial perception of the subcontinental society as a monolith of belief and practice. That there existed a monolith of dominant belief and practice as an aspiration and to a large extent achievement of the uppercaste communities is undeniable and is itself the paradigm of our understanding of the traditional order. However, the trends counter to it, that have increasingly been recognized as important

[13] R.C. Majumdar et al (1978) 'Before the end of 1865 these were 54 samajams (Brahmo) fifty in Bengal, two, in North-West Province one each in Punjab and Madras' p. 869; S.R. Mehrotra (1971) 'By 1884 Theosophical society had over 80 branches scattered all over the subcontinent and the number of sympathisers ran to thousands' p 390.

[14] See J. Leopold (1970). For the wider significance of the discovery of the Aryan see R. Schwab (1984) and L. Paliakov (1974).

in the challenge they posed to the monolithic ideology, were largely ignored during the colonial period.

Faced thus with real and supposed onslaughts on its monopolistic dominance, and having tried different forms of meeting the challenge, such as reform, and revivalism the Brahminic ideology finally settled upon an adequate strategy by reincarnating itself as pan-Indian politi-cal-national Hinduism. The agency through which this transformation was brought about was the small circle of upper caste communities usually centred around the Brahmins in different parts of the country, undergoing the multiple processes of accomodation, unification and empowerment through imperial patronage. This group, as the dominant and leading class reworked and recast Brahminic ideology, from the vantage position of social dominance, to suit the times as an ideology of state power, simultaneous to their claim to appropriate the state itself. The ideology of the old order had to undergo certain modifications before it became the nationalist ideology of nation-al-political Hinduism. The emergent Hinduism was at once Brah-minical as well as national. Nationalism and nationalist consciousness was the context in which the ideology of sacred and secular hierarchy transformed itself into, and articulated itself as, Hinduism. H. Kohn comments: 'Religious renaissance in India became a source of renewed strength of Hindu orthodoxy. All these movements finally merged in India's new consciousness of her unity and her mission in Indian nationalism' (H. Kohn 1924: 56).

Development of the nationalist consciousness in terms of the material interests of the dominant communities closely followed the route taken by ideological Hinduism and in fact the two were deeply intertwined throughout. In other words, pan-Indian Hinduism was the context in which the politico-economic interests of the same social forces transformed itself as nationalism.

The policy of non-interference in religio-cultural matters together with the attempts to strengthen the socio-economic status quo by the British, in a hierarchically organized and segmented society, meant favouring the top echelons to the exclusion of the lower orders. The upper castes, the most favoured part of society, enjoyed enormous expansion of power, status and privilege at the expense of the masses, both in the traditional power arena of land relations as well as in the emergent education and employment-opportunity structure.[15]

---

[15] Note that at this stage of the biased sectional collaboration between the native

The series of land settlements not only legitimized the existing patterns of dominance but also accentuated it by depriving the tenants of their security and occupational rights. Superior tenurial right to revenue were elevated to the status of ownership with the right to eject tenants and dispose of the land unilaterally. The operations of the land records office, lower judiciary and revenue administration combined to remove customary restrictions on the exercise of control over land by the dominant communities. The benefits of decreasing tax on land, instead of being passed down to the lower classes, were grabbed by the landlords themselves.[16] The increasing pauperization of peasants, artisans and labourers was making them restless and agrarian disturbance was raising its head in several parts of the country.

In education and employment too, the same cluster of communities monopolized the opportunities and excluded the masses. Laying down the educational policies during the early decades of the century, the bureaucrats ruled out the possibility and feasibility of either vernacular or primary education for the masses, thus making the new education virtually the exclusive preserve of the traditionally literary and ritually high castes.[17] The Muslims, (being the losers of the colonial take-over) were suspect from the beginning as a possible threat, and their presumed leadership in the revolt of 1857 did not improve the Muslim-British relationship. Thus, the going was good for the upper castes in general, in different parts of the country. They were graduating slowly to the position of junior partners of the regime, in preference over the masses who were far behind in practically everything that mattered. A spirit of camaraderie prevailed between the British and their chosen ones from among the natives. As late as 1894 S.N. Banerjee could say,

---

and imperial elite against the masses, the question or accusation of 'divide and rule policy' did not figure at all.

[16] A. Maddison (1971) notes 'The British had inherited the Mogul tax system which provided a land revenue equal to 15% of the National Income, but by the end of the colonial period land tax was only one percent of national income p 45.' On this point T. Raychaudhuri has commented in R.E. Frykenberg edit. (1969), 'the relatively low and unchanging rate of revenue demand which left a large surplus to be distributed among a numerous and parasitical class' p 168.

[17] 'Education and civilisation may descend from the higher to the inferior classes ..... if imparted solely to the lower classes (would) lead to general convulsion of which foreigners would be the first victim' Lord Ellenborough to the court of Directors quoted in D. Keer (1964) p 52.

We have everything to lose and nothing to gain by the severence
of our connection with England. We owe whatever position or
prestige we have acquired to our English education and culture.
If they were to leave the country our English Education and
culture would be at a discount. We are not particularly anxious
to commit political suicide (J.R. McLane 1977: 68).

The slow but steady widening of the cleavage and polarization
within the social structure, and the beginnings of widespread restlessness
in both rural and urban areas appeared to be too remote to pose
an immediate threat demanding a reversal of the time-tested policy
of non-interference and maintenance of status quo. However, the
fragile nature of Pax Britannica came to the surface increasingly
after the third quarter of the century. Pressure from underneath
was building up on several fronts, demanding intervention in favour
of groups other than the traditionally dominant. When the efforts
at emergence of the hitherto excluded groups met with resistance
and rejection by the socially dominant and the politically articulate
within society, the mass began to look up to the state as its protector
and promoter. The constraints and compulsions of the new political
structure had per force opened up new avenues to the subaltern
masses to sabotage the old order, to bypass its dominance and even
to challenge it openly wherever possible. Both in the rural and
urban areas, the lower classes were pushing ahead with whatever
support they could muster from different quarters, and maximizing
the rivalries between various groups. Much against the will of the
upper castes, the Shudras and untouchables were making forays into
the new education and were aided in this by the missionaries. Caste
disabilities were also being fought against. On the agrarian front
the situation was indeed becoming alarming. With the masses demanding the immediate attention of the government, a series of agrarian
conflicts of uneven consequences spread over the country—the Map-
pilas revolt, Deccan riots, the Pabna league and the tribal revolts
being the more well known. Within the administration too the
Raj, having almost surrendered its freedom to the local native bosses
in return for permanence and profit, was increasingly losing its
manoeuvring space (A. Seal 1968: 345). The time had come for the
policy of blind support to the status quo to be reversed, again in
the interests of the perpetuity of the Raj. This meant that the dominance
of the dominant communities would have to be circumscribed in favour

of other upcoming communities. A process of disengagement from commitment to the upper castes had to be initiated. The earlier camaraderie was beginning to turn cold (S.R. Mehrotra 1971: 115–16). Signs of the changing times could be traced to the middle of the century though they became pronounced towards the end. In 1851 the Madras Government prohibited employment of more than one member of the family in the same department. In 1853 the patronage system of employment was abolished. In 1854 Wood's despatch revealed the fact that education was not percolating and emphasized the need for mass education. In 1861 the new criminal law, based on the principle of rule of law replaced the Varna-based Gentoo Code of 1776, thus ending Brahminic pre-eminence in judicial matters. In 1870 the government decided to give priority to vernacular education. In 1872 Hunter stressed the need for Muslim education. Tired of waiting for upper caste candidates, in the post-Mutiny period missionaries turned their attention to the education and upliftment of the lower castes. By the third quarter of the century the state had ceased to rely on land revenue as the sole source of income and from then on, was not beholden to those with landed interests. In short, the nominal reign of revenue collection was in the process of becoming the serious business of ruling. Towards the end of the century the government had to do something to protect, or at least appear to protect, the interests of the tenants, hence the several half-hearted measures such as the Punjab Land Alienation Bill, the Deccan Agricultural Relief Bill and the Bengal Tenancy Bill, the Revenue recovery Act of Madras, etc. The government now came forward more forthrightly to defend the rights of the lower castes to enter into governmental educational and employment organizations. J. Gordon summarizes the situation thus:

All over the continent towards the end of the 19th century, the government attempted to break the hold of vested interests in the administration by changing the qualifications needed for office and the method of recruitment. Often these exercises were clearly intended to spread government patronage among more social groups .... of course other interests in society were not slow to respond either to the changing structure of the government or to the prejudices of its officers (J. Gordon 1973: 64–5).

By making conscious attempts to move away from its own established practice of support to the status quo and beginning to respond positively, of course in an extremely limited and reluctant way with the selfish motive of ensuring the Raj's permanence, to the pressures of the lower castes, peasants, tribals and Muslims, the colonial rulers were earning the wrath of the erstwhile collaborators. The different measures of the government such as the tenancy measures, the switch to vernacular education, abettment of lower caste conversions etc., were seriously resented and various associations and forums were utilized to vent these grievances. Greater share in policy making—and implementing—bodies were demanded precisely in this context of competing aspirations. B.B. Misra (1976) accurately pinpoints the twin birth of nationalism and communalism to occasions when the government moved away from its patronage of Hindu upper castes. In the process however, he attributes altruistic motives to the colonial government and this need not have been the case for it is more consistent to argue that the imperialist motive has all along been to achieve profit and permanence and that their tactics had been shifting to this end. 'Periyar' explained this in his typical style: 'Thus the Britisher found that by passing loyalty-resolutions in competition with one another (they all) supported him, and he started distributing one, or two, benefits to everybody; when the Brahmins realized that the privileges and concessions—posts, employments etc which they had been enjoying monopolistically, without giving opportunity to others—are becoming less and less, they got frustrated and started passing resolutions against the state. Today's nationalism started only this way.' (V. Anaimuthu 1974: Vol I, 364) The British were no longer considered reliable enough to keep the guarantee of non-interference given in 1858. They had become the enemies of society, its socio-political order, its value system, its traditions and customs, by causing division among the people. Thus, in a series of actions and reactions, the objective contradiction between the British and Indian interests arose. The solution obviously was that the British had to go; the seed of Indian nationalism had been sown.

Judith Brown has a sharp remark to make on Indian society: 'any king was accorded legitimacy who protected caste society' (J. Brown 1984: 146).[18] By implication this meant that legitimacy would be accorded to ruler only as long as he upheld the caste dharma

---

[18] C. Bougle (1971), 'The proof lies in the unparallelled authority with which it (caste system) weighs in India. All that can serve it prospers. All that could hurt it, perishes', p 68.

and the moment he failed in this would be the beginning of his end. By her declaration of 1858 the Queen had appeared to give precisely this guarantee. But by the end of the century, in the estimation of those who mattered in the subcontinent, the colonial rulers had failed to uphold this promise through their various sins of omission and commission. They had in the meantime laid sufficient ground work in the subcontinent so that withdrawal of legitimacy could be articulated within the ideological framework of modern nationalism.

The birth of Indian nationalism as described above unambiguously points out the fact that nationalism in the subcontinent was intrinsically linked with a concern for the continuation of the old hierarchical order of power relations within society. The context is the dichotomous political awakening of groups variously situated in the traditional social structure, drawn apart and differentially sensitized by the material and non-material changes during the colonial rule. Those at the top of the hierarchy—the upper castes—who had a stake within the old order turned from collaboration to confrontation, in other words they turned national, in the context of the emergence of a different and less inegalitarian form of power realization within the social structure. The attempts of the colonial rulers to pre-empt any possible socio-political upheaval and consequent threat to the permanence of the Raj, by de-monopolizing the pattern of patronage and spreading it to other upcoming and competing backward groups, were resented as unwarranted interference in the traditional socio-religious order and value system, as generating discord among the different communities living in harmony by setting one against the other. In short, the Raj was seen to pose a threat to the religion, culture and interests of Indians as a whole. Therefore, the time had come for the seizure of power from the alien culture. The national element thus at its conception and inception sharply stood apart and in antagonism to the nation—the masses' aspirations for homogeneous or equitable spread of power. Nationalism in the sub-continent sought the transfer of power from the alien culture to preserve the pre-nation form of differential power realization within society; and herein lies the basically contradictory nature of Indian nationalism.[19]

[19] The 'reactionary' nature of Indian nationalism has been noted by a string of writers belonging to different schools of thought from the very beginning. As early as 1926, V. Chirol noted that Indian nationalism rose in order to revive the past social inequality; R.P. Dutt (1948) mentions how early Marxists thought the Indian

The Nationalists

Apart from the reactionary context out of which the consciousness and sentiment of the national was born, the organized articulation of the same was also significant. This organized articulation became a fact with the birth of the Indian National Congress in 1885.[20] When certain sectional demands and aspirations were put forward as those of the whole people of the subcontinent, a claim was made by the small assembly of educated men to be treated as representatives of the interests of a much larger collectivity—the nation.[21] Different attempts were made to define, describe and delimit what constituted or what did not constitute this nation that they stood for. There was obviously no unanimity on this point and competing, even contradicting, ideas of the nation were proffered (C. Heimsath 1964: pp 134ff.). However, very slowly, the nation came to mean the pan-Indian nation. These ideas surrounding the national idea were new in the politics of the subcontinent and the early nationalists deserve to be credited for this. However, by articulating their own demands as national and claiming for themselves the status of the representatives of the whole nation (however diversely construed) the early nationalists had become the nationalist group or the class with the burden of leading the other classes of men towards the struggle of wresting power from the alien culture and constituting a new nation-state. Henceforth, their pronouncements and performances would be judged in the light of the nation and not merely of their own community or class. The questions that therefore come to mind are those that relate to the identity of the articulation of nationalism with the aspirations of the nation i.e. the common masses. Did the nationalist class represent the aspiration of the entire national

National Congress was set up by the imperialists themselves to pre-empt the portending mass uprising pp 301, 309, 311; Anil Seal (1968) later gave a sophisticated version of this; K.W. Jones (1976) concludes, 'British administration provided the rules of the game but the game was more with other communities and within Hindu Community than directly with the government', p 252; S.Sarkar (1973) just stops short of labelling as 'Bhadralok nationalism rationalisation' (see chapter 10).

[20] According to D. Argov (1966) the early (moderate) Congress movement cannot be considered as 'the history of freedom movement' because 'they constantly harped on the theme of securing the permanence of British rule in India' and 'reconciled loyalty to England with Indian patriotism' pp.19-20.

[21] Aurobindo (1972): 'It is not justifiable for a self-created body representing only single and limited class to call itself national' Vol I, p 16.

society? Were several competing socio-political forces included in the movement and forged into one whole of common interests and vision? Was the behaviour of the leaders befitting that of a new political entity in which inter-individual and -group relations are to be based on a minimum understanding of citizenship rights and duties?

Throughout the first three decades of its growth, nationalist sentiments were being articulated by a microscopic minority of mostly English educated men in government service or engaged in new professions, drawn more or less exclusively from the Brahmin and upper caste communities of different parts of the country.[22] Though they were anglicized in language and superficial habits, they continued to be rooted in their caste loyalties and orthodox environments (A. Seal 1968: 15–6). They were men who had added eminence to their previously ascriptive high status (J.R. McLane 1975: 157). Inspite of modern ambitions they lived or aspired to live in an old aristocratic style (J.R. McLane 1977 :63–6). They had more fellow-feeling and commonality of purpose with their patron-rulers than with the masses from whom they felt twice removed on account of their ascription and achievement (ibid: 68–71; J.R. McLane 1975: 161). Although they belonged to a multiplicity of caste groups, they were all high caste men having a definite stake in the preservation of the old order and its values (B.B. Misra 1961: 307).

In terms of the new economics and politics, they had commonality of interest among themselves and against the rest; though initially in rivalry with other power groups, both traditional and new, such as landlords and money lenders, they soon developed a symbiotic relationship with them based on interests, for many of them were already well into the process of becoming landlords and money-lenders themselves, as notions of traditional social prestige demanded (J.R. McLane 1977: 179–80). Thus in terms of economic and political interests the nationalist articulators were fairly a well rounded and homogenous group, and in socio-religious terms they were all high up in the ritual hierarchy and were sharply delimited by the informally drawn social boundary of upper caste Hindu fold. Both these characteristics, the politico-economic as well as socio-religious, determined the nature

---

[22] By 1885, the matriculates were approximately 50,000 and according to the 1881 census one out of 3600 belonged to this class, see B.T. McCully (1966), p. 176. See also A. Seal (1968), pp. 97 ff; B.B. Misra (1961), p.323.

of the nationalists, their relationship with the masses and the course
of nationalist politics, then and in subsequent years.

The supplicatory, or later the romantic, nature of nationalist activities, the limited extent of their mobilization and the sectarian,
that is non-national character of their concerns are well documented
and even national or neo-nationalist historiographers do not mystify
this.[23] The nationalists' obsessive preoccupation was the expansion
of their own share in the bureaucratic and legislative power structure;
they were simultaneously careful to see that power did not spill
over beyond their own narrow circle.[24] They demanded only as
much power as could be absorbed among themselves. They quickly
sought to turn the grinding poverty of the masses too to their own
advantage by prescribing increased political and administrative representation for themselves as the panacea.[25] They had very definite
ideas about the emergent political community and the nature of
power within it. They unambiguously repudiated universal franchise,
quite naturally accepted the imperialist prescription of wealth and
education as conditions for the exercise of public authority, and
being both wealthy and educated, claimed to be the natural leaders
and sole representatives of the whole nation to the exclusion of
other possible contestants.[26] Hence they behaved in a manner which
made it clear to others, that they were not welcome to this semi-
exclusive club, without formally barring anyone. This self-image and
the role they aspired to, did not vary much in substance from the
pre-modern pattern of power realization within the subcontinent.

When willy-nilly issues concerning the welfare of groups other
than themselves were brought up, through the pressures of the groups
themselves or the colonial government, the nationalists were quick
to sense the adverse impact such a move would have on their group
as a whole, and were fairly consistent in arranging themselves against

[23] See for example B. Chandra (1979).

[24] The magazine *Bengalee* wrote in 1887 'who has ever asked that the peasantry
should participate in the government of the country and direct the affairs of the
empire ? Not even the most dreamy of our politicians have ever sought to compromise
our cause by committing this outrage upon common sense'. Quoted in S. Ghose
(1967) p.25.

[25] In 1887 masses were addressed by a kind of catechism, 'Give us the educated
classes power and you, the uneducated will be freed from oppression as you used
to be years ago' see B.B. Misra (1976) p.55, D. Naoroji (1990), pp. 561, 577, 580
etc.

[26] S. Ghose (1967) pp.25-6; B. Chandra (1979) p. 125; J.R. McLane (1977), pp.97-8.

intruders both inside and outside the formal forums. When the question of tenancy reform became urgent and could not be avoided anymore, the government half-heartedly initiated some measures; the nationalists as a block tried to prevent them from being passed and some went to the extent of suggesting that 'tenants needed no protection' and argued for the extension of permanent settlement for all the British ruled areas.[27] The situation was similar when the government wanted to introduce labour welfare measures or expand the educational benefits to the lower classes by giving priority to basic and vernacular education.[28] The doyen of Indian economic nationalism R.C. Dutt has sadly commented:

> Rights of the educated natives of the country to the higher government service, rights of the leaders of our community to a place in the legislative councils, rights of the zamindars to an exemption from all land impositions, have been frequently insisted upon in vigorous language; but the right of the ryots to be educated, to be freed from the trammels of ignorance, to be saved from oppression of zamindars—such ideas have invariably emanated from our rulers and not from us (B.T. McCully 1966: 231).

We have noted earlier that one of the processes set in motion by colonial rule is the gradual elevation of social dominance to state power. As socially dominant groups were transforming themselves through the political processes into managers of the bureaucracy and political machinery, they were not giving up their socio-cultural dominance, particularly when socio-economic change under the British had not brought about any significant vertical social mobility. This meant that the nationalists now had two levers of power—one, through the so called national-secular organizations, based on and for the purpose of promoting their own economic and political

---

[27] J.R. McLane (1977), p. 228; B. Chandra (1964) has joined issue with B.B. Misra explaining that when R.C. Dutt argued for permanent settlement, he did not mean Bengal type of Zamindari Settlement. However, as J.R. McLane (1964) points out, this understanding was not common in the Congress and the controversy assumes a new dimension when carried on in the context of Tenancy Bills. All B. Chandra (1964) could establish was that the Congress was not pro-landlord. This is far from saying that it was pro-tenant for the latter was not in the picture at all. Rivalries between landlords and professionals could not by itself be interpreted as pro-tenant.

[28] B.B. Misra (1964) p 75; (1976) p 275 etc. The author's attribution of altruism to the British and their claim for the concern of the depressed can be taken with a pinch of salt.

interests; and two, through religio-cultural organizations based on the traditional, sacred and social hierarchy—either reformed, revived or rediscovered. Most members of the Congress were also members of different religio-cultural organizations—the Cow Protection Society, Hindu Sabhas, Arya Samaj etc.—and passed from one into the other without any sense of contradiction (A. Seal 1968: 15-16; C. Heimsath 1980: concluding chapter; J. Gordan 1973: 48-9). In fact this is how the secularity and 'national'ness of the Indian nationalist movement in general, and of the Congress in particular, was maintained. The socio-cultural levers for the exercise of dominance and control over the masses were utilized largely through these organizations. While the liberal-secular framework of the movement was retained to a certain extent, the inevitable egalitarian fall-out was effectively taken care of and neutralized through the other forums. This was particularly the case with the extremists, but the moderates too were not free from this dubious use of power. A true analysis of the nature of the nationalists therefore cannot be limited to the study of the annals of the Congress party alone.[29] The traditionalist organizations in which many Congressmen participated actively stood, more or less openly, for the re-establishment of the Brahminical order of society; they had more effective contacts with the mass and rural organizations to exercise social control, and restrain them from 'aping the West', which only meant demanding change towards egalitarianism. The main thrust of the trio—Bal, Lal and Pal, of Annie Besant and later of Gandhi—was an unambiguous articulation outside the formal forums of Congress, in favour of maintaining tradition, and yet these were the men who were guiding the destiny of the nation through the leadership of the movement. The pervasive and persistent theme of their socio-cultural world-view is that of going back to tradition, which in the context meant social slavery for the lower caste masses.

Most of the critiques of the early Congress movement are limited to an examination of whether the movement stood strictly for itself or for the whole nation, and whether it articulated only class demands or integrated the mass demands as well. And they all rightly conclude that by and large the nationalist movement upto the War was merely the nationalization of sectional demands. However, this is only half

---

[29] B.B. Misra (1976) p 60 speaks of the dilemmas of the Congress as a movement and as a party.

the story. Such a view is based on the premise that upal the middle of the second decade of the twentieth century the only politicized group was that of the English educated urban population and the rest were inert, apolitical, and stood speechless and helpless, very much in need of someone from among the 'chosen ones' to represent them.[30] This view of colonial political awakening has already been repudiated in Chapter 2. Political awakening in colonial India was variegated and the nationalist form was one among the several competing ones. In this framework the question is not merely whether the dominant nationalist movement spoke *for* the other interests or not but whether its leaders spoke *with* the other leaders, including the latter to form a coalition of collaborated interests. In this lies the critical test of whether or not the nationalist movement and its leaders envisaged a different kind of political community—a polity of anonymous and equal citizenship rights—in other words, the nation. In this test, the first phase of the nationalist movement failed miserably. Instead of behaving as a national class, they consistently, without exception from beginning to end, demonstrated their sectarian character, and competed with other groups on that basis, yet claimed a monopoly on representing the whole nation.[31] They failed to proffer a welcoming hand to the new arrivals in the emerging political and civil society, using the 'national' concept to exclude rather than include. An inclusive category was being pressed into service precisely to exclude.

The result was understandable. The widening gulf between the two segments in political economy became an unbridgeable chasm in political articulation and trajectory. The microscopic minority of nationalists stood away from and almost in antagonism to the majority of masses—the nation. To the latter, the nationalists were but a group of upper caste men all united in economic and political interest, out to protect themselves against the changing circumstances and surging masses.[32]

[30] This is certainly one of those cases where 'the truisms of the Raj becomes the dogma for the historians', S. Sarkar (1983), p.66.

[31] Replying to the charge of microscopic minority R.C. Mitra had said, 'the educated community represented the brain and conscience of the country and were the legitimate spokesman of the illiterate masses, the national guardians of their interests', quoted in R.C. Maiumdar et. al (1978), p.883.

[32] How do we describe the group of communities that gave birth to nationalist articulation? Class—in the Marxist sense, is certainly not appropriate in view of the marginal differentiation that had taken place within the society; similarly 'bourgeoisie' too has more or less gone out of vogue. The loosely used term 'middle class' is of

Moderates and Extremists

The first thirty years of the Indian nationalist movement is usually divided into two phases—the first two decades known as the moderate phase and the third, as the extremist or the nationalist phase—with the whole of this stage coming to end in 1916-17 when the two groups came together to begin what is known as the Gandhian phase.

The differences between the Moderates and the Extremists were real and significant. For the former the British rule was providential; it brought immense good to the country, sunk as it was in anarchy and backwardness. It opened up the country to modernity and its benefits. It was thus necessary not to antagonize the rulers prematurely; the period of apprenticeship of the country under colonial rule was to last for a considerable period of time. All that could be aspired for was greater association with the rulers and a larger share in the administrative and political power till the day we were able to step into their shoes. The great leaders of this persuasion were the early Congressmen—Mehta, Banerjee, Ranade, Naoroji, Gokhale and others. For the Extremists on the other hand, colonial rule was satanic; it destroyed Indian culture and tradition, and brought humiliation and servitude to the Indian people. The sooner the country got rid of this evil, the better. To achieve this aim, one had to give up the policy of mendicancy and take to militant ways based on one's own religion and tradition. The nationalized religion and religionized nationalism was to be the rallying point to drive out the alien intruder. The well known names connected with this orientation were Tilak, Lala Lajpat Rai, B.C. Pal, Aurobindo and others.[33]

The story of the Congress during this period itself can be seen in the continuous rivalry and antagonism between these two groups, struggling to dominate and capture the organization with all the unsavoury details of manipulation that characterize the Indian political

---

limited value analytically. (Note M.G. Ranade interprets 'middle-class' to mean 'Brahmin-Bania Classes' in J.R. McLane 1977, p. 214.). The discussion centres around the term 'elite' with various qualifications, in all the new schools of historiography. Within the social sciences, the term 'caste-cluster' used by I. Karve (1961: pp. 9,10,19), perhaps comes nearest to reality and this is endorsed by R. Kumar (1971), p.14; for an unsatisfactory discussion on the issue see S.Sarkar (1983), pp.65-70.

[33] For a brief but pointed description of the Moderates and Extremists of the early phase of the nationalist movement see D. Argov (1966).

scene today. However, the differences between the two groups can in no sense be considered absolute. Inspite of all the squabbles among themselves, the Moderates and Extremists posed as a unity, in the face of any outsider group(s) (A. Seal 1968: 11). To begin with, the social origin, educational background and to some extent, property qualifications tended to be the same for members of both groups.[34] Their immediate political goals were the same, and they stood also similarly distanced from the masses though the Extremists made some effort, with extremely limited success, to mobilize the semi-rural masses in the name of religion.[35] Especially from the point of view of the masses one group did not have much to commend itself over the other. Both were concerned with the appropriation of power without having to share it with others, and they showed more willingness to settle for less power rather than expand the base of its appropriation. On this they differed in method.

The Moderates basically tended to accept the framework of the polity erected by the British with all its potentialities of democracy and power-equalization, rule of law and citizenship. In this sense, at least by implication, they saw a role for the lower orders of society even if only in the distant future. However, this largely notional democracy was effectively neutralized by their supplicatory demands for minimal power—only so much as could be absorbed by themselves. A louder and more militant cry for power might have alerted the sleeping masses whom they were mortally afraid of, and against whom they expected protection from the British themselves.[36]

The Extremists on the other hand, were more forthright and challenging; they sought to intimidate the British to open up the floodgates of power. Though their relationship with the masses was

[34] B.B. Misra (1976) has suggested the appellation of 'lower middle class' for the Extremists but found that they too behaved in much the same way as the middle class thereby leading one to conclude that the possible economic disparities between the two groups were only of limited relevance to their political behaviour pp.100, 101.

[35] At the height of the anti-partition agitation in Bengal too, this appears to be the case. B.C. Pal said on this occasion that the mobilization could be said to be of 'Nine paise in the rupee' B.B. Misra (1976) p 153. Tilak's atempts to politicize religious festivals in Maharastra too, did not strike much roots in rural mobilisation, see R.I. Cashman (1975), Chapter IV.

[36] A. Seal (1968) p 346; J.R. McLane (1977) pp 68–71; A. Maddison (1971) has called this "step-into-your-shoes nationalism" p-71.

as tenuous as that of the Moderates they sought to control the masses through their socio–cultural dominance with an emphasis on religion, culture and tradition.[37] For them Indian tradition served this double purpose—it was both a sword against the British in wresting power, and a shield against the masses who might want to share it. Whether they actually believed in re-establishing a polity different from that of the colonial era is not very clear. But what is clear is that at least for the masses and their own political purposes they had recourse to tradition.

The dilemma of the Moderates and Extremists has been eloquently put by B.B. Misra:

> It was difficult for the Indians to make a choice. The acceptance of the Western concept of social mobility constituted a real challenge to Brahminism and the exclusive concept of its caste order. Its rejection on the other hand involved the negation of British rule and a reversal of what that rule had achieved over a period of more than hundred years. The aim of revivalism was to restore Brahminism in a modified form by an exclusion of British rule and the influences that operated under it (1961: 377).

In other words, the problem was of achieving the transfer of power without necessarily having to homogenize or democratize it!

Social Versus Political

That the nationalist movement lead by the Indian National Congress was not the sole contending political force but had to contend with several others, in reference to which it had to take a stand, was well demonstrated by the biggest controversy that dominated the Congress in those years—social versus political reform. In the Congress dictionary, social reform represented the entire gamut of social changes thought to be minimally necessary firstly, by the Moderates to bring Hindu society into accord with the new political structure, and second-ly, it included the radical structural changes within the traditional Brahminical order, demanded by the changed times, and being pushed forward by the mass of lower castes in different ways.

Understood primarily in this sense, 'social' does not appear to

---

[37] J.R. McLane (1977) 73-80; B.B. Misra (1976) p 100.

be merely social or cultural, local or regional but truely political and national. Political issues concerning the interests of the masses affecting the monopoly of power within the Brahminical social order were categorized as 'social' and thus excluded from the nationalists' agenda, clearly indicating the latter's support of the status quo power structure. The men who stood for the 'social' among the nationalists themselves were so unsure that they gave in to the opposition rather too easily. This further removed the non-nationalists from the movement, giving them a confirmation of what they had suspected all along—the reactionary nature of the nationalist programme. The questions raised by the leaders of the Social Conference—Ranade, Chandavarkar, Bhandarkar and others—such as widow marriage, women's education, raising the age of consent, and some spillover educational reform among the lower castes were indeed the nationalists' version of a maximum programme of democratic enablement of the weaker sections of society.[38] The nature and extent of these 'social' reform programmes, although nowhere near the collective struggles to pull down Brahminical structures and alter power relations through the emergence of the lower caste masses as new citizens, did indicate the signs of times to come. These weak-kneed efforts continued inspite of the nationalist movement and died out later during the Gandhian era without making any dent in the overall thrust and direction of the movement.[39]

Effective exclusion of the 'social' was achieved step by step in several ways. At the outset, Dadabhoy Naoroji, much to everyone's relief, laid down that only the concerns of the whole nation could be the agenda of the National Congress and local and regional issues were not to bother this august assembly.[40] This policy of the strictly

---

[38] Many of them were acutely conscious of the basic contradictions involved in hierarchically segmented communities aspiring for modern nationhood; See C.H. Heimsath (1964) p 326; and Tagore (1918) pp 125-8; Sankar Ghose (1967) has a chapter specifically devoted to this issue. However, practically all these articulations remained at the level of pronouncements only and they hardly made any dent in the nature and direction of the nationalist movement. The reason was obvious; the position of these well meaning people within the movement itself was only marginal; but more important was the social cleavage that existed between these and the lower caste men who were struggling against the caste system. They could not come together even though their ideals at times coincided.

[39] For a critical reading of the social reform attempts within the nationalist tradition see S. Natarajan (1959).

[40] A. Seal (1968), p.295; J. Gordon (1973), p.35. J. Brown (1984), p.173, J.R. McLane (1977), p.111.

national effectively weeded out any possible discussion on issues that were cropping up in different regions in an uneven way. Thus the concerns of the smaller or weaker segments were not those of the nationalist movement. Not that the early Congressmen were too dull to imagine the possibility or the necessity of making national level policies with respect to these local and regional issues; but the fact is that this formal guide line was a device to keep away many a substantial or material issue. This was considered insufficient and a further decision was taken to the effect that no issue on which there was an absence of unanimity should be discussed, implying that national unity was to be conceived of and erected on the members present and voting; thus the fate of the unrepresented was to be of no concern to the movement. And finally, since 'social' questions tended to divide those present, it was ruled that only 'political' questions of national importance would be relevant. This was tantamount to saying that only questions relating to the transfer of power to the sole representatives, i.e. the Indian nationalist movement operating through the Congress, would be the one point agenda for all time. Questions relating to the relocations of power within society, the emancipation of lower castes, the removal of agrestic bondage etc., became 'social' questions and had to be firmly kept out of the movement.

If nationalism indeed was a double congruence of power and culture, externally and internally, the Indian nationalist movement during its first phase set itself clearly against any form of internal power relocation and pursued the narrow project of transfer of power from the British. Maintenance of status quo in internal power-relations was as important to them, if not more, as wresting power from the colonial rulers. However, these internal problems of the movement hardly caused any ripples among the wider masses who were pursuing their own autonomous project of preparing themselves, in a rather limited and uneven way, for participation in the new political community.

Pan-Indianism, Common Will and Future Vision

In view of the above analysis of the context, birth and growth of Indian nationalism during its first phase, the claims of pan-Indianism, commonality of goals and a future vision of society for the movement can be assessed. Much has been claimed for the new, centralized structure of politics, as being responsible for the birth of pan-Indianism as a sort of 'matching response' and so too for English education and other communicational developments, by both the imperialist as well as nationalist historiographers. However, it is better to consider all these and other such factors as contexts or occasions for at best providing a formal framework for the expression of pan-Indianism. The substance, in large part came from within the tradition itself. The unifying effect of Brahminism and Brahminic culture and religion, at least as an aspiration towards dominance in the subcontinent has already been noted, and the Brahmins, though differentiated into specifically rooted communities, are to be found throughout the country sharing some kind of common tradition and social dominance, making them in a sense national caste. The pan-Indianness of the dominant community is of ambiguous value to Indian nationalism for its very unifying principle is also the basis of social divisiveness and oppression. Even this ambivalent pan-Indianism did not emerge at once or smoothly. The subcontinent's society is not only a caste society but also one divided in terms of linguistic groups, each having some reference to territory. In such a context, nation could mean either one's own linguistic group and thus limited to a particular geographical area, or the pan-Indian nation that was thought to be in the making. This ambiguity too, was present in the thought of those who articulated nationalism during this phase. The areas where the major nationalist activities in the nineteenth and early twentieth centuries took place were Bengal and Maharashtra. For many of the leaders of both these regions, nation was an ambiguous concept referring both to their own linguistic area as well as to the pan-Indian nation. Since nationalism is about power, this ambiguity of the concept itself had adverse implications for the development of a genuine pan-Indianism.[41]

With regard to a common will in the context of the notions of nation and nationalism, it has been seen that political awakening itself was dichotomous, following the polarizing influence of colonial rule on the hierarchically ordered society. Towards the end of the period under consideration, the masses and the elite stood at cross purposes to each other. This polarity of political ideals and aspirations

---

[41] B. Chandra (1984) p 24 notes the 'presidency patriotism' of Bankim C. Chatterjee; this tradition continues within modern Indian historiography too, especially in the 'Bengali school of history wherein Bengali and Indian nationalism are substituted one for the other non-problematically; see P. Dixit (1976).

was well utilized by the rulers to perpetuate themselves. When the different segments of the hierarchical society were in the process of getting dichotomously politicized, according to their own perceived interests and ideals, to speak of a commonality of purpose against the alien culture was something more than dubious. Under such a situation the commonality of purpose could not be based on perceived economic and political interests; it could be based on religion and culture. But in Indian society religion and culture, at least in its dominant and Brahminic form, had a contradictory role to play during this stage of the movement. This leaves the door wide open for commonality of purpose to be based on racism. The British practised and maintained their dominance through racism and racially discriminatory practices, and the response of the Indians was to raise the slogan of objective contradiction with overtones of the same racism, removing the explanation of nationalism from the domain of history.

A vision for future India the early nationalists certainly had, especially of themselves as rulers in place of the British, which eventually became a reality. But what role did they see for the masses in this India of the future? Was it to be different from the one that the masses had played during the long course of pre-modern history? If it was to be different, what was the nature and extent of the difference? These are questions the answers for which are difficult to find within the explicit pronouncements and performances of the early nationalists.[42] Perhaps it is accurate to say that these questions were not of serious importance to them, pre-occupied as they were with their own concerns of expansion of their representation in the civil service and legislative apparatus.

[42] Some indications were there of course; See nos 24, 26 etc.; this was to emerge more clearly during the latter phase of the movement.

V

Nationalism: Competing Ideologies and Contrasting Visions

IDEOLOGY AND INDIAN HISTORIOGRAPHY

Karl Mannheim has pointed out that ideological representation can be considered either as 'false consciousness', 'a deception', and a 'conscious lie', or as the 'outlook inevitably associated with a given historical and social situation and the Weltanschauung and style of thought bound up with it'; and that in concrete situations, these two apparently polar aspects most often tend to 'coalesce' (K. Mannheim 1979: pp. 49ff.). In the context of Indian historiography this differential conception of ideology has provided the basic value-reference for divergent interpretations of the nationalist movement and thought. At one end of the spectrum, we have the nationalists for whom the ideology of nationalism was a great unifying force, an accurate reflection of the objective condition and contradiction—colonial exploitation—that was central to the corporate life of society at large. It was the Weltanschauung at first, of the emerging middle classes, but soon spread to the entire mass of people, welding them towards a corporate will to be a nation.[1] At the other end of the spectrum, however, we have the Cambridge scholars for whom the same nationalist ideology (indeed any ideology) was merely a convenient label to hide what was essentially an unprincipled pursuit of economic and political advantage on the part of the different

---

[1] The most articulate exponent of this point of view is Prof. Bipin Chandra. See particularly (1987).

elite groups, in competition with each other, always in response to and essentially determined by the imperial initiatives. The anti-imperialist nationalism was a 'deception' and 'a conscious lie' as borne out by the middle classes' collaboration, and even collusion, with the colonial state at different levels.[2] These two polar positions based on exclusive conceptions of ideology are themselves obviously ideological and have been found too simplistic in either direction by most scholars.[3] The several intermediary positions apply, in various combinations of both the partial as well as the total conceptions of ideology, to Indian nationalism, and describe it as bourgeois, elite, and communal. As an expression and rationalization of the interests and aspirations of the bourgeoisie, the elite or of the majority religious community, nationalism of the subcontinent, was certainly a false representation in this view. However in its basically anti-imperialist character, it was a true reflection of the objective contradiction between the society as a whole and imperialism. Thus taken together, though imperfect, limited, ambiguous or derivative, Indian nationalism, at least in its later stages, was indeed genuinely national.[4]

Historiography has hitherto highlighted the differences between these various readings of the nationalist ideology and also claimed that these represent the multiple and contesting power positions within society.[5] But for our purpose, it is pertinent to unravel the basic similarities and value assumptions that underlie these polar as well as inter-polar ideological positions. Despite real and serious differences especially between the nationalist and Cambridge scholars, all these historiographical constructions are erected and maintained on certain formal premises, essentialized categories, and conceptual monoliths. The millenia-old dominance of the upper castes in the pre-modern era, their politically successful articulation of the nationalist ideology during

---

[2] While 'Cambridge Scholars' is certainly no monolith, devaluation of ideology as a motor force in history is characteristic of all of them; for a strident formulation of this point of view see D. Washbrook, particularly his earlier writings (1976) and with C.J. Baker (1976).

[3] Nationalist extremism has been met time and again by the Marxist, Subaltern and Cambridge historians; for a criticism of the latter, see R.E. Frykenberg (1978), T. Raychaudhuri (1973), H. Spodak (1979) and other reviews; within the country, see M.S.S. Pandian (1995). Washbrook himself appears to have shifted from his earlier position in his later writings; see for example his (1982).

[4] See A.R. Desai (1948) and recently S. Sarkar (1983).

[5] J. Chaturvedi (1990) would be one such attempt.

the colonial period, their subsequent near-monopolistic assumption of power within both the civil and political societies to the exclusion of the mass of lower castes, Muslims and tribals in independent India, have helped in the historiographical construction, sociological elaboration and political maintenance of a complex nationalist mythical lore, as a master-narrative, of the nation's becoming. Such a lore woven around the now worn out categories of communalism, nationalism and imperialism informs, of course in a differential manner, the different historiographical schools.[6] Parallel to the lines of contestation among themselves in interpreting the details of history, there also runs a not too thin line of consensus on the basics of nationalist ideology in the Indian context. This agreed-upon nationalist myth has hitherto successfully managed to project the formation of a somewhat homogenized, quasi-class from among the scattered, traditionally dominant communities, as the emergence of the nation. In other words, the application of the Mannheimian distinction between the conscious lie and weltanschauung of the age by modern Indian historiographies is somewhat superficial. Underlying such a distinction is a vast area of non-distinction or consensus that is definitely related to the identity of the societal power-position they speak from, *vis à vis* the culturally scattered and presumably inarticulate masses.

The nationalist mythical core that underlies all schools of hitherto elaborated historiographies can be deconstructed into a set of propositions, concerning political awakening in general and nationalism in particular, as follows: Political awakening in the subcontinent was a late phenomenon of the fourth quarter of the nineteenth century. Until the Gandhian phase, political activity was limited to the elites of various description and the masses in general were apathetic and even dormant. Politics itself meant only that articulation and activity which was addressed to, preferably against, the colonial state. Nationalism, in both form and substance, came from the West and was expressed through the sole channel of the middle classes. Outside

---

[6] The Subaltern historiographers, to the extent that they have pointed out the existence of other voices, divergent in trajectory from that of the elite leadership, and have recognized the non-emergence of the nation, indeed represent a breakthrough. But beyond this, they too share with the rest all the other major propositions enumerated below; working within an extremely narrow data-base, worn-out conceptions of nation and nationalism (as anti-Britishism) and refusing to recognize the culture-specific power configuration within society. They have largely failed to interpret the subaltern voices in the field.

of these groups, there was no nationalism. Nationalism in colonial countries is considered to be a special category and in the context of the subcontinent is to be understood only as pan-Indianism and anti–imperialism. Sections other than the middle classes, i.e. the lower castes, Muslim masses and tribals, came to participate in public life at the instance of the divide and rule policy of the British. The somewhat unauthorized and autonomous assertions of these other sections, being neither pan-Indian nor anti-imperialist in form, were not national but its polar opposite—communal whether religious, casteist, ethnic, linguistic or whatever. Imperialism, embodying a well-rounded value system, was another polar opposite of nationalism and hence, of those who chose to call themselves nationalists. The nationalists, the sole articulators of nationalist ideology in the subcontinent, stood equidistant from communalism and imperialism; that any challenge to the nationalism of the middle classes was inspired either by communal or imperialist ideas (the latter being Eurocentric). The Gandhian genius and subsequent political mobilization eventually neutralized all but one form of communalism, brought the masses under the true nationalist hegemony and defeated imperialism. This is the myth at the core of Indian nationalism. This way of representing political awakening and nationalism common to all forms of historiography, if not perceivable as a 'conscious lie', was certainly not the weltanschauung of the age, and this sameness of perspective is related to the identity of the social position they all speak from.

The application in the earlier chapters, of the recent developments in the sociology of nation and nationalism, as elaborated in our theoretical paradigm of double congruence between culture and power, lead us through the historical landscape, to areas not usually recognized as the national. Even a cursory survey revealed that the masses were in no way apathetic or dormant and there was in fact a restlessness all over the subcontinent. It also revealed the fact that political consciousness arose much earlier, was more widespread, and political activities manifested themselves in multiple and contesting ways. Nationalism itself was neither a monolith nor was nationalist ideology the monopoly of the dominant communities.

Outright denial of all these and other facts or de-legitimization of them by branding them casteist, communalist, regionalist etc., is crucial for the elite articulations of nationalism in the subcontinent to be considered the 'Weltanschauung of the age'. To understand however, the real import of the elite nationalist ideology, it is vital to contextualize it within the realm of plural and conflicting political awakenings and articulations in colonial India. The weltanschauung of the age might then appear as more the weltanschauung of an inchoate, emerging coalition of ruling groups, and certainly not that of a nation.

This chapter is therefore intended to analyse and delineate the multiple and contending ways in which nationalist ideology was articulated and the nation imagined.

NATIONALISM AS AN IDEOLOGY

Theorizing on nation, nationality and nationalism in general has proceeded rather exclusively along either the subjective or the objective factors that constitute such phenomena. Nations are presumed to have certain objective characteristics such as language, race, religion, territory or history which either singly or in combination distinguish them from other nations. Protection and promotion of these, in competition and conflict with other nations, then becomes nationalism. Alternatively, nations are considered as collectivities built on the subjective consciousness of identity of kind, commonality of interests, and a will to be a nation. Here political assertion and actualization of such a consciousness or will becomes nationalism. On the basis of such divergent theoretical orientations, nationalisms have been classified as cultural or political respectively. Most scholars see Western nationalisms as political and the Eastern ones as cultural. The alternate classification of the nineteenth century nationalisms as political and the twentieth century ones as cultural, alters the above geographical, dichotomy only marginally. Outright moral evaluation of nationalisms is also noticeable; Western nationalisms are considered genuine, progressive and secular while those of the East, are imitative, conservative and primordial. This is so because, we are told, nationalism is a doctrine invented in the West and subsequently transported to the rest. The terms East and West, originally applied to intra-Europe differences were later transferred to the halves of the globe.[7]

Taking a cue from Gellner, however, our own approach has been to describe the nationalist phenomena as the double congruence between culture and power—a combination of both the streams of

---

[7] See the earlier references to nationalism in chapter I, particularly those of H.Kohn (1965), K.R. Minogue (1969), and L.L. Snyder (1954).

theorizing—the process of homogenization of power within culture as the transition to nation, the transference of power from without, i.e., the assertion of distinction and the demand for self-determination—as the nationalist movement and the congruence between the two processes as nationalism (see chapter I). Such a theoretical elaboration assumes variability of both actualization and occurrence of contestation at every level of nationalism in concrete historical circumstances. Nationalism as a form and manifestation of modern politics is about groups in conflict for power—social, political, and economic—and as an ideology it is always articulated in the context of multiple ideologies (G. Therbon 1980: pp. 41ff.). Excluding therefore, those that stand explicitly for non-congruence of culture and power, all ideologies indeed have nationalistic implications or dimensions variably expressed, whether or not they label themselves as such. What we are suggesting is that nationalism as a modern ideology can never be a monolith within particular cultures; instead, it is always pluralistic and contestingly articulated. Nationalist political awakening, i.e., political awakening that aspires to a new culture-power congruence, is basically a contestation among social and economic groups as to how the congruence is to take place. While the contestation between forces opposing and those supporting congruence under colonial circumstances tends to be exaggerated, the primary contest however remains within culture in the realm of how the nation is to be constituted. The external struggle, its form, duration, nature, and intensity are not unrelated to the basic internal struggle. In this sense, it is poor theorizing, firstly, to club together pre-modern quasi-national movements with modern nationalism and describe all of them as manifestations of primordialism; and secondly, to describe in monolith fashion modern nationalisms of particular geographic regions, or epochs of history, as either cultural or political. It is also inaccurate to set up an entirely new category called colonial nationalism as a sub-monolith outside the general theoretical framework. The variable and contesting nature of modern nationalist ideologies had been pointed out by Carlton Hayes, who found that the so-called political nationalisms of the West, from a different perspective and at certain phases, presented themselves as cultural, and that cultural-national chauvinisms are certainly related to their own internal struggle for power-distribution.[8]

---

[8] C. Hayes (1931) notes the simultaneity of waning of liberalism with the waxing

'Nationalism is a doctrine invented in the West' asserted Khaddourie. Scholars before and after him have taken this for granted, and within the subcontinent too, this is being repeated ad nauseam, both in and out of context. What however this scholarly insight of apparent consensus ignores is the crucial distinction between form and substance in nationalism. If by nationalism is meant the style of thought, its terminology, its formulation including the historically specific form of the nation-state with all its formal paraphernalia, then it was developed in the West. If however nationalism means the coming together of culture and power, a kind of social and societal change in which ascription is challenged and the social power balance in general is tilted towards the hitherto excluded masses within culture, and also an aspiration of cultures for recognition and self-determination then nationalism is neither an invention of the West nor its monopoly domain. Complex agrarian cultures everywhere, to a greater or lesser degree, within their own space and time specificities have expressed both these tendencies of cultural assertion and power homogenization in several spheres of formal life. The emergence, for example of cultural wholes—speech communities—containing the whole range of social classes, is an accommodation of the egalitarian aspiration of the labouring masses as well as an assertion of collective identity. The substantial issues of contestation in the context of modern nationalisms in all societies are therefore internal to their own specific form of development. These are to be traced to their individual histories, in order to grasp what finally determined the nature and outcome of the nationalist struggles as well as to predict their future course. The form and the idiom were certainly borrowed, but primarily to express and resolve the historical dialectic of each society. The determinative power of the imported ideological forms and styles however, is not to be overrated particularly when the culture concerned has a long and continuous history. Viewed from these somewhat tentative theoretical perspectives, the nationalist articulations of colonial India appear to have the following characteristics: One, a rather low level of articulation throughout the entire period under discussion; it is noteworthy that not a single ideologue of stature, not to speak of consensus, emerged in India. Instead, ideology was articulated piecemeal, often shifting positions over time, thus creating enormous

of nationalism, p. 163 ff.

scope for multiple and even contradictory interpretations later. Two, nationalist ideas and forms were appropriated and articulated here, not in imitation but primarily to express local concerns which were in continuity with the history of the subcontinent. Several studies have highlighted the fact that the Indian freedom movement drew its inspiration from one or another of the European revolutions—the French, the American, the English, the Italian, the German, the Irish, the Turkish and the Russian, as well as, from the Fascist and Nazi ideologies. However, the Indian movement cannot be understood in terms of any one or more of these; ideas were certainly borrowed but they were modified and transformed to express substantial issues peculiar to the subcontinent. It is the historical development and the modern historical context that would provide a meaningful explanation of Indian nationalism, not the ideas that are presumed to have come from the West.[9] Three, following in a broad sense the long historical dialectics of the pre-modern era, the polarization process during the colonial period that tended to aggravate pre-existing social cleavages and the subsequent pluralist political awakening, it could be said that nationalist ideology in the subcontinent was articulated initially trichotomously and eventually settled down to a contentious dichotomy. The forms of nationalism described below are distinguished on the basis of the predominance of particular aspects of nationalism rather than exclusive characters. The trichotomy comprised the political nationalism of the lower caste masses, the ethnic and linguistic nationalism of the tribals and regional culture-groups, and finally the cultural nationalism of an emerging pan-Indian upper caste/class elite (C. Heimsath 1964: pp. 132ff.).

While it was freely accepted that India was composed of several nations and nationalities in the rather general sense of culture-groups, castes, communities, tribes and linguistic groups, neither the British nor the emerging pan-Indian elite was willing to see the subcontinent as consisting of distinct, identifiable and territorially contiguous ethnic and linguistic nations such as in Europe, for example. For the British, an admission of similarity with Europe would mean granting of equality to the East as the other. Their actions—piecemeal conquest, the organization of large port-centered presidencies and the erection

---

[9] See F. Giueseppe (1993), P. Heehs (1984), K. Kaushik (1984), M. Sadig (1983) and H. Brasted (1980). S.N. Banerjee (1925) described the situation accurately enough: 'I lectured upon Mazzini but took care to tell the young men to abjure his revolutionary ideas', p. 40.

of uniform administration—contributed much to the denial and disruption of the orderly, though unevenly developing ethnic diversity. This imperial perception and practice suited the emerging dominant-Sanskritic elite group too, as they dreamed of transforming themselves into the pan-Indian successor to the British. Within these multilevel constraints ethnic and linguistic ideology could express itself only marginally and indirectly. The tribal groups, wherever territorially contiguous, did articulate such an ideology. However, these articulations were in general late in being heard, and marginal to the overall socio-political dynamic of the subcontinent. The port-presidencies of Bengal, Bombay, and Madras too were not free of ethnic and linguistic nationalisms; the ascendancy of the Tamil Brahmin groups in Madras created ethnic nationalist reverberations among the Malayalis, Kannadigas and the Telugus. In Bombay and Bengal many of the so-called pan-Indian ideologies could be better understood as Maharashtrian and Bengali national aspirations and these too generated reactions in the Gujarati, Oriya, Bihari, and Assamese areas.[10] However these forms of political awakening and national articulation could not, during the colonial period, spread or sustain themselves in the face of the overarching political discourse of the imperialist–nationalist continuum which was pan-Indian in both structure and ideology. In other words, the overwhelming and pan-Indian horizontal cleavage that developed as a result of colonialism, an interactive process first of both collaboration and then of confrontation between two sets of elite, largely and at least for the time being, overshadowed the historical agenda of diverse ethnic groups and left the field open for the two main contestants—the political and cultural nationalisms both articulated at the pan-Indian level.

Cultural Nationalism

The articulation of cultural nationalism revolves around first, the beliefs concerning the distinctness, integrity, uniqueness and superiority of one's culture and second, the claim that such a culture is the proper and legitimate repository of collective and determinative power. The culture is named and identified, its contours delineated and

---

[10] For the rise of ethnic and regional consciousness in different areas, see S. Chandra (1982a) and (1992), M.J. Koshy (1972), N.K. Arooran (1980), S. Banerjee (1992), C. Heimsath (1964), ch. VI etc.

lineage traced, its rise and fall in history noted and potential threats to it identified. Then this sanctified culture, with its internal power-configuration, is projected as the normative model for the present and future nation. Finally, the demand is raised that collective power congrue with this 'national' culture. Cultural-nationalist articulation is thus a process that sets forth the nation as an ideological-cultural construct. The complex process of selection, rejection, modification and codification of a normative national culture from amorphous pre-modern traditions does not take place in a vacuum. Nations and nationalisms, not only as forms of transition from one kind of society to another, but also as ideological-cultural constructs, need to be situated within one and the same socio-historical context and understood both as a continuity and a break in history. In other words, the nation as an imagined community or as a nationalist invention cannot be detached from politico-economic transitions and understood solely in terms of either modernity or pre-modernity.

Beliefs concerning what the nation is or ought to be, in terms of either culture or power, in the subcontinent began to be pieced together during the early colonial period. Apart from the politico-economic or structural context delineated in the earlier chapters, certain aspects of the ideological context for the articulations of nationalism need to be pointed out here. The first is the set of beliefs and articulations of the British concerning the subcontinent's society and culture. The numerous ways in which 'they' represented India provided the ideological environ within which the nationalist self-perception took shape. The second is the set of beliefs and articulations again of the British, concerning their own national society and culture, i.e., the ideal nation; the number of ideological premises, often implicit, that underlay the new juridico-administrative infrastructure also provided the environ within which the self-perception of the nation took shape. These two sets of beliefs held by the colonial bureaucracy are advisedly characterized as the context or environ, and not the determinants of nationalist ideology.[11] For as we have repeatedly pointed out, it is the substantial issues internal to the subcontinent's history that ultimately determined the social

---

[11] Nation as a cultural construct needs to be contextualized within the nation as socio-political change. Therefore R. Inden's orientalist thesis (1986, 1990) would be incomplete if not seen in the context of actual re-hierarchicalization of society during the colonial period and if orientalism itself is not recognized as a collaborated venture of two power groups.

power-configuration within the nation, albeit in the modern ideological idiom and structural context.

The process of piecing together the cultural nation began during the last quarter of the eighteenth century with the orientalist project in Bengal. It spread subsequently among the emerging middle classes in all the important regions, the process continuing till the end of the colonial period. The historical cultural discoveries of the early orientalists, working in and around Fort William, Calcutta, regarding the Aryan myth, the Sanskrit language, and the sacred texts, laid the foundation for all subsequent cultural, nationalist articulations in the subcontinent. While the precise formulation of the ideology is to be traced to Orientalism, the project itself needs to be understood as a process and product of a collaboration and coincidence between two sets of sources—imperialist and native.[12] Evidence is not lacking to show that cultural pride in the subcontinent pre-dated colonialism and it occurred simultaneously in several regions as a reflection of the social power-position of the articulating groups.[13] Cultural nationalism here, then, is both a break with, as well as a continuity in history. The first significant aspect of this cultural, nationalist ideology was this: ever since the late eighteenth century the cultural core of the nation-to-be, though variously named as the Aryan, Indo-Aryan, Sanskritic, Sanatan, caste-Hindu, Hindu or even Indian, came to be identified with the Sanskritic, textual traditions of Vedic, Brahminism. Civilization itself was supposed to have dawned on this subcontinent with the advent of the Indo-Aryans who were a branch of the master Nordic races of the Northern hemisphere. The two branches of the Aryan stock were non-problematically identified with the present day Brahminic upper castes and the British rulers. Sanskrit, the sister language of Greek, through the Dharmic texts is presumed to have preserved the cultural heritage of the nation and to be the root of all subsequent vernaculars, in terms of both language and culture. The cultural-spiritual soul of the nation

---

[12] See R. Schwab (1984); L. Paliakov (1974); P.J. Marshall (ed.) (1970); J. Leopold (1970); R. Thapar (1975); C. Jeffrelot (1995) and D. Kopf (1969). Vivekananda went to the extent of seriously considering Max Muller as a reincarnation of Sankaracharya himself: 'My impression is that it is Sayana who is born again as Max Muller to revive his own commentary on the Vedas. I have had this notion for long. It became confirmed in my mind, it seems after I had seen Max Muller'. Vivekananda (1965) Vol VI p 495.

[13] See for example Sachau, E.C. (ed) (1914) *Alberuni's India* pp. 22 ff.

to be born was thus identified and baptized. **The second** aspect
was that the territorial spread of this cultural core was supposed
to be co-extensive with the subcontinent itself, though again differentially named the Aryavart, Bharatvarsh, Hindustan, British Empire, colonial state or even India. Vedic Brahminism, through
religio-cultural symbolism and a consensus value system, was supposed
to have given unity and integrity although in an uneven manner
to the entire spread of the subcontinent. The apparent contradiction
between cultural minimalism—Vedic Brahminism—as the nation and
the territorial maximalism—pan-Indian spread—as the state was sought
to be resolved through the mediation of the popular yet nebulous
concept of Hindu/Hinduism/Hindustan. Through this conceptual
spectrum, understood either in religio-cultural or in territorial terms,
Vedic Brahminism as an ideology re-engulfed the subcontinent now
transformed into the colonial state, thus creating a pan-Indian religio-
cultural nationalism on the models of pre-modern Islam and Christianity. The third aspect was that the values and principles of the
social organization of this cultural nation were to be derived and
defined through a presumed polar opposition to those of the West,
Europe, and British imperialism or simply modernity. If the West
was materialist, we were spiritual, if individualist, then we were
corporate, if competitive and conflictual then our culture was organic
and harmonious. And finally, perhaps the most decisive presumption
was that, if western society was based on uniform rights for individuals,
then Eastern society was organized around differential duties for
naturally ordained, stratified groups. Indeed this hierarchical Varna-
based ordering of groups with presumed natural tendencies and aptitudes was hailed as the great national-social synthesis effected by
the so-called Aryan genius that contained the core of the continuity
from the past, through the present, to the future of the cultural
nation. This national-proper, conceptualized differentially as societal
synthesis, social economy, Hindu genius, national legacy etc. was
not only considered the appropriate foundation to build the nation
on, but also the great Indian message to the strife-ridden modern
world. The ideology then called upon the nation to recognize its
uniqueness in these (above) terms, to feel collective, cultural pride
in its heritage, and to unite and oppose everything that threatened
its continuance, regeneration and reassertion in modern times.

   These three dimensions of cultural nationalist ideology; Vedic
Brahminism as the cultural core, a pan-Indian territorial extent, and

an antagonistic polarity with the West/modernity—became the sacred tenets of the new civil religion and informed all further elaborations and controversies. Together they formed a single perspective for the middle class, nationalist movement to view the past, present, and future of the nation in the making. They were also used as a touchstone to test the national-ness or otherwise of persons, movements and ideologies, and they determined the boundary line of exclusion from, and inclusion within, the sacred precincts of the nation that was seen, in Anderson's words, 'to be arising from its hoary past to loom large over the present and to extend into the future'.

Apart from the collaborative nature of the process, particularly the deep commitment and contribution of imperialist and orientalist scholarship, through which cultural nationalism in the subcontinent was constructed, what strikes one is the rapid and steady emergence of consensus approaching unanimity concerning the cultural nation, among the linguistically and regionally scattered, dominant upper castes, who were turning into a pan-Indian middle class. The history of this consensus did have stages, was not always linear and was even contested at times. Initially, controversy raged between the orthodox and the heterodox sections around socio-religious issues. The debate then became political and bifurcated between the Moderates and the Extremists; parallel to these was the disagreement over the precedence of political over social reform or vice-versa. If Bengal's approach to these problems was in general romantic and ideological, Bombay's was pragmatic and action-oriented. At the turn of the century however, as the nationalist movement surged ahead particularly in Bengal, reformism gave way to revivalism which was appropriately re-christened and seen as 'reform along national lines'. Discontentment, however, over the insufficiency of national reform and/or the excessively partisan way in which the cultural nation was defined, did surface time and again within the movement itself. Surely a repeat performance of the past, pure and simple, was not the agenda. The inchoate groups, through their differential formulations of tradition, did stand for some sort of reform and were anxious to absorb what they perceived to be the strong aspects of Western culture, and to that extent were willing to adjust their own culture. Having said this, however, it must be pointed out that the entire range of issues, controversies and debates within the emerging groups was largely peripheral to wider society, particularly in the concrete historical context, which was overcast with much more radical disputation.

Reform or change in the colonial context was looked upon by the native dominant groups either offensively or defensively as moves initiated and abetted by the foreign rulers and not as a demand of the historical dynamics of the subcontinent itself. A progressive stance *vis-à-vis* specific issues was only too easily maintained within a perfectly conservative frame of mind and often enough this vanished quickly when put to the test or was forced to extend to other issues. Taking sides on such issues did not lead to the development of a consistent and distinct attitudinal or ideological viewpoint on overall social and societal relations. The realm of reform and thus controversy, lay well outside the cultural nation in which consensus reigned supreme, and therefore there was no compact imaginable with those who challenged the cultural nation itself in the name of reform. Under such circumstances, it was not the differences, debates, controversies or rivalries among the middle classes but the underlying consensus, explicit or implicit concerning the basic premises of the cultural nation, that came to play a crucially determinative role in the realm of politics and ideology. The silent as well as not-so-silent consensus among the middle classes concerning the three dimensions of the cultural-nationalist ideology as the ideological minimum, and its socio-political implications, permeated the whole range of their modern intellectual activities laying the foundation for the emergence of a civil society specific to the subcontinent. Whether it was the early period in which ideological articulation was the exclusive privilege of the educated of the presidential towns, or the period of transition, when attempts were made with limited success to rope in the rural elite, or the later period in which mass activity finally emerged under Gandhian leadership; at no point of time was the cultural minimum of the nation-to-be challenged from within the movement itself. Across regions too, the same consensus came to mark the political awakening of the upper castes in Bengal, Bombay, Madras and subsequently other areas. This similarity across regions needs to be explained not only in terms of the overpowering imperialist tutelage, but also as a reflection of the identity of the power position these groups occupied within society. Whether it was the progressive Raja Ram Mohan Roy, or the conservative Deb Kant, the moderate Justice Ranade or the extremist Tilak, the fractious groups of the Acharyas or the Ayengars of the south; whether the new civil religion was seen as distinct from the traditional one as by Naoroji and Mehta or as identical as by Aurobindo and Vivekananda; whether Hindu culture was interpreted in a geographical sense as by Savarkar or in a religo-cultural sense as by Gandhi; and whether the ideologies operated formally from within the Indian National Congress as a political body or chose to have their own distinct and at times even antagonistic political platforms such as a liberal party, socialist party or communist party, or socio-cultural forums such as Hindu Mahà Sabha etc, these differences did not affect the essential understanding shared by them all. They all understood what was at stake, what needed to be strengthened and what ought to be fought against.[14]

Articulations concerning the cultural nation-to-be were not limited to those within the narrow realm of formal politics, but extended to all in the different areas of public life that eventually came to constitute civil society in the subcontinent; this included journalistic proliferations, literary imaginations and academic paradigms. While not many critical studies have been forthcoming on journalism during the colonial period, sufficient evidence can be gleaned from the available research to establish that powerful newspapers and journals such as *Tribune, Bengalee, Indian Mirror, Calcutta Review, Bengal Magazine, Hindu Excelsior Magazine, The Arya, National Magazine, The Theosophist, Young India, Harijan, Kesari, Sudharak, Vande Mataram, Hindu, Patriot, Bengal Hurkaru, Jugantar, Amrita Bazar Patrika, The Hindu* etc. played a crucial role in the definition and description of the cultural nation. The impact of these newspapers was generally uneven; some of them explicitly identified themselves with particular groups within the Indian National Congress, others were outside of it but aligned with the nationalist movement in general. Yet others made efforts to clearly stand apart from the political movement as such and give a non-partisan and professional approach to contemporary issues. While the circulation figures of these journals, even taken together, might not have amounted to much in terms

[14] Such a minimum denominator underlies all the writings of the cultural nationalists of the colonial period: Raja Ram Mohan Roy, Bankim C. Chatterjee, R.C. Dutt, Pal, Vivekananda, Aurobindo, Tilak, Lala, Ranade, Motilal Nehru and later Gandhi, and a host of lesser writers. See their writings listed in the bibliography. Gokhale also appears not to be free of this, see S. Chandra (1992) pp. 126. Some like S.N. Banerjee started out differently, yet soon ended up acquiescing with the rest, see his (1925) pp. 367 ff; also G. Omvedt (1976), p 113.

of absolute numbers, they did reach out to a pan-Indian readership among the educated.[15]

The content of these mass cultural organs could be simply described as colonial controversies of all kinds that affected the larger society: reform of religion, culture and tradition, state policy—what they are, should, and should not be, societal contours and construction, actual and ideal; threats to culture and tradition both from within and without etc. Controversies grew around every single socio-cultural issue often instanced by the colonial state; sides were taken and changed, alliances made and broken by individuals and groups, charges were traded and labels stamped on rivals and opponents. However, these contending cultural literary groups, working in and through the various controversies and negotiating continually for an advantageous stance *vis-à-vis* the colonial state through the pages of nearly a century old subcontinental journalism, consciously and/or unconsciously helped construct a consensus among themselves with regard to the site of contestation along with a code of conduct for the same. The overarching moral and ethical tone in which the proponents and opponents argued the issues brought them together towards an accepted ideal of the future cultural nation. Though identified and projected as Hindu, Hinduism and Hindustan, such an ideal was in fact an eclectic construction of Vedic Brahminism in its polar opposition to the West/modernity, was recognized, and was accepted not only by the wrangling groups but also by those contemporaries articulating from outside the movement. Textual Vedic sanction was sought by all the groups either for acceptance or rejection, or for modification of custom or tradition. The Vedic Varna ideal, as the representative of a harmonious society structured on the basis of differential duties as religious dharma, against the 'promiscuous', egalitarian rights of the secularized West, was the consensual aspiration of these groups. Vedic–Sanskritism came to be looked upon as the sacred cultural legacy of the subcontinent paralleling the role of Islamic or Christian traditions elsewhere in the world.

A similar process of consensus and construction around the cultural nation could be identified among the pioneering literati of the colonial period. The role of novelists and those generating other narratives

---

[15] For general information on journalism during the colonial period, see R. Parthasarathy (1989), and S. Natarajan (1962), and for critical information B.T. Mc Cully (1966), S. R. Mehrotra (1971), and S. Chandra (1986, 1986a, 1992).

in imaginative constructions of the national community is being increasingly recognized in social science literature concerning nationalism, thanks largely to Ben Anderson's path breaking book. The subcontinent too has had its share of cultural imaginations of the national community in several of its languages, beginning with the second half of the nineteenth century when prose narrative came into vogue, often imitating that of the western languages. Linguistic and literary renaissance in the subcontinent, like everything else here, has been uneven and took, at least initially, multiple directions. The representations in different languages had a differential determinative impact on the thought and behaviour pattern of society at large. However, underlying this amazing variety and unevenness, it is possible to discover substantial consensus on the ideal, at least among the more influential writers in the major Indian languages. Beginning with Bankim Chandra Chatterjee and later R.C. Dutt in Bengal, including the pioneers of Hindi fiction—Pratap Narain Misra, Harish-chandra Govardhanram, Balkrishna Bhatt, Radhacharan, Kishorilal, Devakinandan Khatri, Gangaprasad Gupta, Durgaprasad, Premchand, Maharashtrians like Harinarain Apte, as well as the Brahmin Tamil novelist Subramaniam and others, the writers of the times either created an imaginary world of consonance with Vedic Dharma or critiqued an actual world of dissonance from it in their work. Their 'voyages of nostalgia' into space and time, with a sense of historic and ethical destiny, invariably tended to strike home where dominant dharma or the traditional social values would be approved and upheld. In their view, the cultural-nationalist ideology comprised mainstream traditional values. Some of them did not grasp the full implications of such a conception, while others were perturbed by it. Yet others were at times severely critical of the nationalist movement which, through its praxis, was carrying forward the sectarian, cultural ideology to its logical conclusion. But with challenges mounting from both within and without, they implicitly or explicitly closed ranks and this helped reinforce the same cultural nationalist ideology.[16]

The cultural-nationalist ideology of the political movement was the dominant and determining inspiration behind the birth and development of modern historiographical and social science paradigms

[16] The basic reading for the cultural imaginings of the narrativists are M. Mukherjee (1994), S. Chandra (1982, 1982a, 1986, 1986a and 1992), S.R. Bald (1982), G. Pandey (1984), and T. Sarkar (1987, 1994). The felicitous phrase 'voyages of nostalgia' is borrowed from M. Mukherjee (1994) p. 63.

in the subcontinent. The three dimensions of cultural nationalism, Vedic Brahminism, a pan-Indian territory and an antagonism to modernity became the basic value orientations upon which the objectivity of modern Indian social science was sought to be established in both its theoretical and empirical aspects. Sanskritic Vedic texts were the source and foundation for a disciplinary diversification. The texts were treated as the main source of information and knowledge in an understanding of how the subcontinent's society was/is constituted, and thus how it ought to be constituted in the future. The unity of the subcontinent was sought to be demonstrated in several ways ranging from the implicit and non-problematic acceptance of it, to the explicit partisan construction of it, using Sanskritic texts. The unity—geographical, political and religio-cultural—of the subcontinent, woven around the symbols, myths and values of the sacred texts, was supposed to have existed both objectively and subjectively from time immemorial, though in the face of contemporary divisions and conflicts it was conceded that the nation was in the making. This primordial unity now took the shape of a supreme and overarching value framework for studies and investigations.

The multiple religio-cultural traditions of the subcontinent were now seen as part of a single coherent religion—Hinduism—which was emerging with all the regular trappings of organized religions such as Islam and Christianity. The intellegentsia, both within and without the political movement, repeatedly felt compelled to define the Hindu person and the content of Hinduism. Their definition invariably revolved around Vedic Brahminic ideals, icons and codes of behaviour as represented in the Dharma Shastras. The culture of the subcontinent was defined and described as Hindu culture and Hindu civilization, and in explicitly political contexts, as Indian culture and civilization.[17]

[17] In place of nation and nationalism, the single most important theme for discussion during the colonial period by the cultural nationalists was Hindu and Hinduism. Practically every one of them was constrained to raise the question, who is a Hindu, and what is Hinduism, and to answer the same in terms of acceptance of the Vedas and other Dharmashastras and the ideals presumed to inform them, most importantly of differential duties to people with differential tendencies, meaning, of course, some form of Varna ideology. By repeatedly defining, describing and debating this twin question, the cultural nationalists indeed created the modern political Hindu and Hinduism and thought these to be the indigenous equivalents for nation and nationalism. See the writings of cultural nationalists listed in the bibliography. Parallel to Hindu and Hinduism, was also constructed 'Hindi' again through a series of exclusions, see K. Kumar (1991, 1993) and M. Mukherjee (1994) pp. 60-61.

A value system, different from that of Great Britain, Europe or the West, was supposed to be embodied in this newly constructed Vedic Hindu–Indian culture, and much effort was mobilized in delineating and elaborating it in the different intellectual spheres—art, architecture, society, culture, philosophy, religion, and the sciences. Such a painstaking construction of real and supposed differences between a monolithic East and an equally monolithic West, and the creation of two irreconcilable and antagonistic cultural wholes, yet again drew its substance from the Vedic content of the Dharmashastras. And this East-West polarity became another value orientation in and through the writings of a whole spectrum of pioneering social, sociological and historiographical thinkers and writers—Vivekananda, Aurobindo, Ananda Coomaraswamy, Radhakrishnan and scores of other lesser luminaries such as R.L Mitra, R.C. Dutt, J.N. Sarkar, M.C. Ranade, Nila Kanta Shastri, R.C. Majumdar, K.K. Dutta, R.K. Mukherjee, C.P. Ramaswami Ayyar—who continually constructed and conjured up conceptual wholes such as India, Hinduism, culture, civilization, etc. in historical and normative categories. Thus the triple dimension of the cultural-nationalist ideology of the political movement transformed itself into the universal intellectual and scientific paradigm of the age itself.[18]

The articulation of cultural nationalism in the subcontinent, approximately during the hundred years preceding the transfer of power in 1947, by almost solely the Brahminic, upper and dominant castes, in precisely the way depicted above, did not exhaust or extinguish several other, even antagonistic articulations, within the emerging class-like formation. The important ones among these have been identified as socialist and economic-liberal nationalist aspirations. The socialist variety of nationalism came to the subcontinent belatedly, after the success of Russian Revolution in 1917, as either socialism or communism. It began to exert some influence only in the 1920s by which time the basic contours of cultural nationalism were already drawn and consensus had been reached. Here, the deviation was

[18] Though full length studies on the partisan nature of most of the social science and history paradigms have been rare, increasing attention is being focussed on the topic at the instance of the rise of communalism. See R. Mukherjee (1979), R. Thapar (1975, 1988, 1989, 1992) and R.S. Sharma (1961). Writing in 1961 R.S. Sharma notes: 'The main trends noticeable in the works of recent Indian writers such as Ketkar, Dutt and Ghurye is to present the caste system in such a way as may help to recast it in response to present requirements'; p. 106; see also R.C. Majumdar.(1961), and S.K. Mukhopadyaya (1981).

with respect to the political and social implications of the dominant
cultural-nationalist ideology in the realm of formal politics, and not
about the basic tenets themselves. The articulators of socialist-
nationalist aspirations, either within or without the mainstream nationalist
movement, were not differentiated from others, in either socio-cultural
or economic background. The socialist-nationalist articulation did
not engender any new form of compact with the larger masses but
by and large continued as another variety of the same elite articulation,
albeit organizing to some extent the peasantry and the workers.
The same could be said of economic–liberalism though this had
a much longer history. The political movement which started during
the last quarter of the nineteenth century had many stalwarts who
articulated economic–liberal nationalist sentiments—Dhadabuoy,
Ranade, Bhandarkar, R.C. Dutt, S.N. Banerjee, and later Nehru
and others. The earlier phase of liberal–nationalism was so far removed
from the masses as well as the non-metropolitan elite, and so deeply
implicated with colonial bureaucracy that it was rarely distinguishable
as a form of nationalism.[19] The drain theory of Dhadabuoy and
the economics of R.C. Dutt, when placed in their historical contexts
could be better interpreted as a continuity with the liberal tradition
within imperialism itself. With the upsurge of cultural nationalism
in Bengal and Maharashtra around the turn of the century, the earlier
phase was quickly done away with, along with any influence it
might have had. Many of the so-called economic-liberals themselves
being of the same socio-cultural and economic background helped
construct the basic tenets of cultural nationalism itself.[20] And any
quarrels they had with the core of cultural nationalists, were about
peripherals at the level of tactics and real politics, and consensus
with this core was easily visible. Later historiography, in view
of the subsequent rise of the aggressive brand of cultural nationalism with all its ugly implications, read back into history the distinction
between communal nationalism and secular nationalism. The

---

[19] Much of the economic writing of D. Naoroji and R.C. Dutt is indeed a continuity
of and a supplement to the liberal traditions within imperialism itself. They rely
heavily on the speeches and writings of colonial bureaucrats on the impeachment
of Warren Hastings and indicate the way to rule the country so that the welfare of
both England and India could be secured and the bond between the two, within
the framework of the British Empire strengthened. See D. Naoroji (1990) and R.C.
Dutt (1960a); See also D. Argov (1966).

[20] See for example R.C. Dutt (1963a), and R. Ranade (ed) (1992).

consciousness that within the nationalist movement some were communal (meaning the exclusion of Muslims from the political arena) and others were secular (meaning the inclusion of Muslims) was a phenomenon of the later half of the 1920s when the foundations of our national society along the lines of cultural nationalism as depicted above had already been laid. This distinctive consciousness could not be attributed to the formative periods of the cultural-nationalist ideology during the entire nineteenth and the first quarter of the twentieth centuries. What we are suggesting by way of conclusion is, that the several, differentiated articulations of elite nationalisms failed to take a different course of development, much less to strike a new path in the nation's becoming because they all shared a minimum consensus concerning cultural nationalism. This was because they all emanated from within the same socio-political locale of society and again because their differences were limited to the level of strategy and tactic in real politics. Instead they trailed along with the chief articulators of cultural nationalism as the acceptable and loyal opposition.

The cultural-nationalist ideology, in its three dimensional form, was articulated by the traditionally dominant, literary communities now emerging under the colonial auspices as a class-like social force. If so, what were the positions of the generally lower caste, Muslim and tribal communities *vis-à-vis* this ideology? The common historiographical position on this issue has been to say that the masses were dormant, and if at all there was any activity or ideology among them it was peripheral and tended to be communal-casteist. There was no pattern much less consensus among them, and that they never exhibited any autonomy of inspiration or motivation and hence followed the lead of the imperialists and missionaries in their antagonism to the nationalists. In Chapter III an attempt was made to systematically analyse the socio-political behaviour of the traditionally subaltern groups and it was found that the above historiographical premises are untenable; it is only by detaching the study of nationalism from its historical context is it possible to hold on to them.

In other words, the differentially articulated anti-Brahminic, anti-hierarchical and pro-democratizing aspirations, the individual and collective socio-political behaviour of the lower caste masses to overcome the traditional ascriptive liabilities and their all-out, somewhat autonomous and unauthorized bid to emerge into the public sphere as equals is the historical context, and therefore the legitimate contemporary consciousness, from which the cultural-nationalist ideology needs to be critiqued in order to grasp its social and political implications for wider society.[21] If the earlier chapter dealt primarily with subaltern political behaviour, the attempt here, is to interpret the salient aspects of the subaltern Weltanschauung with which their behaviour was informed. Excavation and reconstruction of subaltern ideology in any context is an exercise in interpretation, for the crucial area lies between scarce articulations and rich everyday forms of resistances, and the situation in India is complicated by its embeddedness in ethnic and linguistic diversities. However, a reading of the available secondary and some primary sources does warrant a two-stage piecing together of subaltern national ideology: the first stage consists of contestation and hence a deconstruction of cultural nationalism, from within the subaltern perspective, presented here as the political implications of cultural nationalism to the larger society; the second stage comprises the construction of an alternate political nationalism dealt with in the subsection below.

Despite the use of socio-politically integrative categories both foreign as well as native, such as nationalism, civilization, culture, heritage, legacy, Indian, Hinduism etc., cultural nationalism of the dominant groups was perceived with remarkable consistency throughout in the subcontinent as Brahminic, with communal exclusivism rationalized through territorial inclusivism. The historical vision of the cultural nation constructed exclusively with the religo-cultural material of the dominant communities, i.e. the Vedic corpus mediated through the Dharma Shastras, was perceived to have been built on a parallel political vision of a nation constituted by the same dominant groups and communities as again a more or less exclusive power block. This could not be otherwise in the context of nationalism as a congruence between culture and power.

While the masses perceived themselves to be excluded through communal exclusivism, they felt included through territorial inclusivism;

---

[21] The exclusivism of the cultural nationalists needs to be viewed in the light of consciousness that obtained then. Devotees of Rajaram M. Roy, Bankim, and others, are pained that these stalwarts are arraigned for conduct that was considered praiseworthy in their time, and believe they should not be judged in the light of today's understanding of egalitarianism. The effort in this study has been to show that egalitarian consciousness was very much there during the colonial period (and indeed it has been there all along) and evaluation of the cultural nationalists is certainly by their contemporary political nationalists and not by reading back today's conceptions into history, See G. Omvedt (1992).

in other words, if they were not welcome within the nation, they were not expected to abdicate the nation-state of which the cultural nationalists hoped to become the sole heirs. Clearly the demand was then to give consent to the legitimacy of the political and social leadership of the cultural nationalists. This was not all: the third element of the ideology defined the cultural content of the nation as anti-western civil society, modernity etc. In the context of spreading restlessness, political consciousness and socio-cultural organizations of the lower caste masses, the three dimensional cultural nationalism of the dominant groups then came through to the masses not as a call for change towards a new form of society and social relationships, but as a thinly veiled order to revert back to the age old, pre-modern pattern of superordination and subordination with its attendant religio-cultural ideology.[22] Running parallel to the rhetoric of cultural nationalism from its inception during the early nineteenth upto the middle of the twentieth century, the lower caste masses and their spokesmen perceived a consistent line of affirmation in some form or other of the dreaded Varnashrama Dharma as the identifying characteristic of the social synthesis of the nation-to-be. The differences among the cultural nationalists—moderate-extremist, liberal-conservative, heterodox-orthodox, capitalist, socialist etc.—might have been very important for themselves but were removed from the concerns of the excluded communities and their representatives. Here we are not referring only to those subsequently labelled as the Dalits but the entire mass of lower orders—Shudras, Ati-Shudras and other communities differentially alienated in the different regions from the Brahminic dominant caste configurations. These communities were struggling in essence for a principle of egalitarianism as the new norm for social relationships and could not identify in this ostensible diversity a single and significant articulation against Varnashrama Dharma, much less a willingness to join hands on equal terms with themselves to struggle for such an ideal as a vital part of nationalism. Concern for the depressed and the deprived was at first sporadically

---

[22] Straightforward glorification of the caste/Varna system and ideology were also not at all rare; Aurobindo (1972) 'caste..... a supreme necessity without which Hindu civilization could not have developed its distinctive characteristic or worked out its unique mission' Vol.I p. 537; Lala Lajpat Rai, 'The need of restoring the ancient spirit of Varnashrama system with the change dictated by modern conditions of life' V.C. Joshi (ed) (1966) Vol. II p 257; Vivekananda (1965), 'Caste has kept us alive as a nation' Vol.II p 489; for Nehruvian ambiguity towards caste, see below; and for Gandhi's, see ch. VI.

expressed and later in a more depoliticized, religionized form as anti-untouchability, included within the cultural-nationalist programme. It was not acceptable as a substitute for an all-out trans-formation from ascriptive hierarchy to egalitarianism as a social ideology which the depressed communities were aspiring for in historical con-tinuity with the subcontinent's traditions of resistance.[23] The writings and speeches of Joti Rao Phule, Sri Narayana Guru, Mangoo Ram, Gurudas, Chandram, Sonnadhar Das, E.V. Ramaswamy Naicker and of course Bhim Rao Ambedkar and a host of lesser luminaries—some times systematically but often in fragments, less in secular Western categories and far more in indigenous cultural terms—express and embody the above delineated perceptions and posture towards the cultural nationalists and their ideology. Since articulation, and much less ideological articulation, was not the forte of subaltern people, the writings and speeches of their spokesmen are not to be taken as the sole source from which to interpret the subaltern wel-tanschauung. For most of them it is their actions and behaviour that is the most effective articulation of ideology. In the subcontinent of the colonial period, the fact that there was a continuous, consistent and country-wide although uneven, autonomous subaltern political thrust outside the dominant nationalist movement, informed by the above critique of the latter, was dealt with in the earlier chapter. That a similar political thrust and ideology existed within the nationalist movement too is the theme of the subaltern historiographers.

Political Nationalism

Political nationalism has been associated with some form of a democratization process within society and the emergence of the mass into the public sphere.[24] While the specific formulation of this process, the level of mass emergence, the social forces behind

[23] An accurate and the most charitable interpretation of the upper caste concern for the masses is given by S.R. Bald (1982), pp. 4–5. This self-appointed nature of the traditional elite came to a critical point with Gandhi, when he claimed to represent and lead the untouchables 'inspite of them', see chapter on Gandhi. Needless to say, the anti-hierarchy consciousness of the political nationalists had no use for this *nobeless oblige*, and understandably viewed it as the enemy of the new emergence.

[24] For nationalism as democracy, see earlier references to political nationalism, also De Tocqueveille (1970), and R. Bendix (1961). F. Fukuyama (1992): 'Nationalism is a specifically modern phenomenon because it replaces the relationship of lordship and bondage with mutual and equal recognition', p. 266.

it, and its integration into the politico-juridical and administrative structures of the new nation-state might have differed from country to country, the phenomenon itself and its accommodation at least at the level of ideology has been unmistakably identified as the hallmark of political nationalism. The invariable concomitant of such a mass emergence into recognition or new spheres of articulation and assertion is the loss of privileges based on ascription for the traditionally articulate groups—nobility (sacred/secular), and royalty. The abolition of traditional and ascriptive privileges could either mean actual loss of power for these privileged classes or a shift towards a far more flexible and non-fixative basis of power than ascription. In either case, it is a destabilization of the old order of power configuration within society, in favour of the hitherto excluded masses. This loss by the traditionally dominant of their monopoly access to power, combined with the stepping in of the mass into the public/civic arena at least ideologically as equals, lies at the root of the democratization process associated with political nationalism engendering a nation, i.e. a deep sense of comradeship or of equality, expressed through a shared, mediated and much diversified terrain of social power—the civil society. Articulations of political nationalism then are aspiring, advocating, affirming and asserting verbally and through behaviour, such an ideology of socio-cultural democracy.

The successful emergence of political nationalism in Western Europe is mainly attributed to the rise of the bourgeoisie in opposition to manor-based feudalism, at the instance of capitalist expansion, mercantile and industrial, and hence has been labelled bourgeois democracy. Political nationalism is seen here as the ideology of the bourgeoisie rising to power through the market and machines, and thus a result of an antagonism between two sets of elite. However, this transition from serf-feudalism to bourgeois democracy meant liberation of the masses from serfdom, for whom it was a genuine democratization process both in the realm of ideology and political economy, brought about as a compromise or compact between the bourgeois and the proletariate in fulfilment, though only partially, of their age-old aspirations, was not fully realized till recently. Socialist and communist interpretations too contributed to this undervaluing of the democratization process by painting it as bourgeois rather than democracy. These different intellectual constructs have been appropriated by the elite of the colonial countries, chiefly to identify internal democratization as the bourgeois democracy of the imperialist

West, an imposition of the western way of life on the rest and therefore to be resisted in the name of anti-colonial nationalism. In the subcontinent, it was only too easy and convenient for the traditionally dominant communities, now turning into the new middle classes and aspiring for state power, to forget that internal democratization in the minimum form of ideological abolition of ascriptive privileges and the yielding of public space to the hitherto excluded masses was a historical demand of every complex culture, and resistance to this could not be legitimized even if baptized as anti-colonialism. Anti-colonial cultural nationalism in this context becomes a double edged sword enabling the elite to ascend the throne of the modern nation–state while at the same time substantially defining the nation itself as the same old traditional society.

In the subcontinent unlike in western Europe, the ideology of political nationalism i.e. socio-political egalitarianism, or in our theoretical paradigm, homogenization in the sense of equitable distribution of power within culture, was articulated by the masses themselves. In the absence of a bourgeoisie antagonistic to ascription, lower caste, Muslim and tribal masses voiced this as a continuity of the age-old tradition of resistance to the Brahminic ideology of privileges and caste-based feudalism. The difference between the ideology of social egalitarianism articulated by the lower caste mass and the west European bourgeois democratic liberalism as well as the similarity between the two, are crucial to our understanding of the situation in the subcontinent. Here the struggle for social egalitarianism and abolition of ascriptive privileges did not necessarily imply a wholesale appropriation of the juridico-administrative paraphernalia of bourgeois democracy or of political modernization, yet it embodied the same human aspirations towards equality and equal recognition that can be identified in all human collectivities. On the other hand, the bourgeoisie here, whether meaning the new traders and industrialists or the educated middle class both of whom were fast becoming part and parcel of the bourgeois colonial, democratic state, had no use for socio-political egalitarianism. Their antagonism to caste-feudalism, if there was any, was certainly not on this question of egalitarian ideology. Partha Chatterjee, after a long and cautious study of nationalism points out in his latest work:

> What we have here is a desire for a structure of community in which the opposite tendencies of mutual separateness and mutual

dependence are united by a force that has a greater universal actuality than the given forms of the dominant dharma. For want of a more concrete concept of praxis we may call this desire in an admittedly abstract and undifferentiated sense a desire for democratisation where rights and the application of norms of justice are open to a broader basis of consultation, disputation and resolution ... and yet this democratisation fell short of bourgeois democracy (P. Chatterjee 1994: 197).

The ideology of political nationalism in the subcontinent, except for a handful of non-Brahminic leaders of the Madras and Bombay presidencies, was articulated uniformly by the hitherto excluded or exterior communities, whether described as depressed, untouchable or not. Thus: Ayyankali, Sahodharan Aiyappan, Dr Palpu, Kumaran Asan, Narayana Guru, Iyothee Dass, R. Srinivasan, M.C. Rajah, Varadharajulu, E.V. Ramaswamy Naicker, T.M. Nair, C. Sankaran Nair, Yellamma, Manjari Hanumantappa, Jotiba Phule, Shivram Prasad Singh, Ghasi Das, Balak Das, Mangoo Ram, Bhimaboi, Sonadhar Das, Swami Achchutanand were spokespersons among numerous others. The general location of these political nationalists at the lower levels of social structure and their cultural embeddedness determined to a large extent their relationship with the masses and the nature of their articulation. Since they did not belong to the traditionally literate communities, most of them were vernacular first-generation-educated and some of them like Ayyankali of Kerala were not literate at all. Their advocacy, therefore was generally in an idiom closer to the masses often oral rather than written. They are better described as rural than urban and those few who spoke from the urban platform had not yet severed their connections with land, or rather landlessness. The concerns they articulated revolved around the day-to-day issues and aspirations of the communities they came from. In other words, the political nationalists were merely spokespersons, verbally translating the aspirations and socio-political behaviour of the masses. These and other such circumstances differentiated them from their counterparts—the cultural-nationalists—*vis-à-vis* the mass and belie the proposition, recently advanced somewhat aggressively, that both were elite and their articulations could be comprehended from within a common perspective as 'scramble for crumbs'.[25]

[25] The Cambridge Scholars, viewing the situation from without, understandably could not distinguish between the struggle of the hitherto excluded castes from the

The ideology of political nationalism, of abolition of ascriptive privileges and democratization of society in the subcontinent, was at the primary level translated, concretized and diversified into a series of rights for the lower caste masses, intended to facilitate their emergence into different spheres of the new power and opportunity realm—the civil society. These included the following: right to give up traditional/hereditary occupations and to choose any other, right to ownership of land and to organize one's lifestyle, housing, clothing etc., right to education at par with others, right to jobs, government and private, access to public places—roads, markets, offices etc., right to public resources particularly water, right not to abide by customary forms of agricultural bondage, right of access to religious places, symbols and literature, right to protection by the state and its agencies against their social and economic superiors, and above all right to political self-representation. Through the articulation and advocacy of these and several other rights, although unevenly, throughout the length and breadth of the country, the political nationalists sought to bring about an equalization at the level of the ideology of the masses with the classes within culture.[26] These aspirational articulations through concrete struggles did represent the attempt of the masses towards emergence not only in political economy but also into political subjectivity. It is necessary to point out that the specific issues chosen for advocacy, the nature of their articulation and the limits etc. were all substantially determined by the age-old historical dynamics of power as resistance of the subcontinent. This was in continuity with pre-modern struggles for equality against the Brahminic principles of hierarchy, exclusivism, privileges and discrimination rather than by any process imitative of western bourgeois democracy.

At the secondary level, these various concrete rights of the masses were sought to be woven together, integrated and elaborated within the ideology of citizenship and the duties of the state by the more westernized sections. Advocacy of rights for the lower caste masses within society was resisted by the dominant and Brahminic communities in general as being against custom and tradition, and by

power-manipulations of the traditionally dominant. But a view from within would not only show the difference but also be properly historical.

[26] The demand for colonial state protection through separate legal provisions, as has been pointed out earlier, became an obsessive issue during the subsequent stages of the struggles, thanks mainly to the upper caste resistance to the mass emergence in the name of cultural-nationalism.

the cultural nationalists in particular as being an imitative process of western culture. Indian culture was presumed to be spiritual, harmonious and constructed around the notion of duty/Dharma rather than rights. It is precisely at this moment of non-acceptance of and resistance to the new emergence of the masses that political nationalists sought state intervention and protection in the name of equality of citizenship. The political emergence of the masses, was not encouraged nor lead by the rising classes, but was rather sought to be prevented by them and then onwards had to be nurtured by the colonial state along with its typical ambiguities and distortions. The story of protective discrimination of the weaker sections by the colonial state has been told often enough and need not be repeated here. However, the underlying thrust and theory of equality as an aspect of the ideology of political nationalism is hardly noted.

The demand was for equal citizenship as the foundation of all the civil rights movements of the lower caste excluded masses. The intention was to homogenize power and accessibility to power structures within culture, at the instance of the general unwillingness, or resistance by, the dominant communities. This was the central concern of the more educated political nationalists particularly from the Southern and Western parts of the country—Jotiba Phule and Ambedkar, the non-Brahmins of Madras and the Civil Rights League of Travancore. The century-long experiences and struggles of the lower caste masses had convinced them that their fate could not be entrusted to the so-called majority for as majority that dominance was being interpreted. The most clear expression of this came by way of a combined memorandum of Ambedkar and R. Srinivasan, both belonging to untouchable communities, submitted to the Simon Commission: 'The depressed classes must be made free citizens entitled to all rights of citizenship in common with other citizens of the state' (B.R. Ambedkar 1982: Vol II, 69). It was thus precisely the antipathy and aversion of the dominant communities and cultural nationalists to the 'unauthorized' emergence of the masses into the public realm that made the political nationalists demand for special state protection, which was subsequently delegitimized as the new enclave of privileges, the exact reversal of what the lower caste leaders intended and demanded.

At yet another level, the actualization of concrete rights for the masses as aspects of equal citizenship, was conceptualized as the very transition to nation and nationhood, and nationalism was seen as the ideology asserting and upholding this transition and the nation's becoming. Writing in the very same year as the birth of the Indian National Congress, Jotiba Phule challenged the 'nationalness' of the new organization with his counter-concept of the nation:

> There cannot be a nation worth the name until and unless all the people of the land of King Bali—such as Shudras and Ati-shudras, Bhils and fishermen etc, become truly educated and are able to think independently for themselves and are uniformly unified and emotionally integrated. If a tiny section of the population like the upstart Aryan Brahmins alone were to found the 'national congress' who will take any notice of it? (J. Phule 1991: Vol II, 29).

Within the non-Brahmin movement of the south, the idea that nation and nationality meant comradeship based on equality of recognition and acceptance runs through as a steady undercurrent. Ramarayaninger, for example at the Coimbatore Conference in 1917 pointed out that '... the nation-building and nation regeneration ideas of non-brahmins are different from that of the Congress; it is the democratic idea' (V.T. Naidu 1932: 8-9). And later at the Bikkovale Conference, Venkaratnam Naidu wanted to know whether in societies where the higher castes treat the lower castes as less than human beings, 'Can we expect that sympathy which is the ground work of nationality?' (ibid: 33-34).

The most crucial episode in E.V. Ramaswamy Naicker's early public life was the Gurukulam incident at Shermadevi and the controversies surrounding it. The general position of the cultural nationalists—the Congress and Gandhi—on the practice of untouchability in the ashram made Naicker turn away from them and begin a long militant career of political nationalism. He explained in this context:

> 'The Gurukulam must stand for an ideal—for Indian nationalism—and there should be no invidious distinction between man and man' (E.S. Viswanathan 1983: 49).

Coming down heavily on the Congress brand of nationalism which sought to restore to dominance all forms of religious superstition, Periyar indicated in his inimitable popular style the kind of nationalism he had in mind:

If we consider, on what must depend the nationalism of a nation, minimally, the people of a nation, without having to sell or bargain their mind or conscience, should be able to eke out their livelihood. More than this there are several other nationalisms: knowledge should grow; education is needed; equality is needed; unity is needed; self-effort is needed; genuine feelings are needed; cheating one another for a living should not be there; lazy people should not be there; slaves should not be there; untouchables, and those who cannot walk on public streets should not be there; like these several more things should be done. (V. Anaimuthu, 1974: Vol I, 372).

Before all else, however, nationalism requires the total abolition of caste and its discrimination based on birth. (ibid: pp. 371–388)[27]

Finally, it is in the writings and speeches of Ambedkar that the nation-wide civil rights movement of the Shudras and Ati-Shudras is transformed through the concept of equal citizenship into an all-embracing ideology of a struggle and aspiration towards a society built on the modern national principles of equality, liberty and fraternity. Ambedkar's obsession with the liberation of the depressed classes cannot be extricated from his all-important concept of an ideal society in the form of a social democracy; in fact social democracy is the plank from which his concrete struggles and advocacy of untouchables' rights were conducted. Ambedkar had on several occasions talked of the nation, nationality and nationalism not only in the context of the lower castes but also of the Muslims. His concern was obviously for the whole—the nation—of which he hoped the depressed classes would become not only an integral but also an indistinguishable part.[28] His repeated emphasis on nation as comradeship, consciousness of kind, of kith and kinship, of common and united sympathies point to the same direction.

Nationality is a social feeling. It is a feeling of corporate sentiment of oneness which makes those who are charged with it feel that they are kith and kin (B.R. Ambedkar 1990: Vol III, 31).

---

[27] Periyar's ideas on nationalism are collected in V. Anaimuthu (1974: Vol I pp. 371–388).

[28] Note that Ambedkar, M.C. Rajah and other leaders' idea of the lower sections becoming an 'indistinguishable' part of the whole, has been lost in the subsequent struggles for legal protectionism, again thanks largely to the resistance by the dominant communities.

Defining the ideal society or the nation as democracy, Ambedkar points out that 'Democracy is not merely a form of government. It is primarily a mode of associated living, of conjoint, communicated experience' and it is incompatible and inconsistent with isolation and exclusiveness resulting in the distinction between the privileged and the underprivileged (B.R. Ambedkar 1989: Vol VI, 57, 222).

Nation for Ambedkar then, is a new form of social and societal relationship built on the principles of equaltiy, liberty and fraternity. Nationalism is the call given to abolish the Brahminic ideology of privileges and discrimination embodied in the tradition and religion as reinvented by the cultural nationalists. Ambedkar's appropriation of French ideals, far from being an imitation of bourgeois democracy of the West, is merely a modern formulation of the age-old aspiration and struggle of the lower caste masses of the subcontinent towards an egalitarian and democratic society.

NATIONALISM AND THE INVENTION OF TRADITION

> If nation-states are widely conceded to be 'new' and 'historical' the nations to which they give political expression always loom out of an immemorial past ... (B. Anderson 1983: 21).

A crucial aspect of the articulation of any nationalist ideology is the intellectual construction of the nation as a continuity from a hoary past. This conjuring up of the nation-to-be from out of a seemingly endless past, through nationalism has multiple functions: one, to give legitimacy to the nation which is made to appear as having always or nearly always existed; two, to indicate the ideological direction the nation is to take in future with its past as the model; and three, to draw the desired line of inclusion and exclusion within society, culture and history. It is this construction of a continuity from the past, through the present, towards the future that constitutes the identity of a people, the soul or the genius of a nation. This culturo-historical construction is no mere reproduction nor, despite claims to that effect, an objectively true representation of the past. On the contrary, the process by which a people becomes self-conscious of its distinct identity is a political one, related to power–relations within and without, and therefore the present power-configuration is the framework from within which the past of a culture is reconstructed through elision, selection, relation, addition etc. into a desired or ideal nation. In short, the construction of histories and invention of traditions in nationalist contexts are intellectual activities of myth-making in modern times, whose political import far exceeds their factual content. Nationalist myth-histories follow more or less a general pattern: the longest possible genealogy is claimed for the society and culture, the continuity of the present with such antiquity is established non-problematically, antiquity itself is presented as glorious and golden, harmonious and peaceful in comparison with the present that needs to be transformed. The transition from the allegedly golden past to the present fallen state is attributed to factors perceived to be extraneous to the original genius of the culture, and the glorious past is then ideologically transported and projected into the future as the destiny of the people.[29]

While the creation of a political myth-history in the colonial subcontinent too, shared all the above general characteristics, what is of particular importance and relevance to our discussion here is the fact that the myths created here were multiple and full of contestation, and the visions envisaged were polarized and antagonistic. The invention of tradition and the reconstruction of histories based on traditional cleavages within pre-modern society, colonial changes, and political awakening manifested itself trichotomously and eventually settled down to an antagonistic and polarized dichotomy of a meta-discourse and its counter. The meta-narratives of the discovered or imagined India were recited by the cultural nationalists from a position of dominance, in collaboration with British scholars and bureaucrats and these were sought to be challenged and negated through counter-recitals by the political nationalists working somewhat autonomously from the disadvantaged and diversified subaltern positions. The meta-narratives embodying a common vision of the subcontinent's past informs most of the writings of the cultural nationalists—communal or secular, moderate or extremist—and despite differences among themselves, set them antagonistically apart from the counter-vision articulated by the political nationalists.

India Discovered

The following discussion of the reconstructed past espoused by the cultural-nationalist ideologues, is based on Jawaharlal Nehru's

---

[29] See S. Hobsbawm & T. Ranger (ed.) (1983); also B. Anderson (1983).

'Discovery of India', by far the most nostalgic and consciously woven text, written while its author was serving a prison sentence in Ahmed Nagar in 1944. The most striking characteristic of this myth-history is the idea that the nation in the subcontinent is ancient, despite occasional claims to the contrary, and is to be identified unambiguously with the Aryans or Indo-Aryans, later called Hindus, however meaning again, only caste-Hindus. The history of the subcontinent for Nehru starts with the advent of these Aryan races in the remote past. The subsequent historical development is mainly the story of how these Aryans came, saw and conquered this backward land inhabited by uncivilized people and developed a social synthesis by establishing the Arya Dharma, the national religion and culture—'a conception of obligations, of the discharge of duties to oneself and to others'. These ideals embodied in the life and literature of the Indo-Aryan race, despite successive waves of invasion and conquest by Persians, Greeks, Scythians, Muhammadans, remained practically unchecked and unmodified from without down to the era of British occupation, providing stability, continuity and thus identity to the nation.

From these dim beginnings of long ago (the Indo-Aryan literature and philosophy mainly the Vedas) flow out the rivers of Indian thought and philosophy of Indian life and culture and literature ever widening and increasing in volume and sometimes flooding the land with rich deposits. During this enormous span of years they changed their courses sometimes and even appeared to shrivel up, yet they preserved their essential identity (J. Nehru 1946: 80-87).

The conquest of the peoples of the land—the Mlechchas, barbarians, primitives, forest dwellers, Dravidians, etc.—whom a 'wide gulf' separated from the incoming Aryan races and to whom the latter 'considered themselves vastly superior', was unique and characteristic of their national genius. Unlike other conquerors of ancient times our Aryan ancestors did not annihilate or 'enslave' the defeated people but in benevolence civilized them by inclusion within the Aryan fold i.e. the nation, as the 'dasa–shudras' in accordance with their natural tendencies and aptitudes.

... in the ages since the Aryans had come down to what they called Aryavarta or Bharatvarsha, the problem that faced India was to produce a synthesis between this new race and culture and the old race and civilisation of the land. To that the mind of India devoted itself and it produced an enduring solution built on the strong foundations of a joint Indo-Aryan culture. Other foreign elements came and were absorbed. They made little difference (ibid: 138).

And also;

... at a time when it was customary for the conquerors to exterminate or enslave the conquered races, caste enabled a more peaceful solution which fitted in with the growing specialisation of functions. Life was graded and out of the mass of agriculturists evolved the Vaishyas, the artisans and merchants; the Kshatriyas or rulers and warriors; and the Brahmins, priests and thinkers who were supposed to guide policy and preserve and maintain the ideals of the nation. Below these there were the shudras or labourers and unskilled workers other than the agriculturalists. Among the indigenous tribes many were gradually assimilated and given a place at the bottom of the social scale that is among the Shudras. The process of assimilation was a continuous one. These castes must have been in a fluid condition; rigidity came in much later (ibid: 85).

In other words, the Indo-Aryans in the course of their conflict with and conquest of the non-Aryans discovered a unique solution to the conflicts in civilization and culture of all times—the Varna/caste ideology—and succeeded in effecting a humane model, a 'national–typical' synthesis which in its original state of vibrancy and flexibility stood for harmony, stability, continuity and therefore identity of the nation down its long and tortuous history. The other two institutional pillars of this 'national–typical' are the village and joint family system.

All the three pillars of the Indian social structure were thus based on the group and not on the individual. The aim was social security, stability and continuance of the group, that is of society (ibid. 255).

And:

Over and above these (functional units of social structure) a strong and fairly successful attempt was made to create a common national bond which would hold all these groups together—the sense of a common culture, common traditions, common heroes and saints and a common land to the four corners of which people went on pilgrimage. This national bond was of course very different from present day nationalism; it was weak politically but socially and culturally it was strong (ibid. 251).

Though the ideological outlines of this national synthesis were already laid out during the Vedic and Upanishadic periods, the actual working out of the social reorganization was a long drawn-out process that continued despite Buddhist and Jainist challenges till the Kushan period in the third century A.D. The Kushan period was one of 'invasion by strange peoples with strange customs' who 'not only broke up India's political structure but endangered her cultural ideals and social structure also'. In response to this new threat, then, an anti-foreigner resistance movement against the Kushans took shape which was the first nationalist upheaval in the subcontinent, successfully re-establishing the 'nation'.

The reaction was essentially a nationalist one with the strength as well as the narrowness of nationalism. That mixture of religion and philosophy, history and tradition, custom and social structure which in its wide fold included almost every aspect of the life of India and which might be called Brahminism or (to use a later word) Hindusim became the symbol of nationalism. It was indeed a national religion with its appeal to all those deep instincts, racial and cultural, which form the basis everywhere of nationalism today (ibid: 138).

Buddhism, being similarly a child of Indian thought, had a nationalist background but by becoming a world religion, it had abdicated its nationalist role. Thus it was natural for the old Brahminic faith to become the symbol again and again of nationalist revivals (ibid: 138).

The Brahminic nationalist movement of the Kushan period produced a strong anti-foreigner sentiment, brought about a Brahmin-Kshatriya coalition in defence of their homeland and culture, and ushered in a 'revitalised nation' in the Golden Age of the imperial Guptas during which an 'attempt was made to build up a homogenous state based on old Brahminic ideals. The Golden Age of the subcontinent's history was thus a period in which the Brahminic ideals or the Varna ideology was established as state policy, against attempts at disruption/democratization and the Weltanschaung of the age was Brahminic nationalism, or nationalist Brahminism. This pact between, and mutual reinforcement of, Brahminism and nationalism was to repeat itself time and again in history whenever the nation found itself in crisis, for,

> The Aryan faith in India was essentially a national religion, restricted to the land and the social caste structure it was developing, emphasized this aspect of it (ibid: 175).

The great revival of nationalist Brahminism and the cultural renaissance under the imperial Guptas continued for about two centuries, the fourth and the fifth, and eventually declined in attempts to resist the new barbarian invaders—the Huns. In the eighth century Shankaracharya—one among the greatest of India's philosophers—emerged and revived Brahminism/Hinduism by adopting the Sanga tradition of the Buddhists (ibid: 180).

It was not the brilliant Arabs but the Turkish tribes who brought Islam as a significant social force to India (ibid: 227).

> The Moslems who came to India from outside brought no new technique or political and economic structure. In spite of a religious belief in the brotherhood of Islam they were class bound and feudal in outlook. In technique and in the methods of production and industrial organisation, they were inferior to what then prevailed in India. Thus their influence on the economic life of India and the social structure was very little (ibid: 267).

> On the whole, the various types of Muslim tribes that crossed the border—Turkish, Afghan and Turco-Mongol or Mogul—did not seek to change the lives of the people, the customs or the tradition and so they were all eventually absorbed within the flow of the mainstream of native culture.

> What is called the Moslem or medieval period brought another change and an important one and yet it was more or less confined to the top and did not vitally affect the essential continuity of Indian life so many of their predecessors in more ancient times became absorbed into India and part of her life .... A deliberate attempt was made apart from a few exceptions not to interfere with the ways of the customs of the people (ibid: 237-38).

However, the first half of the second millennium was clearly a period of rigidity, stagnation and decay for the subcontinent. While signs of regression were evident even before the invasions, it was during the Mogul period that the social structure and cultural ideals in conflict with the new, foreign and proselytizing culture became more rigid, insulated and stagnant. The incoming culture was not vibrant or dynamic enough to have a vitalizing influence.

The last of the socalled Grand Moguls Aurengazeb tried to put back the clock and in this attempt stopped it and broke it up. The Mogul rulers were strong so long as they put themselves in line with the genius of the nation and tried to work for a common nationality and a synthesis of the various elements in the country. When Aurengazeb began to oppose this movement and suppress it and to function more as a Moslem than an Indian ruler the Mogul empire began to break up (ibid: 265).

Basically, the introduction of an alternative belief system and a philosophy which was found to be crude, or the conversions in large numbers by the lower castes and individuals of the upper castes, did not matter, but 'What was objected to was interference with their own social structure and ways of living'. Thus, the second Brahminic national revival (now termed Hindu nationalism of course) though not as glorious as the first one, Nehru says, took place in the seventeenth century when Aurengzeb offended the sentiments of the dominant and ruling communities, the Rajputs, Sikhs and the Marathas, through religio-cultural coercion and oppression.

All over the widespread domains of the Mogul Empire there was a ferment and a growth of revivalist sentiment which was a mixture of religion and nationalism. That nationalism was certainly not of the modern secular type, nor did it as a rule embrace the whole of India in its scope. It was coloured by feudalism by local sentiment and sectarian feeling ... yet the religion itself had a strong national background and all its traditions were connected with India.

'The Indians', writes Professor Macdonell, 'are the only division of the Indo-European family which has created a great national religion—Brahminism—and a great world religion—Buddhism'....(and) Shivaji was the Symbol of a resurgent Hindu Nationalism drawing inspiration from old classics ... (ibid: 273).

The coming of the British to the subcontinent however, meant a radical change in the social structure and cultural ideals here. Despite their conservative intentions and associations, the imperial British through their new political structure and the economic change they caused had been playing havoc with traditional Indian society and culture, and particularly the hitherto carefully preserved social hierarchy. In this context, the following is how Nehru envisioned the role of the nation:

> The conflict is between two approaches to the problem of social organisation which are directly opposed to each other .... The Caste system does not stand by itself; it is a part and an integral part of a much larger social organisation. It may be possible to remove some of its obvious abuses and to lessen its rigidity and yet to leave the system intact. But that is highly unlikely as the social and economic forces at play are not much concerned with this super structure .... It has ceased to be a question of whether we like caste or dislike it. Changes are taking place in spite of our likes and dislikes. But it is certainly in our power to mould those changes and direct them, so that we can take full advantage of the character and genius of the Indian people as a whole, which have been so evident in the cohesiveness and stability of the social organisation they built up. Sir George Birdwood has said somewhere : "So long as the Hindus hold to the caste system India will be India; but from the day they break from it, there will be no more India" .... But there is some truth in what Sir George Birdwood said, though probably he did not look at it from this point of view. The break up of a huge and long standing social organisation may well lead to a complete disruption of social life, resulting in absence of cohesion.... Perhaps disruption is inevitable.... Nevertheless we cannot just disrupt and hope for something better .... In the constructive schemes that we may make we have to pay attention to the human material, to the background of its thought and urges and to the environment in which we have to function. To ignore all this and to fashion some idealistic scheme in the air or merely to think in terms of imitating what others have done elsewhere would be folly (ibid: 246–47).

The choice of Nehru's text to elaborate the cultural–nationalist vision of the past was not fortuitous. Apart from the fact that 'Discovery of India' is the most systematically and nostalgically written text, Nehru's image unambiguosly has been that of a modernizer and an indiscriminate one at that; and it is rarely realized how close he was in thought and sentiment to the rest of the nationalist pantheon—Bankim Chandra Chatterjee, Gandhi and Savarkar. Therefore contending with Nehru is in a real sense, contending with the meta-narrative of the nationalist vision of the past in its most liberal form. The others embellished, symbolized and to a certain extent simplified the vision for mass consumption: for example, Nehru's ambivalent evaluation of the non-Aryan traditions; pre-Aryan, Buddhist, Islamic and liberal, became more openly devalued and negative in the writings of R.C. Dutt, Bankim, Ranade, Lala Lajpat, Aurobindo, B.C. Pal and others. The Aryanism and Brahminism of the elite Nehru was again transformed in deference to mass sensibilities, into a generalized discourse on Hinduism in most of the works. The harmonious society built on the Brahminic ideals of hierarchy was retailed as Ram Rajya mainly by Gandhi. Despite such a variety of formulations of the past, the common denominator and trajectory in all of them was clear and sharp: the preference for and priority of the Aryan/Brahminic races, their ideology of social gradedness/hierarchy, their constant historical role in developing the identiy of the 'nation', the necessity hence of shaping the nationalist future by salvaging as much of these ideals as possible from multifarious modern attacks. It is precisely this sectarian and select reading of the past, intended to preserve and promote the status quo or rather status quo ante of social power-configuration within society as the scientific history of India, that was challenged and exposed by scores of political nationalists who saw themselves as heirs to other traditions in history.

Alternate Discoveries and Antagonistic Visions

Alternate and antagonistic discoveries of India, challenging the dominant vision of glorified, nationalized Brahminic hierarchy, as we have already suggested, were attempted from the general subaltern position. The implications of this locale of relative powerlessness were several and significant; first of all, unlike the former, these subaltern visions were not an imperialism-sponsored project and under the concrete, historical circumstances were not only autonomous but by implication a part of a broader anti-imperialist agenda of mass emergence. If the colonial project of extraction of economic and human surplus was constructed on the foundational premise of the traditional status quo, the master mythification of the past was its integral part. The subaltern agenda of mass emergence in constructing divergent and antagonistic mythological histories thus challenged the intellectual foundation of colonialism itself. Secondly, the subaltern imaginings failed to develop and transform themselves into one grand meta-narrative counter to the dominant vision, and their episodic nature was due to their general position of subalternity. However, there is more to this; what is pejoratively labelled as fragmentation is in fact rootedness in and continuity with the culturally diversified traditions of the subcontinent. And so it is only through a strange logic of the dominant political idiom that diversity itself has come to be looked upon as fragmentation, an aspect of subalternity. And thirdly, in the face of the colonial–nationalist and oppressive master-paradigm of history and culture, the subaltern search became multi-directional. It included the repudiation of the meta-narrtive, attempts to discover a counter meta-narrative, and constructions of differential and separatist pasts.

The privileging of Brahminic hierarchy as history and legacy by the cultural nationalists triggered off multiple responses from the political nationalists working within the vernaculars in different cultural regions of the subcontinent. What was glorified and upheld as the ideal for the future by the former was now painted as plain horror, to be combated at all costs. Counter-histories of anti-Brahminic egalitarianisms were set up as the alternate nodal points of history. And differential attempts were made to trace out a separatist yet more homogeneous and inclusive history and legacy, at regional and local levels. Thus both in history and by logic, it was the sectarian, exclusive and partisan reading of the past by the dominant cultural nationalists that was prior to all other forms of sectarianism and exclusivism in modern India. These later were responses and reactions to the communal and somewhat racist exclusivism of the leading groups who expected the continuation of the silence and subservience of the masses. Instead, the subaltern-lower castes despite heavy odds made an all-out bid to emerge by creating autonomous myths and histories, challenging the elite dominant vision.

The great political nationalist ideologues of modern India—Jotiba Phule, Ramaswamy Naicker, Ambedkar and Swami Achchutanand—incessantly and systematically exposed and condemned Brahminical Hinduism as a religion and culture of social slavery, and therefore an enemy of the people struggling to emerge as a modern nation. The ideals and values and the customs and injunctions of Brahminical literature—the Vedas, Upanishads, Ithihasas, Puranas and Dharma Shastras—as interpreted and upheld within the competitive politics of modern nationalism appeared to these men as a peremptory call to reinforce and re-establish the Varna ideology of discrimination against the lower classes. Confirmation of this was not lacking in the manifold attempts of the Brahminic and allied classes to prevent mass emergence in the new opportunity structure of education, jobs and political representation. The sacred, national legacy was interpreted as tales fabricated by Brahmins, fantastic, immoral and superstitious, intended to perpetuate Dasa and Shudra slavery. The obvious terrain of contestation was the varna/caste scheme. While an idealized Varnashrama Dharma was found glorious and worthy of export to all other cultures of the world by Tilak, Vivekananda and Gandhi, on the other hand, Phule, Naicker, Swami Achchutanand and Ambedkar considered the Varna scheme to be a plain and painful anachronism that deserved to be dumped, and if it was found to be an integral part of Hindusim then that Hinduism itself *in toto* needed to be given up. Thus Ravan Rajya or Balirajya was preferable to Ramrajya in which Varna would be the national state ideology. In fact one of the major pre-occupations of most political nationalists of all regions was the deconstruction of the emergent Hinduism to reveal its Brahminic form and demystification of it as a new political weapon of the Brahminic and dominant groups. Their writings in the vernaculars, intepreting Hinduism and the epics as carriers of the Brahminic ideology of domination, found its echo among the hundreds of thousands of lower caste men and women and continue to be controversial even today.

For the political nationalists the golden age of the subcontinent was the pre-Aryan epoch when social equality was presumed to have flourished and society on the whole was organized on fraternal and democratic lines. In the south and the west the pre-Aryan era was conceptualized as the Dravidian, Adi-Dravidian civilization. The Tamils for example, considered the Sangam Age to be pre-Aryan, believed that in the era there was no caste/varna system and the present lower caste and untouchables were free men, owners of the land and rulers of the people. The ideology of Adi-Dravida extended itself into Adi-Kerala, Adi-Andhra and Adi-Kannadiga, throughout the entire southern peninsula. In the north however, pre-Aryanism expressed itself as Adi-Hinduism and Adi-Dharmism, particularly in the United Provinces and Punjab. Mangoo Ram of Punjab and Swami Achchutanand of the United Provinces believed in and preached pre-Aryan egalitarian principles of the times in towns and cities. The first statement of Adi-Dharma ran thus: 'We are the original people of this country and our religion is Adi-dharm. The Hindu quam came from outside and enslaved us' (M. Jurgensmeyer 1982: 57). The historical vision of Swami Achchutanand and Ram Charan is paraphrased thus by a scholar:

> The Adi Hindu leaders claimed that there had been ancient Adi Hindu Kingdoms in capital cities, forts and a thriving civilisation. They alleged that when the Aryans invaded the country they conquered these Adi Hindus variously by brute force, repression and treachery.... They then devised the caste system and oppressive social laws, embodied in the vedas and codified in the Manu Smriti in order to relegate the Adi-Hindus to untouchable status and to deprive them of their rights in Society.... The Adi Hindu leaders projected the past not only as a period when the forbearers of the untouchables were rulers but also as a golden age of social equality.... Through their newly constructed history of the original inhabitants of India, the Adi Hindu leaders outlined an idealised vision of social equality, and of the past power and glory that the untouchables had lost and were to claim (N. Gooptu 1993: 290-94).

The point of contrast is only too obvious: while the golden age of cultural nationalism was Brahminical consolidation and social inequality; for the political nationalists it comprised precisely social equality and egalitarianism as a principle of organization.[30] Again, the fall or degradation for the former meant an increase in the influence and authority of non-Aryan races or the mixing of castes and races; for the latter the same meant enslavement to the Brahmin/Aryan cultural and social system.

The political nationalists saw themselves as heirs to another tradition of the subcontinent's history—that of resistance, heterodoxy, protest and egalitarianism.[31] The anti-Brahminic traditions of Buddhism and

[30] Note that what was considered the golden age by the cultural nationalists was the period in which untouchability emerged into social significance, see P. Mukherjee (1988) p. 94.

[31] G. Omvedt (1994) pp. 223-59. A full length history of the subcontinent from the anti-Brahminical view was written by Swami Dharm Theertha (1946). Several

the Bhakti movements of the pre-modern era were appropriated to express the modern socio-political message of equality. The Vaishnavaite Movement of the Shudras—Yadavs, Koeris and Kurmis of Bihar, the Matua cult variation of the same among the Nama Shudras of Bengal, the modern revivals of Kabirpanth, Ravidas Panth etc. among the lower and depressed castes of north and central India are some examples. The renewed interest in Buddhism in modern times is certainly connected with unearthing alternate traditions antagonistic to the Vedic/Brahminic hierarchy. As early as the 1890s, Buddhism was reincarnated among the lower castes of Madras Presidency combined with educational efforts and expansion in the assertion of a new identity. Ambedkar's re-discovery of Buddhism was the most consciously worked out recovery of traditional egalitarianism in the context of modern nationalism. These multiple discoveries,

> had either created a new symbol or modified the existing ones. For instance, the animal sacrifice was substituted by coconut sacrifice; the sacred thread was replaced by Kanthi (rosary of basil bead); the pattern of diacritical mark was modified; the temples were replaced by monasteries or Gurudwaras; the Vedas were replaced by Guru Granths (sacred texts of Gurus) or living Gurus or by both. They also created their own myths, rituals and practices etc. (N. Gooptu 1993: 104).

If Gandhi was enthralled with the possible re-establishment of the self-sufficient and harmonious little republics in oceanic circles, Ambedkar had nothing but contempt for pre-modern Indian village life.

> In this republic there is no place for democracy. There is no place for equality. There is no room for liberty and there is no room for fraternity. The Indian village life is the very negation of a Republic (B.R. Ambedkar 1989: Vol V, 26).

Attempts were even made to rework the Vedas and Vedantas: although Vivekananda did not find any contradiction between non-dualist philosophy and discriminatory caste practices, the same Advaita became

---

other 'histories' lie buried within vernacular traditions, embodying alternate and antagonistic visions, for example, 'the history of the country of Indirars' (Tamil) by Pandit Iyothee Dass of Tamil Buddhism. For an alternate evaluation of tradition particularly of religion, see B.R. Ambedkar (1987) Vols. III & IV.

the philosophical foundation for struggle against all social differences and the caste system in the writings of Sri Narayana Guru. The common import of all these variegated reworkings of the resistance tradition was clear enough: if the cultural nationalists claimed continuity with hierarchical Vedic traditions and traced the history of the nation as one of ascriptive gradedness and inequality, the political nationalists claimed continuity with egalitarian heterodox traditions and traced the history of the nation as one of identity of human worth or equality.

Origin myths proliferated among the lower castes in general during the colonial period: the common refrain discernable among them was how they were all equal in the beginning and how they were subsequently deprived and depressed. 'Equal in the beginning' was meant to counter the 'natural' inequality of human beings that the cultural nationalists believed in, preached and practised. Sri Narayana Guru conducted a practical test to demonstrate the 'natural equality' of all men: he taught the Vedas to a group of students and chose a high caste person to select the best Vedic-recital from among them. When the judge pointed out to a boy, the Guru revealed that he was a Pulaya by caste—the most polluted by Brahmin standards. The contrast here again was the natural versus the historical explanation of the so-called differences of merit among the castes. The contentions of the political nationalists were in the realm of history and their praxis was an agenda to be realized within history.

Alternate discoveries and antagonistic visions by the generally subaltern masses were attended with frantic attempts to overcome their inherited disabilities and they were more often than not beset with desperation and frustration. Their aspirations and socio-political ambitions were not making sufficient and satisfactory headway either with the British or the cultural nationalists. The selfish and imperial calculations of the former and the monopolism and exclusivism practised by the latter in the context of skewed economic change, generated a solid and combined fortress which precluded mass access. Frustrated mass emergence was beginning to look for other avenues when it was increasingly becoming clear that within a unitary form of society and state it was nearly impossible to realize the age-old dream and tradition of socio-political equality. Ambedkar was satisfied with making a symbolic gesture of religious separatism by renouncing the Hindu fold and becoming a Buddhist. In the north the political nationalists Swami Achchutanand, Ram Charan and Mangooram toyed with the idea of a separate quam and Achchutistan. The Sikhs too raised the demand for a separate Punjab, and in the south, anti-Brahminism transformed itself through the demand for self-respect into a Dravidian Movement for a separate Tamil region. The tribals, wherever they found themselves in numerical strength and occupying contiguous territories, raised the slogans of Adibasi/Munda/Birsa Raj. While these separatist rumblings, religio-cultural or politico-cultural, were largely contained within the level of society at least during the colonial period, the same was not true of the Muslim demand for Pakistan.

The Muslim middle class, or what went by that name among the Muslims, for it was never appreciable in size and shape, struggled for a long time without working out an alternate vision for themselves. Their demand all along had been political nationalist in nature, demanding acceptance and encouragement of their emergence as much as the other lower castes, yet they were participating in the political activities of the cultural nationalists, struggling within them for a fair share of social and political power. However, when it became clear that integration within the nation–state was pre-conditioned by the acceptance of a peripheral position within the nation they began their search for greener pastures using their rich religious traditions, myths and memories.

The main ideologues of Muslim nationalism—Syed Ahmed Khan, Iqbal and Jinnah—all started out as staunch pan-Indian nationalists and only subsequently turned separatists. The first articulations of the separatist Muslim national consciousness, by consensus, can be traced to the 1860s when Ahmed Khan's ambiguous statements were expressed when the demand for replacement of Urdu by Hindi in the UP administration was raised. Khan's concept of 'quam' too, varied from time to time. But what is of significance is his stress on education, much in the same way as that by the lower classes and castes in general. Iqbal's dream of a homeland for Muslims was pretty late in coming during the first decade of the present century, and revolved around the northwest region although the status of the region as province or nation remained ambiguous. Jinnah's term of struggle with the cultural nationalists was the longest. Without however, minimizing the inherent ambiguities of the colonial situation, the growing power and territorial spread of Islam and the later virulence of the Muslim 'communalists' themselves, it could still be said that during the pre-Khilafat period the thrust of the Muslims in general was power sharing and progress through education. Their separatist imaginations and visions, riddled with several ambiguities, never managed to mobilize the culturally scattered Muslim masses at the subcontinental level, but continued to be a phenomenon of certain areas only and as such were very much within the power of the cultural nationalists to contain and hegemonize.[32]

Later historiography, due to contemporary political compulsions, sought to apportion equal responsibility and blame to both Hindu and Muslim communalisms or exclusivist visions. But at the level of society it was the social and cultural separatism of the dominant castes that was prior both logically and historically. Aspirations for political separatism on the part of the Muslim elite was truly a fall-out ·of their inability to secure an honourable place within the sectarian national vision of the cultural nationalists.[33]

Gandian political philosophy and praxis attempted to collapse these antagonistic and alternate·visions into a unitary societal form in consonance with the unitary state structure erected by British Imperialism. Did it succeed in its historical mission?

---

[32] Basic readings for Muslim political/cultural imagining are the writings of S.A. Khan, Iqbal and Jinnah; and also see K.K. Aziz (1987), A. Aziz (1967), S.N. Ahmed (1991), F. Malik (ed) (1971) etc; and B.R. Ambedkar's (1990) Vol 8.

[33] While the theme 'Hinduism in danger' was at the very root of nationalist political awakening, the slogan, 'Islam in danger' was raised only during the last decade of the colonial rule, see B. Chandra (1984) pp. 163 ff. .

VI

Nationalism and Nation: The Gandhian Synthesis

Transitions

The overall impact of colonial rule on the hierarchical society had been to bring together similarly positioned castes and communities in the social structure, and to widen the already existing cleavage between the higher and lower castes, thus initiating a process of double horizontal polarization. Such a transformation, depicted above in ideal-typical fashion reproduced itself in political consciousness, which was similarly seen to be largely dichotomous or disjuncted.[1] Within the sociological paradigm of nationalism as congruence between culture and power, the two strands of consciousness represented the two aspects of congruence—one, of the lower castes, tribals and largely Muslim masses aspiring for homogenization or equitable distribution of power within culture, and two, the upper caste-cluster centred around the Brahmin communities, demanding transfer of power from without. Within the long span of the subcontinent's history, the cleavage as well as the consciousness represented in their bipolarity a continuity, albeit in modernized form, with the age-old power-realization as dominance of and resistance to ascriptive inequality. With reference to the old order, the destruction of which constitutes the minimum pre-condition for the emergence of the

---

[1] See S.K. Ghosh (1989), p 1. In fact a trichotomous political awakening including ethnic-national could be identified, which eventually collapsed into a contentious dichotomy, see chapter IV.

nation as the modern political community, these two streams and the social forces representing them stood antagonistically related to each other.[2] The masses were clamouring for the demolition of the Brahminical social order and the upper castes were struggling to reincarnate it as nationalist ideology through liberal western categories.

The antagonistic totality of political awakening within the constraints of colonial dominance is extremely significant, given the fact that pursuit of political economy and construction of civil society had become the new overriding ambition of the masses for the first time in the history of the subcontinent, and that this project was seen as a challenge not only for a select few but for everyone; hence the need for engaging in the process collectively and competitively. In other words, this conflictive awakening is about hard, material and worldly realities—the economic and political, whose structure within society is no more pre-ordained or fixed (as within the traditional order) but is to be shaped and reshaped continually in collaboration and competition with other fellow human beings, in terms of changeable and changing positions and alliances. This whole set of new realities is even more significant for the masses of lower castes whose position within the socio-political structure till recently had appeared to be immutably fixed at the bottom rung through the formidable doctrines of Karma and Dharma. The ascendancy of the economic and the political as a civic project for the entire society, and more so for the lowly placed communities is being stressed here as a new emergence because during the second phase of political mobilization, to be analysed below, it's very *raison d'être* was sought to be challenged, and the process to be contained.

Till about the First World War, the growth of political consciousness had been antagonistically bifurcated reflecting the material interests of the different social groups. The lower caste groups, tribals and the Muslim masses in general were spreading and escalating their attempts to get past the different disabilities that had been their lot under caste feudalism in various ways, in the hope of actualizing and appropriating the new socio-political order. However their multifarious attempts could not be unified, generalized or raised to the

---

[2] In modern times, doing away with ascriptive, social hierarchy is considered the minimum and not the maximum requirement for the emergence of new political community. In history the maximum has been formulated as the communist ideal, with other forms such as welfare state, liberal democracy etc. thrown in between.

pan-Indian level. They remained instead, fragmented and uneven due not only to the limited nature of economic change that had taken place but also due to the plural nature of Indian society itself.[3] The upper caste group on the other hand, were getting unified at a pan-Indian level on the strength of common religio-cultural traditions and new-found educational and economic well-being. Their preoccupation was the transfer of power from the British exclusively to themselves. However, being a 'microscopic minority' and lacking the necessary sanction in their struggle, their repeated supplications for more share in power had hardly produced any response. Within these two polarities, the Muslim elite's attempt to carve out a unified Muslim political identity too proved only a limited success. The Montagu-Chelmsford proposal for further devolution of power accelerated the processes of political mobilization of these contesting forces, and contradiction among them sharpened further. The Home Rulers tried to extend their constituency through the use of religious symbols and by concluding a pact with the Muslim elite in 1917 (I. R. Cashman 1975; B. Southard 1980). Such attempts at demonstrating their 'national' character only further alienated the non-Brahmins and the masses in general. In their view the nationalists were Brahminic and their impatience for power was aimed at excluding the traditionally excluded masses.. The nationalists' ideological response was to delegitimize lower caste struggles by describing them as job-hunting, casteism, communalism, pro-imperialism etc.[4] The foreign rulers pretended neutrality in these wranglings and were trying to utilize the resultant antagonisms towards their continuance.

Such an impasse in the nascent political life of the subcontinent was not to last too long. Changes in the international scene, combined with the arrival of Gandhi, no doubt a charismatic figure, effected far reaching changes in the political mobilization of the country. The success of the Communist revolution in Russia and the advocacy by the Leninist International of the principle of self-determination for colonies had universalized its earlier limited application at the Versailles Treaty. This offered a sense of freedom and politico-moral

[3] The subcontinent's society is not only a hierarchical one but pluralist as well with several unevenly formed linguistic/ethnic communities. Ethnic pluralism as a political problematic however came up towards the very end of the colonial period and became a major political agenda during the post-Independence era.

[4] S. Kumaraswamy Reddy, 'If we ask for a ministry it is job hunting; and if Congressmen ask for it, it is patriotism' quoted in C.J. Baker (1976), p. 306.

legitimacy to nationalist struggles all over the world and especially in India. The rise of pan-Islamism too had its fall-out here, with the provision of a lever for the Muslim elite against the British who imposed an 'unjust' war punishment to the Caliph in Turkey. Very soon (by 1921) the Communist movement also was to become another reality that had to be reckoned with in the political life. By the time Gandhi entered the scene, politics in the subcontinent had become intensely competitive. The nationalist movement as represented by the Indian National Congress, composed of several streams of thought and social groups, was only one among the many competing forces, albeit the most dominant. The public and political postures of the nationalists were increasingly being determined not only with reference to the colonial rulers but also to the competing groups in the field. Two developments in particular tended to blur the earlier dichotomized, political consciousness: one was the local agenda of pan-Islamism, to create a pan-Indian Muslim political identity; and two, the birth of communist, socialist consciousness at different levels. Muslim political mobilization along with its counterpart Hindu Mahasabha movement were explicitly vertical mobilizations aimed at cross-cutting the interest based, class-like cleavages that had developed earlier. The success of both was severely limited and their trend largely reversible in the pre-Gandhian era.[5] The advent of socialist consciousness also created complexities though at a different level, for both the political polarities; suffice it to state here that this was no simple strengthening, either of the lower caste struggles for power homogenization within, nor a unilateral support to those who aspired for transference of power from the British.[6]

GANDHI AS AN EVENT

The Gandhian era (1920–1947) of the Indian nationalist movement

[5] See G. Minault (1982), for the formation of a pan-Indian Muslim identity.

[6] The rise of the proletariat in India from a hierarchical society that had not undergone any significant level of industrialization or social mobility, the caste background of the working class as well as of the Indian Communist leadership, the implication of these to the new politics as well as its postures *vis-à-vis* the dichotomous political awakening etc. are questions that still await exploration. B.B. Misra (1976) suggests that ideas of Socialism, Marxism etc. were appropriated 'not so much from ideological considerations as from political compulsions', p. 152. See also the specific area studies such as G. Jha (1990).

is understandably seen as the period in which the nationalist movement became multi-class and mass-based, gained politico-moral legitimacy, achieved enormous power due to its indigenous tone and style. Thus by effecting a national and nationalist synthesis it succeeded in wresting power from the British. The following pages are intended to scrutinize these processes from the point of view of the fading out of the traditional order and rise of the 'nation'.

Gandhi returned to India from South Africa in 1915, toured around the country, involved himself with the tenants and their problems in Champaran and Kaira and the industrial workers in Ahmedabad, organized an all-India movement which was only partially successful against the Rowlatt Act (1919). He was instrumental in setting up the Central Committee on Khilafat, and became virtually a dictator, for life, of the Indian National Congress since 1920. Combined with the pan-Islamists, he launched the first historic non-cooperation movement but withdrew it prematurely in 1922, in the wake of Chauri Chaura incidents, subsequently engaged himself with constructive programmes with an emphasis on Khadi, allowing the Congress to wield partial power in the legislatures. The Bardoli Satyagraha in 1928 brought him back to national attention, from where he went on to his second great movement of civil disobedience. He represented the Congress in the Round Table Conference of 1931, and deprived the untouchables of the advantage of additional representation granted to them by the communal award through an indefinite fast. The second period of his withdrawal from politics is marked by his emphasis on Harijan upliftment; 1942 saw him leading the Quit India movement, followed by frantic efforts to bring about Hindu-Muslim unity. In 1947 he walked away leaving the Congress to celebrate Independence Day. During this quarter century or so, Gandhi set up several organizations for the promotion of specific causes—Cow Protection Society, One Language, One Script Society, All India Spinner's Association, Harijan Sevak Sangh, All India Village Industries Association etc., carried on voluminous correspondence, wrote on practically everything under the sun, conducted prolonged experiments on sex, food etc., and was in general involved with several other activities which he thought would lead to the moral regeneration of society. A man of extraordinary energy, Gandhi influenced the course of pre-Independence politics as no other individual had done.

However, the Gandhi-Event from the twenties upto forties of

this century is much larger and more complex than the person of Gandhi and his activities. Though centred around the charismatic leader, the Gandhi-Event is a product of several socio-political factors. First of all, there was the Congress, which was related to Gandhi symbiotically yet ambiguously; secondly, the colonial rulers who played no small role in magnifying the Gandhian image;[7] thirdly, the unique support of the Gujarati and Marwari business communities that Gandhi alone enjoyed;[8] fourthly, the private army of Ashram members and volunteers owing personal allegiance to Gandhi and performing the specific function of providing a spiritualist aura to whatever Gandhi did or said; and fifthly, the multiplicity of local interpretations of the Gandhian national message. An analysis of Gandhi as an Event has to be sensitive to these and other dimensions.

Our view of the Gandhi-Event would see Gandhi radically contextualized within contemporary politics which had become intensely competitive, with new dimensions being introduced in the post-war period. This meant that Gandhi and the nationalist movement had to compete with several other forces simultaneously, in their struggle against Imperialism.[9] Gandhian actions in particular, always had this double reference—one vertical, relating to the rulers, and the other horizontal, relating to alternate national contestants.

Gandhi wrote voluminously on almost all matters and as a tireless activist was engaged in an amazing variety of activities. All these did not have a uniform bearing on the movement: a large part of what he said went by the way side, some had a fleeting or partial impact while other parts were manipulated by different people for their own purposes. Within all these limitations, however, he did manage to carry through his main message. Understanding Gandhi as an Event means the unearthing of the Gandhi that had a determining role on the course of the nationalist movement. Finally, we need to ask whether Gandhi was a saint or a politician. That the Gandhian

[7] See J. Brown (1977), p 12; S.K. Ghosh (1989), pp 113, 116, 188, 190. Ellen Williamson thought that 'Gandhi was the best policeman the Britisher had in India', quoted in S. Sinha (1963) p. 57.

[8] C. Markovits (1985) 'The link between Gandhi and a large section of the business Community was a link between Hindu banias with a Hindu political leader rather than a link between an emergent capitalist class and a national leader', p 189; for examples of the kind of financial resources that Gandhi had at his disposal, see G.D. Birla (1968).

[9] And hence the limitation of all approaches to study Gandhi and the nationalist movement entirely within the nationalism-imperialism dichotomy.

discourse is a combination of two kinds, religious and political, has
been generally recognized. But few have pointed out the ambiguous
or even contradictory relationship between the two, and fewer still
the differential impact such a combination had on groups located
unequally and related antagonistically within the traditional social
structure.[10] Within the Gandhi-Event a running discourse on renun-
ciation and moral regeneration is carried on with another, of ruthless
pursuit of monopoly, political power. The elaborate agenda of wresting
moral authority from the British is but a prelude to investing the
same on a set of power-driven politicians. The different Ashrams
as part of constructive programmes, though intended for moral
regeneration of Hindu Society at large, were also propaganda centres
for Congress politics. All of these, and other similar contradictions,
are not reducible to the enigmatic relationship of Gandhi with the
Congress. Gandhi himself seems to carry this seed of contradiction
within his person: his seeming poverty was built on Birla's plenty,
his life of Brahmacharya was based on obsessive sex experiments.[11]
His project of the recovery of the human body from medical tyranny
was conducted while he was under continuous care of allopathic
physicians; his posture of humility was coupled with the claim for
exclusive access to Truth; he preached a politics of powerlessness
and non-possession that did not brook rivals in leadership. His sen-
sitivity to the spiritual equality of all men was coupled with an
insistence on Varnashrama Dharma as the social ideal.[12] For Gandhi,
politics is the means and moral regeneration the end; Satyagraha
and constructive programmes mediated the two; he wanted power

[10] The combination of religion/ethics and politics in Gandhi has been largely acclaimed
as unique and a sign of Indianness and is sought to be analysed 'sui generis' outside
the parameters of ordinary social sciences, by writers of neo-Brahminical orientation.
While this method of analysis of Gandhi and the Gandhian, may increase its saleability,
especially in the West, it hardly helps to understand the real nature of Gandhian
leadership of an interest-based political movement in its competitive context.

[11] Sarojini Naidu, 'If only Bapu knew how much it cost, to keep him simple',
quoted in P. Spear (1969), p. 302.

[12] The disjunction within the Gandhian discourse has been noted by several people.
The British thought that Gandhi always acted with an 'ulterior motive', see J. Brown
1988, p. 271; Edgar Snow, 'the dual role of Saint for masses and champion of big
business which was the secret of Gandhi's power', S.K.Ghosh (1989), p. 93. Even
a sympathetic writer A. Nandy (1986) is not unaware of this problem in Gandhi,
p. 99-100. In this context Gandhi's own view of himself may be revealing, 'There
are people who may call me visionary but I tell you I am a real bania and my
business is to obtain Swaraj', quoted in J. Brown (1988), p. 271.

for the Congress so that it could serve the masses effectively. But within the hard world of real politics which is what the politics of contesting nationalism is all about, the means-end relationship did not appear so simple nor so stable, at least in its praxis. A realistic analysis of the national movement during its second phase has to gather up these two contradictory discourses within the Gandhi-Event.

Cow Protection, Khilafat and Untouchability

Gandhi's entry into nationalist politics towards the end of the World War I had far reaching consequences for the subcontinent as a whole; by all appearances it changed the very face of political awakening itself. Within an incredibly short period of five years Gandhi became the most prominent nationalist leader. His all-India tour, forays into the world of tenants and workers in Champaran, Kaira and Ahmedabad, and an all-India preliminary of the Rowlatt Satyagraha all conducted largely outside the formal domain of Congress politics, had already helped to weave the myth of a saintly activist out to set right the wrongs perpetrated by a satanic government. The year 1919-20 however saw him busy forging a new national formula of political alignment, with a sharper weapon, to initiate the new politics of wresting moral authority from the colonial rulers.

The affirmative orientalism of earlier days had prepared the platform of ideological antagonism between upper caste Hindus with a stake in the socio-cultural traditions, and the rulers who exploited the hegemonic possibilities of negative Orientalism.[13] However this alone was insufficient without the effective sanction of the masses whose agenda, as we saw, was unfortunately anti-Brahminic. A consensus therefore was imperative. Khilafat seemed to be a windfall for the pan-Islamic elite struggling to create a distinct political constituency. Finally, the anti-Brahminic agenda of the masses could not proceed beyond a certain limit at the pan-Indian level due to its inherent constraints such as its culture-linguistic rootedness. The dilemmas of these various political formations opened up possibilities for the charismatic new entrant—Gandhi.

His South African experiences with the Muslims helped him in the process of bringing the Ali brothers around to non-cooperation

---

[13] For a treatment of Gandhi's ideas as a continuation of affirmative Orientalism see R.G. Fox (1989), pp. 107-28.

against the government on the question of Khilafat; the quid pro
quo ban on cow-slaughter was accepted gratefully.[14] In return Hindu,
presumably meaning Congress support was promised. It was happily
believed that Hindu–Muslim unity, or more specifically the Ali-Gandhi
combine, could effectively set right the Khilafat wrong. The subsequent
process of getting the Congress to fall in line, though tortuous was
not very difficult (the Punjab wrong was added as an afterthought)
for the Congress had no other alternative. A bigger gulf, however,
existed between the caste-Hindu nationalists and the Shudra, Ati-
Shudra masses challenging or sabotaging Brahminism. Gandhian genius
searched for the appropriate Hindu counterpart to Khilafat and found
it in anti-untouchability. Within Gandhi's calculation, the caste-Hindus could not settle for less and the masses could not, ask for more.
Thus a new nationalist synthesis was conjured by bringing together
the different warring groups—the caste-Hindus, the Muslim elite and
the lower caste masses—on a twin programme of Khilafat and anti-
untouchability for the sacred cause of nationalism.

The Indian National Congress, under its newfound 'permanent
super president', answerable only to his own 'inner voice', thus having
forged together a new political formula, was thoroughly overhauled
(J. Nehru 1936: 132). The changes included a new constitution
and formal structure parallel to that of the British Raj, linguistic
divisions to ensure effective transmission of the message, four anna
membership etc. The war machine was then set to motion with
the slogan 'Swaraj within one year', and intense political mobilization
with stage by stage implementation of non-cooperation was carried
out.

Resolution no. 11, para 25, of the Nagpur Congress Session read
thus:

> Finally in order that the Khilafat and the Punjabi wrongs may
> be redressed and Swarajya established within one year, this Congress
> urges upon all public bodies, whether affiliated to the Congress
> or otherwise, to devote their exclusive attention to the promotion
> of non-violence and non-co-operation with the government and
> in as much as the movement of non-co-operation can only succeed

---

[14] 'The way to save the cow is to die in the act of saving the Khilafat without
mentioning the cow', M.K. Gandhi, (1922) p. 814 and p. 831; see also G. Minault
(1982) p. 78 and G.R. Thursby (1975) p. 130. For the Muslim offer to 'Save the
cow', see Gandhi (1924) pp. 141 ff.

by complete co-operation amongst the people themselves, this Congress calls upon public associations to advance Hindu-Muslim unity and the Hindu delegates of this Congress call upon Hindus to settle all disputes between Brahmins and non-Brahmins, wherever they may be existing and to make a special effort to rid Hinduism of the reproach of untouchability and respectfully urges the religious heads to help the growing desire to reform Hinduism in the matter of its treatment of the suppressed castes (All India Congress Committee 1924: 31-2).[15]

The actual extent, the success or otherwise of the Non-Co-operation Movement have been described variously depending on the orientation of the individual historian; however it cannot be denied that it was here that political mobilization itself became an actuality for the first time in nationalist politics in serious fashion. Several new groups such as the educated elite of the backward areas, (UP, Bihar and Gujarat), the trading communities, the landlords, and to some extent the rural elite were mobilized in the cause of nationalism, and an atmosphere of mass participation was created. But it was soon found that wherever the masses came in, violence threatened to overtake the movement, and when this became unbearable to Gandhi, he withdrew the movement in 1922.

As the first major effort at nationalist political mobilization, (self-conscious) and (well thought-out) by the Gandhian leadership, the Non-Co-operation Movement is extremely significant in several respects: the changes it sought to bring about in the existing political alignment of forces, the tone and style of the movement, the processes of mobilization, its fall-out etc. Analogous to a trauma at birth, all these aspects were to play determining roles in subsequent political mobilizations in the subcontinent.

The first phase of the Gandhi-Event not only transformed Congress but also destablized and threw out of gear other political formations as well. Gandhi's initiative in founding the All-India Cow Protection Society and One Script, One Language Conference effectively took the wind out of the sails of the Hindu Mahasabha which ceased

---

[15] Significantly Gandhi was not the first one to realize the need for bringing in the Muslims and the lower caste masses into the nationalist movement. The pre-Gandhian attempts were a continuation of the interest based politics: the Lucknow pact of 1916 and the same year's Congress resolution on removal of 'all civil disabilities imposed on the depressed classes by custom' stand in sharp contrast to the Gandhian religious synthesis. See E. Zelliot (1988), pp. 182-97.

to meet between the years 1920 and 1922. With the ascendancy of the Khilafat Committee lead by the Ali brothers and legitimized by Gandhi, the Muslim League practically faded out of existence (1918-24). The Indian Social Conference, which had a distinct but a limited agenda of the welfare of the depressed classes had a serious setback. Lower caste organizations were thrown into confusion and some splits did take place in their ranks although they escaped major onslaught. Thus the Gandhian attempt was to start with a clean slate of national politics, and to this end was considerably successful.

The Non-Co-operation Movement has had certain long-term effects that did not prove beneficial to the political advancement of the country in general and did a lot of harm to the struggles against the traditional Brahminic order in particular. First of all, the entire Gandhian confabulation took place within the presumably sanctified realm of God, Truth, Sin and Punishment—in short, the realm of religion. It was sinful to co-operate with the government, not to support Khilafat, not to work for the abolition of untouchability etc. Gandhi went about as a religious preacher, accompanied by adoring and Bhajan singing devotees, very much like a medieval saint or a harbinger of a new millenium. The leader was peddled to the masses as a miracle-worker who would conjure up Swaraj from out of nowhere.[16] And Swaraj itself was left 'delightfully vague'.[17] It was apparently everything for everybody, without actually disturbing anybody.[18] The net result was to deflect the course of political awakening from the hard world of the economic and political to that of the nebulous and mysterious.

Gandhi's prescription for the Muslim masses who were engaged in struggles for educational betterment, job reservation and adequate political representation was Khilafat—an ambiguous and anachronistic religious symbol even for them.[19] On the other hand, Khilafat rep-

[16] For the religio-millenial nature of the Gandhi-Event see S. Natarajan (1959), p. 138; D. Hardiman (1981), p. 240; K. Kumar (1983); J. Pouchepadass (1974) and particularly G. Shah (1974).

[17] Nehru (1936), p. 76. D. Keer (1973) has noted that Gandhi had more than twenty definitions of Swaraj p. 355.

[18] Gandhi (1947), 'It is as much for the prince as the peasant, as much for the rich land owner as for the landless tiller of the soil', pp. 9, 33.

[19] See A. Hamid (1967) p. 10 and G. Minault (1982), p. 1. That Gandhian politics attempted to deflect the Muslims from pursuing political interests with a view to

resented political interest for the pan-Islamic elite. The agenda of anti-untouchability played a still more ambiguous role for the lower caste masses whose current concerns were social mobility, education, diversification of occupations and the like (see chapter III). Their interest in anti-untouchability was largely from the point of view of escaping the civil liabilities imposed in the name of religion. On the contrary, Gandhian anti-untouchability was out and out a religious issue and when pursued, appeared to counter their own idea and struggles for emancipation.[20] Cow, Khilafat and Untouchability were the three Mantras which sought to bring down the surging bipolar political consciousness and change the emerging new alignment of social forces. Khilafat as a pan-Islamic agenda threw the Muslim groups into confusion by deflecting them from their present course of action. It gave them a rarefied religious issue in the place of the concrete Lucknow pact. It also differentiated the Muslim masses from lower castes and tribals by reminding them of their religious identity. The Muslim demand for economic and political reservation was primarily based on their experience of being backward and marginalized in the new civil society. The Gandhian counter-agenda for them was based primarily on their religio-cultural identity. Anti-untouchability in its turn reduced a total and substantial agenda consisting of the struggle against ascriptive hierarchy of the mass of lower castes, to a nominal symbolic struggle for a minority of untouchable castes. Here too, the intended shifting of planes and cutting of alliances was clear enough; the terrain was now that of the religio-moral. More important however, was the weakening of struggle of the majority of lower castes who did not suffer from the crudest form of aparthied but none the less stood against ascriptive power relations. The mass was now divided into untouchables and touchables! If the Khilafat and Untouchability movements peremptorily demanded change in the agenda of the respective social groups, Cow Protection signified only a change of heart on the part of the caste-Hindus. And most often, since Gandhi was the ideal Hindu change of his own heart was considered sufficient for the purpose.

---

protect the Congress monopoly pursuit of power, is the argument of S. Sinha (1963), p. 6, 24, 27 and 64.

[20] 'For me the question of these classes is predominantly moral and religious. The political aspect, important though it is dwindles into insignificance compared to the moral and religious issue' and 'I want to save them against themselves', Gandhi quoted in B.R. Ambedkar (1945), p. 78 and p. 70.

This conscious and calculated attempt to displace the secular and political by the religious and symbolic is commensurate with the Gandhian understanding of the Hindu-Indian ethos as distinct from and even contrary to the materialist West. The Indian genius is presumably spiritual and hence all our competition should be restricted to the attainment of Moksha.[21] This overarching religious discourse, for the benefit of the Muslim and lower caste masses, was simultaneous with the process of strengthening the bargaining power of and the addition of sanction to the power struggle of the upper caste-lead nationalist movement (S. Natarajan 1959: 145). Religion thus, whether or not intended by Gandhi, coincided with the giving up of the political for the masses, while strengthening the same for the classes.

Gandhian political conduct within the so-called superior framework of religion or ethics operated differentially on people whose interests had already become bifurcated and who had contradictory political agendas. The old and new classes that were in the leadership of the nationalist movement, though often embarassed and puzzled by Gandhian eccentricities, always acquiesed in the end to the new politics for they understood very well that herein were secured their future economic and political interests. The religious discourse of Gandhi within the new political praxis, in short, meant religion for the lower caste masses and politics for the uppercaste nationalists. A disastrous fall-out of this is the instrumental and mostly hypocritical use of religion to cover up power pursuits, degrading both religion and politics (A.N. Das 1983: 90-100). Whether Gandhi himself intended this or not is of marginal value here; what is of relevance is that this way of conducting politics was the first and therefore to some extent determinative of the nature of mass awakening within nationalist politics that spread all over the country and percolated downward to quite an extent. What is specifically 'modern' in Indian mass politics has seen the light of day.

Pre-Gandhian political awakening was not only interest-based but also a reflection of the horizontal cleavage between the upper castes and lower caste masses in general, a cleavage that had widened as a result of colonial policies and practices. While this social disjunction, in the absence of large scale industrialization and social mobility, did not come anywhere near the Marxian concept of class, it did unambiguously point out the direction in which economy and politics

[21] For 'spiritual' as specifically Indian, see R.G. Fox (1989), p. 39-40.

were moving. Propertied classes in the subcontinent came to be perceived as upper casteist (with a handful of the Muslim elite thrown in, of course), and the Shudra, Ati-Shudras, tribals and Muslim masses represented the dispossesed. The class-like formation was clearly horizontal, cutting across so-called religious unities. Particularly remarkable was the fact that the Muslim masses, most of whom were converts from the lower castes, stood within the social structure as near equals to their Hindu counterparts exhibiting unmistakeable signs of unity of interest with them. Together they were antagonistically poised towards the upper castes/classes.[22]

This scenario, being opposed to the supposedly organic nature of Hindu society, alarmed Gandhi a great deal; the closure of this fissure was also a political need of the leading nationalist castes (R.G. Fox 1989: 40-1). The Non-Co-Operation Movement based on Cow Protection, Khilafat and Untouchability was aimed precisely at arresting this development and reversing this trend of political movement. The tragedy of modern Indian politics lies in direct proportion to the success of this first phase of the Gandhi-Event.

The professed agenda of Khilafat was setting right the wrong done to the Caliph in Turkey. The Sultan, being the Islamic counterpart of the Pope, was not at all unambiguous within British India. Secondly, the Arabs had raised the banner of self-determination against him. Finally the Turkish people themselves were fast casting aside the Caliphate as anachronism; nor did the local Khilafatists hope to ever check the changing global scenario. The real agenda of Khilafat had to be located within the subcontinent in the political need of a section of the Muslim elite for a separate constituency. In this project of the setting up of a vertical pan-Indian Muslim political community, under the leadership of the Ali brothers, Gandhian Khilafat and Non-Co-operation played a major, if not a decisive role.[23] In several senses this coming into being of a pan-Indian Muslim political consciousness is a logical sequel and a necessity to the previous rise of pan-Indian Hindu political consciousness.

[22] B.B. Majumdar (1965) points out to the similarity of political awakening between the lower castes and Muslims p. 259; S. Bandyopadhyay (1989) points out the interest-based unity between the East Bengal Muslims and Nama Shudras, p. 194; see also B. Hettne (1978) pp. 131-57; J.B. Brown (1984), p. 152.

[23] That the creation of Muslim political identity under the leadership of the Ali brothers was the real political agenda of Khilafat is the basic argument of G. Minault (1982); see also J. Brown (1972), p. 220.

Participation in and enablement of the maturing of a fellow religious community into political adulthood yielded several incidental benefits to upper caste Hindus of the Congress, and specially to Gandhi. The fact that the Congress itself would represent the political interests of the Hindus, that Gandhi, being the model Hindu, would act as a supreme Hindu leader and that both sets of elite would take care of the mobilization of 'their own masses' without interfering in each other's domain, were silently agreed upon by the colluding elite of both communities, and forcefully imposed upon the masses who were on the 'dangerous march' towards unity based on new secular political interests. Khilafat and Non-Co-Operation, though ostensibly intended to bring about Hindu-Muslim unity, prevented the maturing of the masses into a whole in terms of secular politics, and brought about an ephemeral elite unity in terms of symbolic religious categories, to deflect the mass agenda of subverting the traditional social order. The vertical mobilization of the two communities that followed, quickly replacing the tortuous growth of horizontal mobilization was the new politics of the emerging ruling caste-cluster and their response to the nascent mass upsurge of the emerging nation. The direct result of Khilafat and Non-Co-Operation was to tear asunder the lower caste-Muslim unity, bring the respective masses under the leadership of the traditional elite of the two communities, using the newly fabricated idiom of pan-Indian political identities, both Hindu and Muslim. It is in this context that Gandhi's fearful utterance, at the instance of the Communal Award gains omnious significance and indicates the direction in which his mind was working: 'Untouchable hooligans will make common cause with Muslim hooligans and kill caste Hindus' (M. Desai 1953: 301).[24] The Gandhian nationalist agenda here is unambiguous: the replacement of the emerging mass unity, based on economics and politics, and the arresting of the class-like polarization process by the creation of two vertical communities based on religion and religious identities, and placing them under the presumed elite unity of the respective communities. This shift from the secular to the spiritual, politics to religion, was presumed to be in accordance with the Eastern genius and a part and parcel of the erection of the nationalist moral response to imperialism. While the fixing of sole responsibility of

---

[24] Note Gandhi's plea, 'I am here today to ask for a reprieve for my caste Hindu brethren' in Pyarelal (1932), p. 70.

Hindu-Muslim communalism and Partition on the person of Gandhi acting consciously or wilfully, is not the aim of this analysis, the role played by the Gandhi-Event in the process cannot be exaggerated.[25]

The Brahminic nature of the subcontinent's nationalism was thus sought to be covered up by Khilafat on the one hand and anti-Untouchability on the other. The first phase of the Gandhi-Event did succeed at least partially in this. But the price was formidable: the negation of the emergence of the masses into a new interest based political community. Since Khilafat and Non-Co-Operation, vertical mobilization of Hindu and Muslim communities became the dominant discourse of nationalism, submerging the struggling discourse of social mobility, education, diversification of occupation by the lower castes. In this nationalist counter-discourse the advocates of Hindu-Muslim unity as well as those who stood for antagonism, both had a remarkable identity of function: to prevent the nation from emerging. The autonomy of the lower caste masses was to be denied at all costs and their differential and modern political agenda to be submerged. The nationalist version of the nation was now composed of two vertical communities presumably run on the basis of the pre-modern social order, of course with the necessary expansion of power and a political role for the upper caste elite.[26] In Gandhi's hands nationalism too went through a subtle metamorphosis. Pre-Gandhian nationalism was a coalition of interests of different regions (M. Edwards 1986: 203; J.H. Broomfield 1968: 147). The nationalist leaders were men rooted in the culture and language of respective ethnic communities and they brought such cultural differentiation to bear on their nationalist enterprises. Their leadership was limited to the regions they hailed from, and hence at the centre the form of the high command was to an extent collective, co-operative and consultative. This was no doubt made easier because the political nation was then small and strictly comprised elites only.

In contrast to this, Gandhian leadership was a truly nationalist one, in the sense that Gandhi was the first leader of all-India stature, having a direct link with different regions. Negatively speaking, he never had a home constituency in the true sense; he was a Gujarati

---

[25] See P. Spear (1969), p. 299; S. Natarajan (1959), p. 133; also S.K. Ghosh (1989) p. 248.

[26] No doubt, viewing Indians as Hindus/Muslims, originated within Imperialism and was also found during the early nationalist phase, see D. Naoroji (1990), p. 183; but with Gandhi this became an effective determinant in politics.

bania and this gave him enormous support from his kinsmen and region. However, here too, his leadership was through assistants only (J. Brown 1972: pp. 186 ff; R. Kumar 1971: 100). As the dictator of an all-India body, Gandhi was possessive of his monopoly control of all the organizations he headed, and was answerable to none but to his own 'inner voice'. He was also almost completely insensitive to the cultural differentiation, uneven historical and social development of the different communities within the subcontinent.[27] To him India represented a monolithic religio–cultural community having the same cultural and social characteristics everywhere. He was attuned to the 'unifying' or the 'uniformising aspects of Indian culture only, while ... diversification was to an extent considered an aberration'.[28] All these aspects of the new leadership led to a concept of nationalism that was at once rarefied and both ideological and symbolic. The vested interest that could form the basis of this uniformized and to an extent abstract nationalism could be the thin dominant, upper caste strata of different linguistic regions, unified not in terms of their own ethnic cultures and symbols, but the presumed Indian culture. Gandhi had to struggle with both the Maharashtra and Bengal leadership and to relocate the gravitational centre of nationalism to the cow belt (U.P.) where cultural differentiation was at its lowest.[29] Gandhi also found that local circumstances and issues distorted Non-Co-Operation beyond all recognition. The issues hence, of the new nationalist struggles were chosen so as to avoid representing any regional, local interests and to signify the so-called national-symbolic: Hindu-Muslim-unity, Khaddar, Untouchables, Rowlatt, Salt etc.

Unity and diversity in the concrete context of the socio-cultural development of the subcontinent are not two value neutral aspects of what constitutes pan-Indian society; they are not apolitical terms. Unity represents the dominant and uniformizing culturo-ideological and mythical Brahminic factors and is thus oppressive: Vedic-

[27] A. Nandy (1986), p. 20; D Keer (1973) pp. 239 ff; M. Edwards (1986) p. 201; B. Parekh (1989) p. 51.

[28] The Gandhian vision of radical decentralization through Panchayat Raj and village economy is also a piece with this; decentralization here is economico-administrative, and the eternal village is supposed to be reproduced in all its monotony all over the subcontinent; the centralization on the other hand, of Gandhian ideology, is culturo–ideological.

[29] See D. Keer (1973), p. 379; S. Sinha (1963), p. 94; J.H. Broomfield (1968), chapter II.

Brahminic Hinduism as the only acceptable form of Hinduism, Sanskrit as the basis of all languages, Brahmins as the caste to be found all over the subcontinent, and Varnashrama Dharma as the traditional order, representing the dominant and oppressive, ideal social order of the ruling and vested interests. Diversity on the other hand, stands for the movement away from these uniformizing factors, the tendencies of resistance of the subaltern and the locally rooted castes and communities in general; the growth of the vernaculars and their cultural communities, and the scores of attempts at creating culturally specific non-Brahminic myths and popular religions, are, in a sense, the defiance of the commoners against the imposition from above. Finally, the actual and attenuated realization of the Varnashrama Dharmic ideal in the different regions of the subcontinent represent a history of resistance and uneven success.

Understood this way, the subcontinent's history, tradition and inheritance are composed of both these distinct yet often dialectically united streams, and together in an imaginative and creative synthesis, would ideally inform the nationalist political awakening and mobilization. Now, elevating one trend and that too the oppressive one, in favour of the other/others, to the sacred position of nationalism, the Gandhi-Event seriously prejudiced the political emergence of the social forces that historically represented the subaltern and the suppressed. This fact is all the more unfortunate particularly because under the changed circumstances the masses were making significant efforts on their own to come into the new political community. Here too, the idea is not to place the burden squarely on Gandhian shoulders, for seeds of this process existed within the Congress itself; as we have seen the nationalist movement was considered upper casteist and even Brahminic by the major counter movements of the colonial period. But to the extent that the Gandhian vertical mobilization extended down to the masses successfully, nationalism has to be seen as vanquishing the nation itself.

Constructive Programme

The Khilafat and Non-Co-operation experience was followed by a period of withdrawal from active politics for Gandhi who now concentrated on the Constructive Programme. Gandhi's interest in the Constructive Programme dates from his **South African** days and in India it was an alternative to the **westernized programme** of social reform. Within the Gandhian scheme, the Constructive Programme is midway between the goal of moral regeneration of Hindu Society and that of attaining Swaraj; at times the Constructive Programme itself became either moral regeneration or Swaraj. Hence its unique importance in the Gandhian scheme of things.

Gandhi himself enumerated a thirteen-point agenda for the programme: communal unity, removal of untouchability, prohibition, Khaddar, village industries, sanitation, new or basic education, adult education, upliftment of women, health and hygiene, Rashtra Bhasha, love of one's own language and economic equality through trusteeship (M. K. Gandhi 1941). In order to implement the programme Gandhi set up a series of all-India organizations over which he had supreme control; the resource base to run the programmes was generated via the generous donations by Bombay businessmen and Ahmedabad mill-owners who had become committed supporters of Gandhi, but not necessarily of the Congress. Of the thirteen items only three Hindu-Muslim unity, the removal of untouchability and Khaddar—came to have an all-India significance, while the rest were largely limited to Gandhi's home province, Gujarat; within the province itself the work done in Bardoli appears to be of special significance. Gandhi's concentration on the three chosen items seems to have a chronological pattern to it: the Khilafat years are full of activities around Hindu-Muslim unity; Gandhi spent the second half of the twenties boosting the Charkha and Khaddar; after the civil disobedience movement and the Round Table Conference, the removal of untouchability became the obsession; and the forties saw him return to Hindu-Muslim unity.

Several of the programmes do have a socio-economic reference and appear to be intended to bring about a certain measure of socio-economic change in society. In fact they have often been treated as a blueprint for the future society. Looked at from this point of view, Sumit Sarkar's evaluation of their implementation and effect as 'clearly a failure' seems to be accurate (S. Sarkar 1983: 230). But a more appropriate point of view would be to look at the Constructive Programme as a means of Gandhian political mobilization.

Gandhi himself saw Hindu-Muslim unity and the removal of untouchability within the political context of power devolution through the Government of India Acts. The dichotomous political awakening by which the Muslim and lower caste masses stood opposed to the Congress was a serious impediment to the latter's pursuit of monopoly power:

> The Hindus must realise that if they wish to offer successful non-co-operation against the government they must make common cause with the Panchamas even as they have made common cause with the Musalman (M.K. Gandhi 1924: 467).[30]

Secondly, the basis of the dichotomy, the widening gulf between the rich and the poor had to be bridged, if only to avoid widespread social revolution. And the Gandhian scheme to do so was aimed again at consciousness and not the socio-economic infrastructure: 'There are numerous examples extant of the rich and the poor living in perfect friendliness. We have to multiply such instances' (M.K. Gandhi 1970: 19).

While it is possible that Gandhi himself might have actually believed in making 'common cause' with the lower orders, most of his followers obviously did not; for them giving an appearance of common cause was sufficient for the purpose. Of this Gandhi himself was aware: 'Many Congress men have looked upon this item (removal of untouchability) as a mere political necessity and not something indispensable...' (M.K.Gandhi 1941: 6). And Swami Shraddhanand reports that many Patidars who mixed with the untouchables in the presence of Gandhi, went and took a bath later with their clothes on (Swami Shraddhanand 1946: 148). In spite of this, Gandhi did not apply 'his high pressure technique' to change the heart of his followers and hence his responsibility in the matter cannot be absolved (S. Natarajan 1959: 138).

The context of the Muslim question too was equally clear. Gandhi himself was constrained to 'buy their friendship' for the sake of the cow, and Non-Co-Operation (D. Keer 1973: 319; J. Brown 1972: 152). It was a 'marriage of convenience' on both sides for some time in the beginning, and since the nationalist movement became enshrouded in the Gandhian religious discourse the Muslims became suspicious (S. Sinha 1963: pp. 65ff.; G. Minault 1982: 11).

That the lower caste masses and the minorities were being sought for political expediency and nothing more and that the nationalists sole purpose was to gain for themselves national legitimacy and to grab monopoly power was not lost on the former, and accordingly

---

[30] See S.Natarajan (1959), p. 145; T.K. Ravindran (1980), p. 11.

they learned to use their position as a lever to demand their own share of power.[31] As a mainstream historian reports:

> The interest that the Congress showed after 32 years of neglect in social reform was intrinsically political in the worst sense of the term and its espousal of the cause of the depressed classes an expedient which was not seriously implemented. It is worth noting that from this half-hearted manoeuvre sprang the painful process by which the depressed classes passed into a mood of distrust (S. Natarajan 1959: 145).

Obviously the masses were no more the 'dumb millions' that Gandhi took them to be, but a community of men struggling to emerge into a political nation.

Flowing from such an ambiguous intentionality, the implementation process of the constructive programme did not escape the serious limitations of the Gandhian vision itself. Hindu-Muslim unity was on the top of Gandhi's list of priorities and presumably he died for it. However, the nature and substance of the unity he envisaged in the context of the nationalist movement leaves much to be desired. We have already noted that against all saner advice both from Hindus and Muslims, Gandhi shifted the unity discourse from the realm of interest-based politics to religion and community-based mobilization during Khilafat.[32] After this Hindu-Muslim antagonism reached a point of no return. That the Gandhian method of direct pursuit of Hindu-Muslim unity itself was widening the gulf between communities and increasing the very antagonism it sought to remove has been noted by many and sundry.[33] A discourse on the universal truth

---

[31] Swami Shraddhanand (1946), reports a revealing incident: 'The Secretary of the Delhi Congress Committee called the Chowdharies of the Chamars and requested them to give to the Congress as many four anna paying members as they could. The reply of the elders was that unless their grievance as regards the taking of water from the public wells was removed, they could not induce their brethren to join the Congress. The Secretary was a choleric man of hasty temper and said they wanted Swarajya at once but the grievance of the Chamars could wait and would be removed by and by. One of the young men got up and said—'Our trouble from which we are suffering for centuries must wait solution but the "laddu" of Swaraj must go into your mouth at once. We shall see how you obtain Swaraj at once' p. 133-4.

[32] S. Natarajan (1959), p. 133; D. Keer (1973), p. 312; R. Kumar (1983), p. 28.

[33] G. Minault (1982), p 162; R, Gordon (1975), p. 177; B.B.Misra (1976) 'Between 1923-26 there were as many as seventy-two communal riots against sixteen in the course of twenty two years from 1900' p. 188; also K.N. Panikkar (1989), p. 189.

of all religions not withstanding, Gandhi firmly believed in the distinctness and separateness of religious communities; he also believed that the communities themselves were monolithic. His lack of understanding of the new political reality of a nation made him see national unity as merely composed of religious communities with a distinct cultural ethos.[34] He was especially obsessed with the presumed organic nature of Hindu society based on Rigvedic Varnashrama Dharma and appointed himself the guardian of its integrity. Thus the Gandhian vision of national synthesis was basically communal. The more he preached Hindu-Muslim unity the more conscious the communities became of their distinctness and separate identities from each other. Efforts to forge a unity in the realm of religion, simultaneous to the nationalists pursuit of monopoly power appeared to the Muslims as an attempt to depoliticize them and hence, they understandably became more and more antagonistic. As has been rightly pointed out, the Hindu-Muslim communal problem was basically a regional problem of Punjab, Bengal and the United Provinces where the Muslim masses were near-equals of the lower castes and were in majority. Within the new structure of politics, when numbers became politically significant, the caste-Hindus there could not bring themselves to accept their own reduced political significance. Instead of solving this problem by containing it, the Gandhi-Event enlarged and nationalized it and further complicated it through mystification.[35] Antagonism grew unabated between the two communities in spite of all efforts, so much so that when Gandhi launched his civil disobedience programme, Shaukat Ali, the comrade and soulmate of Gandhi during the Khilafat years, preached against it saying that its goal was Hindu Raj. And Jinnah, once an ardent nationalist, became an inveterate advocate of a separate homeland for Muslims.

Removal of untouchability and Harijan upliftment did not fare any better within the Gandhi-Event. Gandhi himself started at a high pitch, including an untouchable in his Ashram, but soon had to succumb to the pressure of his financiers and say goodbye to the unfortunate family (D. Keer 1973: pp. 224 ff.). Since then his

---

[34] S. Sinha (1963), p. 62; 'I am a Hindu first and nationalist after...so it should be with every religiously minded man' Gandhi quoted in S.K. Ghosh (1989), p. 248; Gandhi was also acutely conscious of the religious identities of individuals in public life which was often embarrassing and even insulting, for example, see S. Wolpert (1984), p. 38.

[35] S. Sinha (1963), pp. 150ff.; B.B. Misra (1976), pp. 162, 250-1.

understanding of the nature and scope of the Harijan Programme
was cautious so as not to antagonize the all-powerful uppercaste
sources of material support. Whenever he spoke of the removal
of untouchability he qualified his statement by adding that he did
not mean interdining[36] In fact the entire programme looked like
one for arresting the process of the mixing of all castes that had
been going on in several parts of the country and to extend the
practice to those areas where it was not heard of till then. No
wonder then, that the extremely narrow understanding of the
programme had practically nothing to offer the depressed classes
who through their own associations were clamouring for their share
of political power. Furthermore the Gandhian religious approach
to the problem determined the methodology which drove away
the intended beneficiaries. Harijan upliftment was basically intended
as an expiation of the upper castes' sins and hence the Harijans
themselves were only marginal to it. 'We have to obtain not the
salvation of the untouchables but ours by treating them as equals...'
(D. Keer 1973: 238). Although this was meant to persuade the obstinate
upper castes, it showed the limitation of the Gandhian approach.
Harijans were not to have any say in the running of the different
programmes because it was the duty of the upper castes, and more
importantly the finance came solely from them. In this approach,
the depressed classes were merely objects to be exploited for the
political salvation of the upper castes here on earth as much for
their sprituaI salvation in heaven (B. Parekh 1989: 211). The Harijan
Sevak Sangh was also an agency for Congress propaganda.[37] The
scope of the programme was limited to temperance, cleanliness and
discipline and no change in their socio-economic, much less, political
situation was intended. Sure, items such as entry to temples, schools
etc. were included in the programme. However, the implementation
was tardy, reluctant and half-hearted.[38] Results, even to a limited

---

[36] Which he termed 'promiscuous', see Gandhi (1935) pp. 464–5.

[37] Swami Shraddanand (1946), p. 190; B.R. Ambedkar (1945), p. 143; J. Brown (1977), p. 357.

[38] Gandhi's attitude towards temple-entry was at best ambiguous. He started with opposing it. 'How is it possible that the Antyajas should have the right to enter all the existing temples?' B.R. Ambedkar (1945), p. 107. Further, 'when the untouchables put forth a demand for political rights he changes his position and becomes a supporter of temple entry. When the Hindus threaten to defeat the Congress in the election, if it pursues the matter to a conclusion, Mr. Gandhi in order to preserve political power in the hands of Congress gives up temple entry', p. 125.

extent, could not be achieved within the Gandhian stronghold Bardoli.[39]

Gandhi was aware that the direction of development most of the depressed classes had taken was at variance with what he had envisaged for them, and realized that their autonomous growth would bring disaster to his understanding of a harmonious society. Hence the Gandhian agenda was to 'save them against themselves' (B.R. Ambedkar 1945: 70).

While some agriculture-bound depressed communities under the dominance of upper caste landlords came under the spell of Gandhi, that too rather ambiguously, and a minusculae of non-Brahminic well-to-do clean Shudras who had reached positions of security in public life capitulated to the Congress, the vast majority of the more politicized Shudras and Ati-Shudras got further estranged from the nationalist movement. At the time of the Simon Commission, out of eighteen representations from the depressed classes sixteen demanded a separate electorate.[40] The antagonism came to a critical head at the Second Round Table Conference.

Charkha, Spinning and Khaddar were the other great items in the Constructive Programme. Khaddar was the symbolic representation of Swadeshi and Swaraj. And Gandhi occasionally spoke of it as a significant economic enterprise that would provide clothing for the millions. However, it appears Gandhi set more store by its mobilizational value than anything else.

'If cooking had to be revived and required same organisation I should claim for it the same merit that I claim for Khaddar' (J. Bondurant 1988: 181).

After his release from jail in 1924, Gandhi's obsession with Charkha and Khaddar came to a point where he wanted spinning to be imposed as a condition for membership in the Congress. Ambedkar has rightly

---

[39] 'One of the 'national' schools of Bardoli Taluka of Gandhi's period of Satyagraha was prepared to close down permanently by Gandhi's trusted lieutenants rather than allow an untouchable boy to sit in the class with others' Swami Shraddanand (1946), p. 147-8.

[40] D. Keer (1962), p 115: 'the minorities always claimed they would be oppressed unless they had special representation. By the time you added up all the special representations they wanted, the majority ended up with about 5%'; Lord Attlee of Simon Commission quoted in S. Sinha (1963), p. 49.

pointed out, that Gandhi was not willing to consider a similar approach for the removal of untouchability.

Tagore could not understand how the mechanical rotation of Charkha could bring about Swaraj; he missed the point Gandhi was making, that the very meaninglessness of the activity had the potentiality to yield a maximum catch and generate euphoria without bringing in any issue vital to the life struggle of the masses. Khaddar and Charkha succeeded in mobilizing the peasants to the extent that they were given something to be occupied with, which did not threaten the status quo but helped to contain the antagonism between communities. The masses were expected to weave their way to Swaraj while the upper classes played politics (S.K Ghosh 1989: 215).

In Pursuit of Monopoly Power

The spearheading of the Constructive Programme during the latter half of the second decade was not without its political benefits. Gandhi was called upon to lead the Congress formally once again, in the wake of the new Government proposal for power devolution in 1928 (J. Brown 1977: 40-1). The events, circumstances and controversies surrounding the years between 1928 and 1932 are crucial to our understanding of the relocation of power within culture. As and when instalments of power were released from the foreign culture, its appropriation by the local culture came to be bitterly contested revealing the fact that nationalism is not a smooth one-way traffic of power from the British to the Indians. The various forces representing different interests within society were grouping and re-grouping themselves and stood sharply poised against one another, in order not to allow the transferred power to sink back to the status quo ante, which appeared to be the main agenda of the nationalist forces. From its inception during the last quarter of the previous century the nationalist movement, composed of the traditionally dominant castes and communities, represented largely in and around Indian National Congress, maintained that it, and it alone represented the whole nation, and others in the field were merely casteist and communalist. The doctrine of nationalism was thus requisitioned in order to continue to exclude the hitherto excluded masses from the new political nation.

Was the Gandhi-Event a continuity or break in this tradition of monopolizing the pursuit of power? The Gandhian image, his saintliness, his constructive programme and his apparent identity with the Indian rural masses were all hard-earned assets to be used in the bargain for power by the nationalists (J Brown 1977 pp. 12 ff.; R.P. Dutt 1970: 358-9). Gandhi himself, in his own person, represented a tradition of wielding power which could hardly be described as democratic. For more than a quarter of a century since his ascendancy in the Congress in 1920, Gandhi reigned supreme, though challenged now and then by individuals, but always obeyed unconditionally in the end. Gandhian leadership of the nationalist movement, far from signifying the emergence of a new style of co-operative, consultative and consensual politics, was in fact a return to the autocratic, inspirational (and irrational to many) and private style in which he was accountable to none except to his own 'inner voice'.[41] The entire movement was in fact reduced to an order-obeying machine (S. Sinha 1963: 28). The history of the movement itself could be a revealing study in the process of the concentration of power in the high command, at a time when the Raj itself under various constraints was becoming more and more decentralized (B.B. Misra 1976: 352). Though the professed aim of Gandhi and the nationalist movement was the destruction of the Raj, in actual practice, the movement was transforming itself into another Raj to replace its predecessor in due time. This process was under the so-called religio-moral leadership of Gandhi himself (A.D. Low 1977: 33). During his dictatorship, Gandhi demanded unquestioned obedience from Congress claiming that as the ideal Hindu he represented the nationalist movement, which in turn stood for India itself which was Hindu. Since Satyagraha was the main weapon of the movement and Gandhi was the self-appointed expert on that subject, the others, mere foot soldiers, need not know the dynamics of the entire war and it was enough if they unconditionally and sincerely obeyed the commands of the general.[42] To this general position, however humiliating it was at times, the stalwarts of the movements acquiesced, for Gandhi alone held the sword of moral sanction and the following

---

[41] 'Mahatma will not play a second fiddle to anyone' S.C. Bose quoted in J. Brown 1977, p. 6; S. Sinha (1963), 'His politics remained personal politics to the end, a matter of private arrangement between himself and the British Government', p. 62, and 99, 112, 162. A.T. Embree (1971), p. 67; D. Keer (1973), p. 286, 331 and S.K. Ghosh (1989), p. 267.

[42] 'I am the expert in this Satyagraha business'. S. Shraddhanand (1946) pp. 150-1.

of the masses. The dissidents sooner or later met political oblivion; money, power and patronage played no small role in this process of power concentration (S.K Ghosh 1989: 95). These dynamics within the nationalist movement during the Gandhi-Event played enough havoc in legitimizing a tradition of wielding power that was more like the monarchy of yore rather than that of a modern political nation. But when transferred to the relationship of the nationalist movement with the other contestants of power, it proved to be an utter disaster to the true national agenda of power homogenization within culture. The Indian nationalist movement always held that it alone was truly national, for it alone represented the entire nation; so any settlement of power had to be solely with it.[43] This meant the nationalist movement had taken a clear position *vis-à-vis* the two referral points of power re-location: it stood for the transfer of power from the British to the Indians, but having defined itself as the only true Indian it had to appropriate the transferred power solely to itself to the exclusion of others. Thus, most nationalist activities were intended as much against the British as against the masses, who had a different agenda altogether. In fact, very often it did happen that the first enemy became the fellow Indians, while the British could be relied on to rally behind the elite nationalists, for the interests of the latter two almost always coincided and were consistently antithetic to those of the lower caste Muslim and tribal masses (S.K. Ghosh 1989: 87, 209). This particular configuration of circumstances became more vivid and was thrown into sharp focus especially during the years of civil disobedience, Round Table Conferences, the so-called epic fast and the Poona Pact.

Right from the days of Non-Co-Operation, Gandhi made it very clear time and again that non-violent Non-Co-Operation was intended as a 'safety valve' a 'restraining force' to prevent terrorism, revolution, disorder, and Bolshevism (ibid: 111, 113, 116, 188, 192, 201, 209). The need here was to edge out the perennial threat of the revolt of the mass of lower caste peasantry and the challenge of more radical ideologies both within and without the Congress. Left alone, the masses were likely to go astray. Hence one had to engage them in some innocent pre-occupation or another, until they were called upon to demonstrate to the alien rulers their solidarity with the

---

[43] B.R. Ambedkar (1970), p. 21; B.B. Misra (1976), p. 352, 355, 501 and 645; D. Keer (1973), p. 553.

nationalist movement through their sheer passive, inactive presence.[44] At the announcement of further devolution of power a whole range of interests outside the leadership of the nationalist movement presented themselves as potential locations of power within culture. The most obvious ones were the Muslims, the untouchables, tribals, Sikhs, Christians and other minorities. Conceived and consolidated within colonial rule, some of these minorities were ambiguous political entities, but with all their limitations still represented the masses outside the nationalist movement. Traditionally these groups were termed as creations of the imperial policy of divide and rule, set up by the rulers to thwart the nationalist movement. Nothing could be farther from the truth; the lower caste, tribal and Muslim masses in general, as we have tried to point out (in chapter III), were ranged together in terms of economic and political interests and were heirs to a pattern of awakening that was distinctly at variance with the social base and political agenda of the nationalists. To term the entire mass of people who did not fall in line with the Congress as pro-imperialist, as the nationalist propaganda would have it, is nothing but absurd. Without absolving the colonial ruler's hand in exacerbating the already existing cleavages the story of Indian nationalism is not how the British divided and ruled over us but how the nationalists united and defeated the British.

Gandhi launched his civil disobedience movement just as negotiations for power devolution were about to begin. The timing of the programme as well as the subsequent incidents clearly showed that the intention was double edged: to pre-empt non-nationalist national forces in the field and to demonstrate to the British that if any settlement was to be reached at all, with whom it had to be. In this regard Gandhi was in no hurry; if power was not to be had *in toto* immediately, it was better for it to remain in British hands till such time as it could be had solely and wholly.[45] Gandhi, as an experienced acrobat, was walking a tightrope with admirable skill and dexterity: he generated a controlled mass mobilization for purely demonstrative purposes, never allowing the masses to take over the leadership (or in the accepted parlance 'to turn violent') and at the same time constantly sent feelers to the rulers for negotiations.

[44] S.K. Ghosh 1989, p. 210; S. Sinha (1963), p. 158, 169; R.P. Dutt (1970), p. 353; S. Sarkar (1983), p. 179; B. Chandra (1976), p. 18, Ibid., (1979), p. 128.
[45] J. Brown (1977) pp. 233 ff and p. 246; also S. Sinha (1963) p. 172.

Obviously for him the terms of negotiations themselves were secondary; the fact that the highest official of the Empire personally negotiated with Gandhi was recognition enough of the latter's position as the monopoly bargainer with whom power had to be settled. It has to be acknowledged that Gandhian political astuteness won the day; Viceroy Irwin fell for it and the pact was made.

By all appearances, the British seemed to be convinced: if ever a power settlement was to be made, it had to be with Gandhi, the sole representative of the Indian National Congress, in turn the biggest conglomeration of interests. But not so easily convinced were the fellow Indians, both those represented and those non-represented in the Second Round Table Conference (J. Brown 1977: 260). Needless to say the dichotomous political awakening of the previous century had undergone considerable changes thanks to the Gandhi-Event. The horizontal cleavage was being relegated to the background as the vertical cleavage of religious communities gained importance; several rural communities who would otherwise have been politicized within the dichotomy, were effectively held back by the communal and top-to-bottom mobilization effected by the Gandhi-Event, and some non-Brahmins were co-opted. However, with all these distortions in the picture, the political representation of the minorities and the majority did preserve the essence of the initial horizontal cleavage: the nationalists supposedly a majority claiming monopoly representation, and the different minorities challenging it. (Indeed the construction, in the colonial period of the categories, majority and minority, was itself a political anomaly of a serious kind. 'Majority' in fact referred to the dominant minority and 'minorities' of all kinds ranged together in terms of their interest against the former were in fact the resisting majority). Most sharply thrown in relief were the untouchables represented by Ambedkar; the Muslims were both a religious minority as well as a part of the excluded masses; the Sikhs once again were an ambiguous community sharing the characteristics of both. Not all were represented of course; for instance there was apparently no effective tribal representation.

The crucial test was how nationalism as represented by Gandhi positioned itself *vis-à-vis* the nation, the so-called minorities, who when put together represented the majority of the population. And what the attitude of the traditionally dominant castes and communities composing the nationalists was towards homogenization of power, or relocating of power within the social structure differently from that during colonial rule as well as that during pre-colonial times.

It is common knowledge that Gandhi, in the Round Table Conference, utterly failed to bring together his countrymen or to accommodate their demands as a nationalist ought to (S. Sinha 1963: 95; B.R. Ambedkar 1945: 55). Instead, peeved at being treated as one among the many, he set one community against the other, and passed crude remarks at the unworthiness of other representatives, all this in the presence of the alien rulers.[46] He was concerned more with being the sole recepient of the power settlement instead of, with the terms of the settlement itself.[47] He obsessively claimed that he, in his person, represented everybody in India and no other representatives were required to bargain for power. Gandhi's main purpose of attending the Round Table Conference appeared to be to gain monopoly power, or to let the power remain in alien hands. On no count could power be shared with those who had the temerity to sit as equals with the traditionally elevated and privileged. For Ambedkar on the other hand the problem was diametrically the opposite: under the specific historical development of societies in the subcontinent and in the context of the traditional ascriptive hierarchy, enabling the depressed classes to enter the new political community would mean special protection. Not to insist on this, meant surrendering hard-won rights and accepting once again the Brahminic ascriptive hierarchy as the principle of social organization.[48] What Gandhi could not understand was that the days of ascriptive hierarchy as a principle of social organization were gone for ever, that a nation was being born and that as a nationalist he was being called upon to assist in the process by taking the lead (S. Sinha 1963: 24, 189). Instead his conduct unambiguously revealed his unwillingness to accept this change; he tried with all his might to prevent the new western monster of a competitive and socially mobile political community

[46] D. Keer (1962), pp. 178ff. D. Keer (1973) reports an incident in which Gandhi went to Aga Khan with a copy of the Koran asking him to swear not to support the depressed classes' demand for special protection in return for conceding all the Muslim demands; see also B.R., Ambedkar (1945) p. 74.

[47] B.R. Ambedkar (1970), p. 21. The Gandhian claim to protect untouchables was described by the Madras Adi Dravida Jan Sanga as a 'Cobra seeking the guardianship of the young frogs' quoted in D. Keer (1962), p. 33.

[48] 'Speaking for the servile classes I have no doubt that what they expect to happen in a sovereign and free India is a complete destruction of Brahminism as a philosophy of life and as a social order', B.R. Ambedkar (1945), p. 213.

from being born which thus meant a vivisection of the Hindu body politic. When some sharing of power appeared to be inevitable he acquiesced. In his view, instead of a single nation of equal individuals, several religious and vertical communities are preferable: Hindus, Muslims and Sikhs (B.R. Ambedkar 1945: pp. 58 ff.). But he fought till the end any sharing of power with the depressed classes with whom he would never advocate social union. Nor would he allow them to leave the Hindu fold, instead peremptorily demanding political unity at the level of subservience. The Muslim leadership, quick to rise to the occasion, drove a hard bargain and could get away with it. The estrangement and embitterment of the lower caste masses and especially the untouchables was complete. Though some kind of bargain was struck subsequent to the Poona fast, an historic opportunity in the lifetime of the nation for forging a unity on the basis of equitable sharing of power with the new entrants to the political community was lost.[49] Jinnah was now bent upon the creation of Pakistan and Ambedkar started thinking of renouncing Hinduism altogether. It is not the argument here that Jinnah and Ambedkar represented the nation, while Gandhi, nationalism. But within the limitations of the legal arena, nationalism as represented by Gandhi failed to grasp the very essence of nation as a new and equitable form of power sharing within culture and to seize the opportunity to hegemonize the contesting groups, inadequately represented by the other leaders. It could perhaps be argued with some truth that the dichotomy was not all that sharp nor complete and Gandhi did represent a nation of some sort. Whatever be the truth of such an assertion (the kind of consent that Gandhi had secured from the masses is dealt with below) the point being made here is that this nationalist failed to see the new emergence, much less to lead and further it, and instead did his best to prevent and distort it.

---

[49] The purpose of the fast was described succinctly by an imperialist bureaucrat writing to Gandhi, 'As I understand your attitude you propose to adopt the extreme course of starving yourself to death not in order to secure that the depressed classes should have joint electorate with other Hindus, because that is already provided, nor to maintain the unity of Hindus which is also provided but solely to prevent the depressed classes who admittedly suffer from terrible disabilities today from being able to secure a limited number of representatives of their own choosing to speak on their behalf in the legislatures which will have a dominating influence over their future', quoted in B.R. Ambedkar (1945), pp. 85-6. Note the kind of protection awarded to the depressed classes was not similar to that granted to the Muslims; the former's was an 'additional' one but the latter's 'separate'.

The truncated political benefits that the Scheduled Castes and Scheduled Tribes reaped in the eventual settlement were wrung out of the unwilling nationalists' hands by the masses. The bifurcation of Bengal and Punjab to create Pakistan failed to solve the problem of Muslims as a whole, leaving them instead at the mercy of vengeful upper caste Hindu communalists. Subsequent events during the post-Independence period would show how inadequate and distorted these doles had become, calling forth new political manoeuvres. With the high drama of power-sharing settled, much to the chagrin of all the parties involved, the basics of the Indian nationalist synthesis were well laid out. Gandhi now retired to do Harijan work. However, he was always alert, even in subsequent years when especially through the constraints of the working of juridical democracy some power had to be devolved to persons and classes who were not traditionally powerful, he intervened to prevent it.[50]

GANDHIAN POLITICAL MOBILIZATION

The oft-repeated statement that at the touch of Gandhi Indian nationalism turned into a mass movement, if it is taken to mean that Gandhi brought the political consent of the masses to his leadership, hides several ambiguities: who were these masses and how were they mobilized? Was there an identity of purpose and interest between themselves and the Gandhian organizers? What was the nature of consent, if any, the masses had given the new nationalist leadership? These and similar questions require to be looked into closely in order to examine the explicit Gandhian claim of representing the entire nation in his person. The earlier nationalist claim that Gandhi awoke the sleeping masses to political consciousness cannot be taken seriously anymore, but it would still be true to say that Gandhi 'brought' the masses to nationalist politics.[51] The experiments in isolated places like Champaran, Khaira, Ahmedabad, Bardoli, the

---

[50] Note the Khare episode and also B.R. Ambedkar (1945), p. 98 and B.B. Misra (1976), p. 355. Also note the first Congress ministry, in 1937, against popular opinion avoided forming coalition ministries in the states. And again they all resigned in 1939 because Congress was not accorded monopoly position in the Imperial Council.

[51] Chapter III analysed the situation and it was found that the masses had their own agenda of political struggle. Gandhian politics deflected the masses towards nationalist politics in which process the British too helped; see S. Sinha (1963), p. 57 and A.T. Embree (1971), p. 68.

country-wide mobilizations around the Rowlatt Acts, Khilafat and
Salt tax and the overt mass flexing of political muscles during Non-Co-
Operation, Civil Disobedience and Quit India Movements were to
transform politics, which were limited to a microscopic minority
till the First War, into a mass movement. Crowds did gather now
at the nationalist meetings and programmes, and the colonial rulers
were thus made to understand, where the sanction of the masses
lay. Did all these amount to conscious political consent by the masses
to the nationalist leadership under Gandhi?

Earlier we had noted that Gandhian mobilization was carried on
within an overarching religio-moral discourse often using religious
or religionized issues as against the interest-based political awakening
of the masses. And to this extent Gandhian mobilization was an
attempt not to bring the masses into politics but to divert them
from their own autonomous or semi-autonomous political agenda.

The tactical nature of mobilization is also to be noted—i.e. mass
mobilization was sought again, not primarily to solve any of people's
problems, but to gain their sanction for Congress politics. This is
not to say that the removal of the British from the scene was not
also in the interest of the masses. However, there were a number
of intermediary and immediate economic and political interests of
the masses in which the elite, native as well as foreign, were ranged
against, and on several occasions the British were in a position to
open ways for the masses in their struggles against the old order.
In Marxist terms, the mass agenda was anti-feudal, the pursuit of
which would necessarily have lead them to the anti-imperialist position.
But the elite anti-imperialist posture was of dubious nature in view
of their strong pro-feudal social base.[52] Mobilization within such
a context meant the use or the exploitation of the masses; here
the mass was not the subject of the mobilization, people were called
into the arena purely for their demonstrative effect. Their role in
the programme was passive, to aid the elite, to follow them and
to boost them whenever required.[53] This meant wresting the masses
away from their own agenda of destruction of the Brahminical social

[52] S.K. Ghosh (1989) argues with strong evidence that total removal of the British
from the scene was never the agenda of the nationalist movement whose leaders
and particularly Gandhi expected the British presence to continue indefinitely to
protect the 'so many interests which the British have brought into being, see p. 87.

[53] S.K. Ghosh (1989), p. 23, 210; S. Sinha (1963), p. 158, 161; J. Brown (1977),
p. 340; B. Chandra (1979), p. 128; B. Parekh (1989) p. 211.

order, and reducing them to the level of political show-pieces in the power bargain between two sets of elites.

Thirdly, Gandhian mobilization was vertical instead of horizontal; it took the endogamous and hierarchical structure of the communities as it was, and the traditionally dominant individuals and groups within this hierarchy were expected to organize and lead the traditionally subservient classes. Gandhian mobilizational success was, to no small extent, due to this. Gandhi was acutely sensitive to the traditional pattern of power-spread within the communities and exploited this to the maximum.[54] He never approached the masses directly but always through the regional and local elite, who in the process tended to gain importance, which they then owed to the supreme leader (J. Brown 1969: 338; R. Kumar 1971: 100). This had a double benefit for the traditionally dominant communities. On the one hand, the mobilization itself was determined by the needs and aspirations of the local exploiter, and the exploited were kept well under control (D.N. Dhanagre 1975: 47). On the other hand, more serious, was the regressive spin-off such a mobilization caused: the slowly yet surely eroding traditional hierarchical structure of social authority-through Gandhian intervention, gained in the name of nationalism another powerful lease of life. Gandhi's mobilizational tactics helped the traditionally dominant classes who were being challenged on all sides to regain a quasi-religious and secular national legitimacy through association with the charismatic nationalist leader (D.N. Dhanagre 1983: 107). In this sense, Gandhian nationalism did strengthen the traditional social order by containing the mass initiative against it. The apotheosis of non-violence by the leadership has to be interpreted in this context. The endemic tendency of the masses and the perennial preaching of non-violence both reveal the fact that the masses had already been driven to a situation in which violence had become inevitable for even a marginal amelioration of conditions. Hence the need for sacralizing non-violence and situating it at the heart of the so-called Hindu Indian tradition.

Fourthly, inspite of the much vaunted Gandhian identification with the masses by the established schools of historiography, Gandhi's own evaluation of and attitude to them, was certainly ambiguous. He needed them for his purpose yet he did not trust them and

---

[54] J. Brown (1972), p. 285; R. Kumar (1969), p. 363 ff, D. Keer (1973), p. 313; D.N. Dhanagre (1975), p. 63; G. Shah (1974), p. 107.

even feared them. Gandhi's opinion of the masses was not very high; he thought they were dumb millions who did not know their own interests and were hence incapable of deciding their future on their own.[55] Not only this, he appeared to have a positive fear of them: 'I know, the only thing that the government dreads is this huge majority I seem to command. They little know that I dread it even more than they'.[56] Meticulous search for an issue that would provoke the least controversy, half-hearted beginnings of movements, hedged in by several pre-conditions, almost simultaneous attempts at compromise, withdrawal at the slightest sign of initiative slipping into the hands of the masses, are but a few of the indications of this Gandhian dilemma of how to 'unleash just enough of the mass movement in order to drive a successful bargain and at the same time to save India from revolution' (R.P. Dutt 1970: 359). Partial solutions to this dilemma consisted in systematically blocking out the vital interests of the masses from mobilization, appeals to the traditional village order, harmony and community-based morality, and in general the mystification of the entire political exercise.

Another ideological invention to prevent the eruption of mass initiative against the traditional social order is myth-making about the peasant. (D.N Dhanagre 1983: 97; B. Chandra 1976: 15). Fabricated within the nationalist, mobilization strategy the peasant was a mystical category intended to hide the caste and class cleavages which were ripping apart the subcontinental rural society. The nationalist movement created this mythical figure *ex nihilo*, hallowed him as the heart-beat of the nation and peopled the entire countryside with millions of them cast into one mould of ignorance, laziness, proclivity to mischief, yet with the capacity to respond to faith and religion. In fact the proverbial stupidity of the Indian peasant was a highly valued asset for the Gandhian mobilizers.

> It is fortunate there is no intellectualism in the people of Bardoli as they do most of the work on faith, otherwise they would not have followed us without questioning.

---

[55] Note his desiring to 'save them against themselves', quoted in B.R. Ambedkar (1945), p. 70; S. Sinha (1963), p. 175.

[56] Gandhi, in *Young India*, 2 March 1922, as quoted in A T Embree (1989) p. 170.

Kuvarji, one of the lieutenants of Gandhi, enlightens us about the secret of his successful mobilization in this nationalist laboratory— Bardoli (G. Shah 1974: 94). No wonder political education of any kind for the masses was anathema.

Gandhian mobilization since it was from top to bottom, was not without its coercive aspect. The peasant movements were carefully pre-planned in every detail. Areas were chosen for their low political consciousness among the servile castes where conditions approximated semi-bondedness. The issues were usually of minor importance affecting the interests of upper tenantry against the colonial government. Within such a context, caste loyalties were manipulated to get the movement going and traditional coercive methods such as authoritarianism, social boycott, eviction and religious sanction such as divine punishment, Brahminic curses etc. were used to round up the lower caste mass of agricultural labourers to demonstrate social cohesion and mass unity.[57] Such a command performance of the docile and adulatory masses at times bordered on the pathetic: the Kaliparaj got themselves renamed as Raniparaj, for example, in return for their support of the Ujalalok's struggle against the government.

Finally, Gandhi wanted to leave nobody in doubt. He clearly outlined the limits to which peasant mobilization under his leadership would and could go:

The Kisan Movement must be confined to the improvement of the status of the kisan and the betterment of the relations between the Zamindars and them ... and scrupulously abide by the terms of their agreement with the Zamindars whether such agreement is written or inferred from custom (M.K. Gandhi 1924: 741-2).

Gandhi's insistence on custom is not without its import. The custom imposing Abwabs, Begari etc. in the old system of feudal land relations was part and parcel of the overall Brahminic social order, specifically against which the Shudra and Ati-Shudra masses had raised the banner of revolt.

The limited and ephemeral nature of Gandhian mass mobilization has been increasingly explored by scholars of different schools of

---

[57] K. Kumar (1983); R. Guha (1989) draws attention to the inter-connectedness of the two categories Dharma and Danda with the clear indication of consequences for those who do not follow the Dharma, pp. 238, 9.

thought. It has been found patchy and uneven, intended to arrest mass initiative, romantic or faction based. Some are of the opinion that Gandhi brought the masses but sent them empty-handed, that it was curiosity that drew crowds to him, that mobilization was akin to that of a medieval caste preacher, and that the mass had its own distinct or even contrary agenda within the movement. All these different ways of describing the Gandhian mass mobilization are saying the same thing: mobilization was ambiguous both in intent as well as content (J. Brown 1972: 345). Mobilization cannot be said to have corresponded to the mass political and economic aspirations and hence the mass's response can in no sense be described as political. Gandhi's and the nationalist's claim either to have secured the political sanction of the masses to the leadership or to their representation of the mass interest does not appear to have been based on ground realities.

Varnashrama Dharma, Trusteeship and Ramrajya

Gandhian political praxis flowed out of a weltanschauung that is articulated fairly consistently through his writings. In fact, as a highly self-conscious activist, Gandhi's world-view and his political practice have to be related dialectically for a proper interpretation and evaluation of the intent as well as import of the Gandhi-Event within the nationalist movement. Gandhi, for example, spoke of self-sufficient villages, cottage industries, panchayat and village democracy etc. Quite a few have interpreted these to mean a clarion call for a new social order and a blueprint for New India. But what is not said is that this economico-administrative decentralization is to be situated and severely circumscribed within the traditional politico-ideological order—Varnashrama Dharma. The Gandhian critique of the status quo was a call for a reversal to what he thought was status quo ante (S. Sinha 1963: 7).[58] The colonial imposition of modern political structure on the traditional social hierarchy, in the absence of in-dustrialization and social mobility, had introduced serious distortions within the Brahminical socio-economic order, such as exaggerated notions of purity and pollution, increased distance between upper

---

[58] In the words of C. Geertz (1973) this was not a call for a 'return to naive traditionalism but ideological retraditionalisation, an altogether a different matter' p. 219.

and lower castes etc. Gandhi was acutely sensitive to this and suggested that a reversal to the old order would solve the apparently new problems. His much publicized antagonism and critique of the orthodox is limited to this. But what Gandhi did not realize was that the new political structure at the same time occasioned the bursting asunder of the Brahminical prison-house, demolishing the 'archmyth' of harmony, interdependence and consensus within the Varnashrama Dharmic order of society. The erection of the new political structure was apparently the last spark that ignited and set in motion the liberative processes in society. The lower caste masses have had millenia-old traditions of struggle against the oppressive Brahminical division of labour. However, lack of any change in material and economic conditions often prevented these struggles from spreading beyond the realm of philosophy and religion. Such a seemingly peaceful situation was the foundation of the well-orchestrated myth of consensual village harmony in pre-modern India. The edifice of Gandhian social philosophy is built on the false premise that the Varnashrama ideal represented consensus of all concerned; that the 'Bhangi', for example, loved to scavenge just as the Bania loved to amass wealth, that it was the materialist West that brought greed to all the classes and that a reversal to our tradition would make the 'Bhangi' understand that his scavenging is as noble a work as that of the Brahmin (M.K. Gandhi 1927: 649, 1935: 463). This is nothing but an ideological reconstruction and distortion of Indian tradition itself, which is much greater than merely Brahminic oppression. Gandhi's construction of the ideal-typical tradition is composed of the worst elements of the subcontinental history, elements that kept the masses under social and cultural tyranny. An integral component of such a reconstruction of tradition is the view of egalitarianism, and any other form of aspiration to socio-cultural equality, as foreign imported, Western, and hence to be repudiated ruthlessly. The Gandhian method of such repudiation of egalitarianism is also typical.

Nor do I believe in inequalities between human beings. We are all absolutely equal. But equality is of souls and not of bodies. Hence it is a mental state. We need to think of and to assert equality because of great inequalities in the physical world. We have to realise equality in the midst of this apparent external inequality (M.K. Gandhi 1970: 18–19).

From a moral and religious preacher this would have been appropriate, but for a man caught in the vortex of struggle for monopoly power between several contestants, this cannot but be interpreted as a pseudo-religious cover for the pursuit of power.

Gandhi rightly observed that 'Bhangis' and Brahmins were ubiquitous phenomenon and not peculiar to India, in the sense of the graded inequality of classes. This being so, why was it that in India alone the notion of superiority/inferiority seemed to plague the communities. What Gandhi failed to grasp was that within a social context which makes the socio-economic position ascriptive, and as long as the Brahmin never sees the possibility of having to be a 'Bhangi' for the sake of earning his livelihood, notions and behaviour patterns of superiority and inferiority are bound to remain. The Gandhian core of the Varna ideal is precisely to preserve this ascriptive division of labour in society. The Gandhian discourse on equality and inequality gets confused as it addresses two distinct discourses counter to itself; one, against the ascriptive social hierarchy and two, for radical economic equality. When Gandhi observed that inequality among men cannot be removed, he was responding to the socialist critique which during his time was becoming increasingly strident, as it too emanated from a section of the elite themselves. But what was specifically the mass agenda during the colonial period was not so much the radical economic equality (although not totally absent) as social equality based on non-ascription and social mobility as Ambedkar had perceptively pointed out:

> Speaking for the servile classes I have no doubt that what they expect to happen in a sovereign and free India is a complete destruction of Brahminism as a philosophy of life and as a social order. If I may say so, the servile classes do not care for social amelioration. The want and poverty which has been their lot is nothing to them compared to the insult and indignity which they have to bear as a result of the vicious social order (B.R. Ambedkar 1945: 213).

And Gandhi was upholding precisely this ascriptive social order by dubiously pointing out the impracticality of radical economic equality. Admittedly Gandhian views on caste changed from time to time, but only within the extremely narrow spectrum of untouchability, interdining and intermarriage (D. Dalton 1967: pp. 159 ff.). These issues were marginal to the existential life struggles of the lower caste masses. Their agenda was the attempt to escape the humiliating ascriptive social identity by diversifying occupations and assuming a new anonymity of membership within a larger whole through competition and achievement. Gandhi was set against exactly this, and the labelling of these aspirations of the masses as non-indigenous, western and materialist itself was an ideological weapon liberally, and often unfortunately successfully, used as part and parcel of nationalist thought resource.

The entire edifice of the Gandhian order—social (Varnashrama Dharma), economic (trusteeship), and political (Ramrajya), all of one piece powerfully informing his social praxis, is expressive of the political interests of the old dominant castes and communities who were engaged in the process of transforming themselves into a cohesive ruling elite. Hence this had a lasting and determining role to play within the nationalist movement irrespective of any occasional counter-ideas Gandhi might have expressed under different concrete circumstances. Varnashrama Dharma as the principle of social organization meant to establish 'certain spheres of action for certain people with certain tendencies' which had the effect of avoiding 'all unworthy competition: servile labour to the Shudras and Ati-Shudras, accumulation of wealth for Vaisyas, ruling, teaching etc. for the Kshatriyas and Brahmins, all classes in their own station according to their natural tendencies (G. Bondurant 1988: 169-70). Under the idea of trusteeship the have-nots will believe that the haves have it all for the benefit of everybody, and in Ramrajya the ruler rules for ever and is not changed every now and then (M.K. Gandhi 1938: 28). Nothing could be clearer and more direct, and nothing could be more clearly against the political emergence of the masses as equal citizens of a nation. Gandhi was of course not against the lower castes getting educated and becoming lawyers for example, but they could do so not to earn their livelihood but to serve society (M.K. Gandhi 1962).

Indian nationalist thought since its inception was always ill at ease with the constant reminder of the traditional ideology—Varnashrama Dharma. Though as an ideology, nationalism here stood for the reincarnation of the same principles under changed conditions, it always sought to cover it up and camouflage it in secular nationalist terms. Some leaders felt the contradictions between the old Brahminic order and the new nationalism more acutely than others and took some hesitant steps to change the situation while others, tended

to ignore the underlying contradiction. Yet others sought to explain
it away in unorthodox ways suggesting that ascription was not inherent
in the Varna ideal. Gandhi alone was unique in that he sought
to establish the nation itself on this decadent Varna ideal (D. Keer
1973: 313). That the emergence of nation and nationalism as a modern
phenomenon was preconditioned on the demolition of the Varna
ideal was not lost on him and yet he sought to establish a nation
on an anti-national principle. He unabashedly defended an anachronistic ideal in its most obscurantist aspect while the masses were making
all out efforts against all odds to do away with it. The carefully
built up moral legitimacy and saintly image enabled Gandhi to battle
the masses and even get away with this, with no small help from
the colonial rulers themselves. Gandhi knew of no other way of
welding together the disparate castes and communities except in
the same old way of material and social hierarchy, of course with
a belief in the equality of the souls of all men added to this. A
change of heart and not social change was demanded. When change
of heart need not be validated by actual social change, then the
former becomes a way to counter the latter under concrete circumstances (M.K. Gandhi 1947: 66). If nation is the political emergence
of the masses as a multiple and potentially equitable locale of power
within culture, grasped in the concept of socio-political citizenship,
then Gandhian nationalism was unambiguously set against this and
did unfortunately succeed in its agenda.

Truth and History

That which is permanent and therefore necessary eludes the historian
of events. Truth transcends history'.[59] 'To Gandhi then, truth does
not lie in history nor did science have any privileged access to it.
Truth was moral; unified, unchanging and transcendental' (P. Chatterjee
1984: 172). Gandhian political practice and his social philosophy
proceed from such ontological views of truth, history and society.
Gandhi sets up a dichotomy between truth and history. Truth which
is beyond scientific and historical enquiry, is eternal and immutable;
it alone can be a guide to action and life in general. On the other
hand, all that history can reveal is changing and transitory and hence

[59] Gandhi in D.G. Tendulkar vol 2 p. 111 as quoted in A.T. Embree (1989) p.
162.

cannot be made a basis of life or the construction of a society. The philosophical and political implication of such a dichotomy and the preference for unchanging truth over changing history for the nationalist movement is fairly clear. The Gandhian nationalist movement was engaged in a struggle on two fronts: to wrest moral authority from the British, and to delegitimize the forces of change within, threatening to blow apart the Brahminical social order. This was the political context of Gandhian ontology. The Brahminical social order or the Varnashrama Dharma establishing 'certain spheres of action for certain people with certain tendencies' as we have noted, represents the ageless, timeless and unchanging natural order, the truth of which is the proper foundation for the future Indian society; it had preserved the same society from unhealthy competition and conflict. The harmony it had engendered within society had freed individuals from material greed and worldly comfort to pursue the spiritual goal of salvation. Such is the uniqueness of Indian civilization. Change and history on the other hand are the curse of the modern West that has brought about conflict between classes and disharmony to life in general whose main goal now was the pursuit of worldly comforts. Imported into India and imitated by the Indians, change and history has had the evil effect of denying the Indian genius and betraying the inherited tradition and legacy. Such a formulation was an effective philosophical and ideological weapon to wield against forces that work for the destruction of the Brahminical order as well as against the imperialists whose continued presence seemed to abet and encourage such a process.

Gandhi's insistence on the immutability and eternity of truth against the deluge of changes threatening the status quo has nothing original about it. Immutable and natural order against reason and change had been the banner of counter-revolution throughout history within the East and the West.[60] On the other hand, change, revolution and history have been the slogans of the excluded and deprived masses who hope to come into their own in the future by wrenching

---

[60] 'Aristotle justified slavery in psychological and institutional terms when he observed "that by nature some are free, others slaves and that for these it is both right and expedient that they should serve as slaves"', R. Guha (1989), p. 216. In the context of the French revolution the very same sentiments were used by philosophers opposed to it, see J. Blum (1978). During his own lifetime Gandhi's objections to equality and socialism were likened to those of 'Church divines and philosophers of the old order in Europe at the dawn of the industrial revolution' by Jayaprakash Narayan, see I.P. Haithcox (1971) p. 220-2.

away the ascriptive privileges of the dominant classes. Within the subcontinent during the colonial times the agenda of the mass movements was not so much doing away with economic inequality as the destruction of ascriptive social inequality. This struggle, far from being inspired by the colonial rulers, was in fact a continuity from the history of the subcontinent. The emergence of the nation and the articulation of nationalism was but another critical juncture in this history, in which the forces ranged for and against the traditional 'natural' order came to challenge each other, in the context of the erection of the new political structure of the nation-state. The question was whether nationalism would articulate the political aspiration of the masses and become an ideology promoting and encouraging the emergence of the modern nation, or on the other hand, ally itself with the traditionally dominant elite and become an ideology to devise ways to prevent, subdue or sabotage the new political emergence. Gandhian nationalism in its philosophical dimension too, set itself against the nation's emerging; its success lay precisely in the fact that it deflected at least a part of the mass movements from their autonomous agenda, by bringing the masses under its non-political and non-secular mobilizational process and effectively demoralizing the rest through its high-flown moral rhetoric of truth against history.

Gandhian nationalism, premised on unchanging truth is a nationalism without social change, perhaps even anti-social change, and hence against the nationalism of the masses.[61] Transition within society, or the emergence of a new society in history is an anti-nationalist project according to this view of nationalism. Such is the contradiction of Gandhian nationalism. As noted by Ambedkar:

> Instead of surrendering privileges in the name of nationalism, the governing class in India is using or misusing the slogan of nationalism to maintain its privileges. Whenever the servile classes ask for reservations in the legislatures, in the executive, and in public services, the governing class raises the cry of 'nationalism in danger' (B.R. Ambedkar 1945: 226).

All appearances to the contrary notwithstanding, the Gandhian era of Indian nationalism represents a continuity with, rather than a

---

[61] B.R. Ambedkar (1945), p. 290-1; R. Kumar (1971); A.D. Low (1977), p. 34; D. Keer (1973), p. 313; see also J. Nehru (1936) p. 511-36.

break from, the earlier nationalist movement (B. Chandra 1979: ch. 4). Throughout its history the Indian nationalist movement was led by the traditionally dominant castes in the traditionally dominant way (G. Krishna 1966: 413-30). Its construction of nationalism was not based on the varied economic and political interests of the local or regional masses but was highly rarefied and based on Brahminic cultural symbols which had the dubious quality of unifying yet dividing the social interests. The Congress continued to be obsessed all along with the idea of monopoly representation of the nation, of excluding the others especially the new entrants from the political nation. It also continued to maintain an ambiguous posture towards the presence of the British, requiring them to protect the nationalists against the masses and the nation. Just as nationalism arose during the last quarter of the nineteenth century at the breakup of the Brahminical order, the Gandhian critique of civil society during the first and second quarter of the twentieth century was intended to re-establish the same old order. In fact what was sought was nationalism with minimal or possibly no social change. Gandhian changes envisaged in the nationalist movement were more formal than substantial. Instead of effecting any significant change in the structure, style and direction of the movement and its leadership, its earlier weaknesses and limitations were successfully transformed into new strengths and vantage points. Armed with a truth and morality discourse the new leadership apparently put an end to the dichotomous distance between nation and nationalism at least for the time-being, not by fusing the different interests but by vanquishing part, and alienating the rest, of the nation through a rhetoric of nationalism.

VII

Nationalism without Nation

INVENTING OR PREVENTING THE NATION

The nationalist political movement in the Indian subcontinent looked upon itself as the sole legitimate representative of the nation, and its political practice was sanctified as the historic moments of bringing forth the new nation. The early Congressmen had no doubt on this score, that they were the nation-builders. Around the turn of the century, the situation and the nationalist claim was expressed thus by Aurobindo:

> ...We believe that the time has come and that by a common resistance to a common pressure in the shape of the boycott inspired by a common enthusiasm and ideal, that united nationality for which the whole history of India has been a preparation will be speedily and mightily accomplished (Aurobindo 1965: 10).

In historiography we have the authoritative statement of this process of nationalist political activity forging a nation, from Professor Bipin Chandra:

> Colonial India has to be studied as a nation in the making both as an objective process and as the subjective cognition of this process...the national movement was the process through which the Indian people were formed into a nation and a people...it was the existence of a common oppression by a common enemy and the struggle against it which provided important bonds uniting the Indian people...the nation was not a datum prior to the nationalist movement. A nation is a process of becoming and

national movement is a process through which the people or a population of a colony are formed into a nation or a people and through which they acquire a vision of their society as a nation and of themselves being a people or a nation(B. Chandra 1986: 210).

As an expression of belief in an almost mechanical process by which nationalism invents the nation, the above statement leaves nothing ambiguous. In this ideology of nationalism all politically successful nationalist movements are credited with the founding of nations. All that is required is that a particular nationalist movement be politically successful i.e. wrest power from the alien rulers and form a state, and this is considered equivalent to the bringing forth of a nation. However, the becoming of a nation and setting up of a state system are two different things; the transposition of nation with state is one of the confusions that recent sociological scholarship has sought to dispel. With regard to the commonality of oppression and struggle based on objective contradiction between the British and the Indian, it should be pointed out that an extremely complex situation of conflicting interests and differential perceptions is sought to be reduced to a presumed overarching antagonism between two conceptual monoliths—the British and the Indian—an antagonism that appears to transcend concrete history, and attempts to evoke semi-racist sentiments. The existence or otherwise of common oppression under the British, of a unified perception of them as the common enemy, of a united struggle against the rulers are matters for historical investigation and cannot be presumed a priori simply because one segment was British and the other Indian.

It is often suggested that nationalist mobilization is primordial, atavistic, and irrational. If this be really so, what is modern about this process? In modern times there have been mobilizations which from an outside view could appear atavistic and irrational; to the extent that they are, they are pre-modern movements in modern times. However, one needs to be cautious in judging movements especially in other cultures and countries. What is specifically modern in nationalism is a particular form of fusion between culture and power. The movement and mobilization takes place in the consciousness of a commonality of purpose and collective self-interest. The atavism, if any, of nationalism in modernity consists in the limit set by culture—why should commonality of purpose limit itself to one's own culture, why must cultural differences between communities become salient in the realization of power, and why should the sense of deep and horizontal comradeship or fellow-feeling stop with the boundary of the culture. However, within culture itself there is contestation in consciousness, and an enemy becomes common to all not merely because of skin colour, or language differences, but because his removal from the scene must mean enhanced and equalized power for all within culture. Thus an implicit or explicit understanding, or some kind of contract among the members of culture, underlies nationalist mobilization concerning the future forms of power distribution within. In other words, the commonality spoken of, in the context of modern nationalism does not refer merely to past or present cultural affinity, but also to a perception of power-sharing in the future as destiny. This perception is existential, rational and very much interest based.

An analysis of the political processes in colonial India (chapters III, IV, and V) showed that political awakening was dichotomous in an ideal-typical sense: the traditionally dominant communities of Brahmins and allied upper castes, brought together in terms of newly created economic and political interests, raised the slogan of nationalism when the British attempted to withdraw their exclusive patronage; the masses of lower castes, tribals and Muslims on the other hand, quick to grasp the implication of the new political structure were pushing their way ahead, away from the traditional forms of caste and religious slavery, effectively utilizing to their own advantage the growing disaffection between the native and the foreign elite. Such a situation could hardly be described as that of a commonality of interests or a common perception of the British as the enemy. Of course, there was commonality of interest in the sense that all the parties concerned were interested in appropriating power, but unfortunately the nationalists were more than ordinarily interested in appropriating monopoly power, in depriving others of their share of pow   In this sense there was an antagonism between the microscopic minority of nationalists and the masses. The imperialists on the other hand, with a view to perpetuate their rule doled out some fringe favours to the lower castes, Muslims and tribals, which appeared to the nationalists as commonality of interest between the masses and the imperialists. Obviously until the First World War there was neither the commonality of interest nor the experience of facing a common enemy among the Indians. A national level contradiction, instead of being automatic and meta-historical, had to be developed within the harsh world of politics and political interests on the basis of sharing of power and accommodation of the various social forces. It is to Gandhi's credit that he was sensitive to this impasse and saw clearly the danger of the potential nation of masses taking an antagonistic posture towards the nationalists. During the second phase of the nationalist movement under his leadership, Gandhi did attempt to bring together this nation and nationalism. The mobilizational success of the nationalists after the First World War, leading to the expulsion of the British in 1947, became the basis for the claim that Indian nationalism under Gandhian leadership did invent the Indian nation.

But a focus on the Gandhi-Event indicated that this mobilization was brought about, not in terms of modern political economy or the politics of equality but by harking back to the very elements of the old social order, religion and tradition which had kept the majority of the masses in social and political limbo throughout pre-modernity. And this atavistic form of mobilization took place, and to some extent succeeded, counter to the initiative of the masses to reach up to a community of enhanced and equalized power distribution. This was clearly not a situation of nationalism inventing the nation and the nation failed to emerge.

To National-Popular Via Hegemony

Forging commonality of purpose and of programme among people differentially located within the power structure in the national context has been discussed by Antonio Gramsci through the twin concepts of 'national-popular' and 'hegemony'. The historical context within which the Italian Marxist developed his ideas is obviously different from that of Indian nationalism, and hence the use of these concepts to understand and evaluate the political processes in colonial India can only be selective and the conclusions reached, relative and elucidatory.[1]

For Gramsci, the class that seeks to create a national synthesis around its leadership ought to hegemonize the other classes of the population; its present or future rule has to be, and genuinely appear

---

[1] See D. Forgacs (1984), for a historical introduction to the concept of national-popular, pp. 83-97.

to be, not merely class rule of one class over the others but a national-popular rule. This means that class rule is to be transformed into a national one through the active and collaborative consent of the masses. The crucial concept within this set of ideas is of course hegemony which refers to the nature of the relationship between the leading class and the masses. While the concept of hegemony is not entirely unambiguous in Gramsci and one can trace a development in its meaning as it is used throughout his writings, it is possible all the same to isolate the elementary and important aspects of the concept for our purpose.

At the most preliminary level, hegemony for Gramsci meant simply an alliance between classes '... it is a system of alliances which enables it to mobilise the majority of working population' (A. Gramsci 1968: 30). But class alliance is only the first step in the elaboration of the concept of hegemony. At the next level, hegemony is the articulation of interests by the leading class within its own unifying principle, by sacrificing some of its economic corporate nature, in a synthesis of a higher order.

> The fact of hegemony undoubtedly pre-supposed that the interests and strivings of the groups over which hegemony will be exercised, are taken account of, that a certain balance of compromises be formed, that in other words, the leading group makes some sacrifices of an economic-corporate kind (ibid: 154).

These two stages mark the operation of hegemony at the level of the economy or base. But this is not all. From class alliances through synthesis of allied interests, the concepts are now expanded to include leadership of a moral and intellectual kind. The hegemony of the leading class now becomes an all-pervading and unifying force and principle through persuasion, education and organization, and proceeds well beyond the economic-corporate stage to the realm of super structure.

> An important part of the modern prince will have to be devoted to the question of intellectual and moral reform that is to the question of religion or world outlook ... (ibid: 139).

When the fundamental class, passing beyond its primary economic or corporate stages enters the realm of complex superstructures in hegemonic advances, articulating around its own hegemonic principle a vast number of subordinate and allied social groups and their interests, it can be said to be in a leading position, in moral and intellectual dominance, or in other words in the world of state and politics. At this level, the ideology of the hegemonic class universalizes or nationalizes itself and is no more mere class ideology.

> The particular form in which the hegemonic ethico-political element presents itself in the life of the state and the country is 'patriotism' and 'nationalism' which is popular religion, that is to say it is the link by means of which the unity of leaders and led is effected.[2]

The culmination of this process is the formation of a new national-popular collective will. The fundamental class thus succeeds in creating a new nation or an 'integral state' which is composed of both political and civil societies. Gramsci in another instance, recaptures the different moments of hegemony in a succint passage:

> The first and most elementary is the economic-corporate stage: one trader feels that he must be solid with another trader ... A second stage is in which consciousness of the solidarity of interests among all the members of the social groups is reached but still in the economic field ... A third stage is that in which consciousness is reached that one's own corporate interests in their present and future development transcend the corporate circle of the purely economic group and can and must become the interests of other subordinate groups. This is the more strictly political phase which marks the clear transition from the structure to the sphere of complex superstructures ... (A. Gramsci 1968: 168).

Thus, the Gramscian concept of hegemony leading to national-popular will, unfolding itself in three stages, is built into the relationship between the different social classes at both levels of economic base and superstructure. Its lowest manifestation is simple class or group alliance based on perception of their own interests; at a higher level it demands some sacrifices from the leading class in order to articulate the different interests into one unifying principle. Finally it manifests itself as a complete fusion of economic, political, intellectual and moral objectives universalized into a national ideology. Admittedly, the Gramscian notion of hegemony has more complex features not all of which are free from ambiguity. However, it is not intended

---

[2] Quoted in C. Mouffe (ed.) (1979), p. 194.

to survey them all here since our purpose is limited.[3] The above delineation of the hegemonic relationship is sufficient to deconstruct it into its elementary building blocks to compare them with the later phase of the Indian nationalist movement when the masses were apparently mobilized under Gandhi's leadership for the common struggle of ejecting imperialism.

Hegemony or False Consciousness

For Bipin Chandra the Indian nationalist movement is the

> only movement where the broadly Gramscian theoretical perspective of a war of position was successfully practised; where state power was not seized in a single historical movement of revolution but through prolonged popular struggle on a moral, political and ideological level; where reserves of counter hegemony were built up over the years through progressive stages; where the phases of struggle alternated with "passive" phases (B. Chandra 1987: 13).

Sumit Sarkar though, concludes, 'Thus there was no breakthrough from the economic-corporative' to the 'hegemonic' phase of the bourgeois class movement...' and would thus consider the Indian freedom struggle as a form of 'limited hegemony' parallel to that achieved in Italy (S. Sarkar 1983: 71-3).

Our analysis of the Gandhian phase of the nationalist movement (chapter V) highlighted the fact that the later phase was a continuity and elaboration of the earlier one, at least in effect, as far as the masses were concerned. The Gandhian leadership devised new tools to effectively blunt the thrust of the popular militancy and agenda in general, and to diffuse the mass struggle against the old Brahminic social order in particular. These were used with high efficacy to liquidate some, alienate many more, and subdue the rest, to serve its own agenda of a variety of nationalism, of a mere change in ruling personnel, devoid of any serious social change. The rhetoric of moral reform, search for truth, critique of Western civilization and restitution of our own traditional ways of life, whether intended by Gandhi himself or not, drove away a substantial portion of the Muslim masses along with their leaders, caused embitterment and

---

[3] See for a critical introduction of the concept, C. Mouffe (ed.) (1979) Chapter 5.

thus antagonized a vast number of depressed classes and their representatives, and finally managed to persuade the rest of the rural masses to give up their own weakly articulated and unorganized anti-caste/landlord agenda in favour of the immediate elite agenda of apparent anti-imperialism.

The masses were indeed seen as part of the nationalist political mobilization under Gandhi though the extent of this is highly exaggerated in nationalist historiography.[4] However, what is not examined is the depth and nature of commonality of purpose and commitment to the programme of the leadership, among the people so mobilized. Can Gandhian political mobilization be described as a process of hegemonization of the popular masses by the leading elite of the nationalist movement? That there existed an unambiguous and serious disjunction of purpose within the nationalist mass mobilization between the subaltern masses and the elite leadership is the single most important theme of the Subaltern School of historiography and hardly needs repetition. Our own line of argument would be to suggest that first of all, there did not exist the necessary pre-condition for a hegemonic process to take place—an understanding and acceptance of the ideal of socio-political egalitarianism, the foundation of political citizenship. What came to be looked upon as the nationalist class was nothing but the disparate and traditionally dominant castes and communities gathered together in their interest to preserve their traditional dominance on the one hand over the lower caste masses, and to enlarge their area of dominance in the new political society on the other. Their new-found national-secular ideology was neither a replacement of nor antagonistic to, the old Brahminic sacral ideology of ascriptive superiority, but on the contrary, a combination with it, and infact a transformed version of the latter, due to historical reasons. Within this politico-social environment, it is no surprise that the seeds of political citizenship could hardly germinate. Whatever sense of egalitarianism eventually came to inform our nationalist movement came either as the inevitable adjustment to be made to the new political structure, or as a concession wrested out of its unwilling hands by the pressure of the subaltern forces. The dominant understanding among the leadership was that they were there because they were born to it, and that they did not require any other sanction

[4] See B. Chandra's earlier estimation of the Gandhian phase (1976, 1979).

beyond this.[5] Thus mass sanction itself was looked upon as a tactic, a tool for political expediency to demonstrate to the imperialist leaders. The question of alliance does not arise in this context, for alliance is premised on a notion of partnership which in turn is based on acceptance of the equal claims of the partner(s) one is allying with.

Secondly, consolidation with other interest groups on the basis of concessions was consistently foreign to the policy and practice of the Indian nationalist movement which, composed as it was of Brahminic and other upper castes, claimed from its inception monopoly representation of the nation and later, sole succession to colonial rule. In this aspect too Gandhi was a true Congressman and fought in every available forum that it was with the Congress alone that the British should settle power. In fact the nationalist movement was at least as preoccupied with how to exclude other groups from power, as how to appropriate it from the British. Eventually when the nationalists were compelled to concede some kind of recognition to the existence of claims other than their own, it was done in such bad grace, that even such an inevitable step could not be converted into an opportunity to develop a historical bloc. Within such a context the issue of sacrificing of some of their own economic-corporate interests does not arise at all. It is a fact that in the name of the nation or nationalism, and in the process of national hegemony, the nationalist movement never felt itself called upon to sacrifice any of their own class, caste, or community interests in favour of their own fellow Indians. Ambedkar has rightly commented that the slogan of nationalism was being raised not to sacrifice anything but to reinforce the nationalists' own traditional and ascriptive privileges.[6]

Thirdly, Gandhian political mobilization—or hegemonic process

---

[5] R. Guha (1989) in passing points out that pre-modern politics had no need for the consent of the masses; it dominated, it did not hegemonize, p. 281.

[6] Not that attempts towards sharing of power based on an understanding between parties were totally absent; note the Lucknow Pact of 1917 and later the regional power sharing arrangement of Swarajya Party in Bengal, (see Sasadhar Sinha (1963). However, these attempts were limited to the inclusion of Muslims only and they too on the whole, could not hold against the dominant trend within Congress; note also when, in 1936 Congress came to power in the provinces, much against saner advice, and despite pre-election co-operation, it refused to form coalition ministries. Finally, refer to the Khare incident in which Gandhi was against the inclusion of depressed class member in the ministry, as it would give 'absurd ambitions' among the communities, B.R. Ambedkar (1970), p. 16 ff.

as was pointed out earlier—was not economic interest based. While the agenda of the Muslim and lower caste masses was education, jobs, political power, social mobility through diversification of occupation and escape from traditional ascriptive civil liabilities, the Gandhian agenda for them was Khilafat, a religionized version of untouchability, moral reform through the Constructive Programme, obedience to the customary laws of land relations, social fixity and in general a reversal to the old order, however differentially understood. Here instead of the nationalist agenda accommodating the mass agenda as a minimum national programme within a process of hegemony, it sought to divert the masses from its own agenda of economic and social interests to a religionized agenda in the name of the uniqueness of Hindu/Indian civilization. This in fact was to further the monopoly economic political power interests of the nationalist elite. Gramscian hegemony is solidly founded on economy and economic and political interests of the contending parties. When the nationalist mobilization attempted to move the masses away from economic and political pursuits by delegitimizing them as imitations of the West, and to bring about a form of national unity based on religion and allied notions, it clearly revealed that the nationalists were taking a definite position of pro-status quo in economic and political matters, and the consequence was that such a political mobilization turned out to be false consciousness or camouflage for the masses whose political and economic interests were sought to be excluded. The Gramscian hegemonic process of building the national-popular is certainly not a process by which the masses are lead into believing something that is not in fact there. Hegemony is a conscious and consensual political process for all the parties involved; it is a process of dovetailing the different interests in the realm first of economics, politics, then, and only then, of culture and superstructures. It is for the same reason that the highest form of Gramscian hegemony, moral and intellectual leadership by the leading class is not to be equated with the Gandhian call for moral reform. The former is a process by which the economic and political interests of different contending parties are unified and universalized into a new form of secular–national morality or popular religion. The latter, on the other hand, was a call to revert to the community-based morality of traditional Indian society with hierarchical ascription, denying the crucial role of the economy and politics as the universal arena of all individuals equally.

Indian nationalist political mobilization within its partiality and patchiness did give an appearance of the emergence of a national-popular will; the masses did appear on the scene, and they seemed to give their consent to the nationalist agenda (perhaps a good portion of them did); however since this consenting process was not built on the solid foundation of even the minimum social and political programme of the masses—the destruction of the old order of ascriptive inequality and acceptance of social citizenship, it was so ephemeral and momentary that it could not even bear the weight of Independence. The conclusion is inevitable: nationalism succeeded but the nation failed to emerge.

Nationalist political mobilization is at once vertical and horizontal and integrative and divisive. The attempt here is to bring together the individuals within one culture on the basis of equal power sharing on the one hand and to effectively exclude the non-members of the culture from such a sharing, on the other. The whole process, takes place within the realm of power as an access to scarce resources—social, cultural, religious, political, and also economic. Shying away from the rush of power in the wake of nationalism under whatever pretext (e.g. the spiritual and immaterial nature of one's own civilization) is a refusal to step into modernity.[7] In the Indian context, the masses were indeed clamouring for facing, sharing and handling this new power, while the elite however was not ready for this changed situation. The latter insisted on the traditional socio-political order first, then elaborated this insistence into a quasi-metaphysical critique of civil society, change, history etc.; the result was the same—preventing the national mass emergence into a new political community.

Gellner did speak of nationalism inventing the nation; but he also spoke of industrialism and universalization of clerisy as a precondition, the changing of society from one kind to another. Anderson wrote of imagined communities but based nationalism on the emergence of print capitalism and a sense of deep, horizontal comradeship. Industrialism or print capitalism are by no means production's inventions or imaginations—they refer to the concrete emergence of new kinds of communities. Studies of nationalism in historical sociology

---

[7] That modernity itself has its limitations is the post-modernist theme. The use of such a post-modernist discourse against social egalitarianism as modernity is nothing but another form of neo-Brahminism.

are coupled with the study of the emergence of the nation. Nationalism does not mechanically engender the nation.[8] In the absence of actual change within society, in our case the destruction of the Brahminic social order, nationalism's relation to the potential nation becomes ambiguous at best. Here the process of invention is displaced by one of prevention; when imagination is limited to a minority of the elite, it turns out to be an illusion to the masses—the nation.

That nationalism won in the subcontinent but the nation was not emerging, was not lost on the very person who, more than anybody else, single-handedly contributed so much to bring about such a situation—Gandhi. In 1947, instead of being the star of the occasion, he walked away in sadness commenting, 'we have now seen it and are disillusioned'. Ironically the sentiments were reciprocated by another person, working from within the other polarity, spending a good part of his public life challenging, debunking and contesting the nationalist forces, especially as they were represented in Gandhi—E.V. Ramaswamy Naicker, the social revolutionary of the South. Periyar celebrated 1947 with a black flag demonstration.

What these two stalwarts from the two polarities of the subcontinent's dichotomous political awakening feared so much in 1947 appears to be increasingly becoming a reality in our body-politic: the rise of communal-nationalism, (communal with reference to not only other religious communities but also the mass of lower castes) of a brutal kind, and on the other hand multiple reactions to it, ethnic nationalisms and group ideologies threatening the very existence of the new nation-state.

THE FAILURE TO EMERGE

Historians, political observers, social scientists and others of varied persuasions have noted the generally backward-looking and reactionary nature of the nationalisms of the East or the Third World.[9] Seen within the ideal-typical dichotomy of the progressive, genuine, political nationalisms of the West and the reactionary, derivative, cultural nationalism of the East, these blanket observations often emanate from ethnic or Eurocentric orientations to the study of nation and

[8] B. Chandra (1986) himself recognizes this, see p. 210.
[9] See for example, E.H. Carr (1939), B. Moore (1967), J. Breuilly (1982) and L.L. Snyder (1954).

nationalism.[10] The nationalist reaction within the subcontinent has predictably concentrated on this aspect and asserts that nation and nationalism are unique constructions, and any comparison that would show Indian nationalism in a pejorative light is necessarily orientalist or imperialist. While such patriotic sentiment is indeed praiseworthy, it does not however advance the understanding and knowledge of our immediate past. Moreover, when patriotism is not founded on the solid rock of critical history, it tends to flounder sooner or later as contemporary events are increasingly demonstrating. Within the subcontinent a good many opinions, not by any means reducible to the imperialist argument have pointed out the negative character of Indian nationalism. The most important of such an evaluation being that of the subaltern historiographers who have set themselves the task of analysing the 'historic failure of the nation to come to its own' (R. Guha 1982: 7). Our own foregoing investigation, of the colonial period of modern Indian history has been a differentiated elaboration of this subaltern position. Taking off from the sociological distinction between Nation and Nationalism and scanning the colonial period for the aspirations for change of power positions within and without culture, we found a divergence between the aspirations of the nation and the nationalist movement.

If the coming into its own of the nation meant a rejection of the traditional socio-political order and a desire of the people for self-government, economic betterment, and social status among peers etc., this transition could be identified both in the West as well as in the Indian subcontinent. Despite its political failure, the process within the latter was truly extraordinary given the limited nature of economic change, the ethnic and linguistic diversity of the area, and the antagonism of foreign rule. But if the ideology and movement of nationalism meant an affirmation of the mass aspiration towards the nation—a equal socio-political community—as a minimum agenda, the phenomenon here was indeed reactionary. While the historical conjuncture in the West favoured a convergence between nation and nationalism, it did not do so in the subcontinent. Nationalism here largely diverged from the nation and advanced towards the formation of a state-system. The Subalternist explanation of the situation that the Indian bourgeosie failed to speak for the nation is too general

---

[10] Typical is that of H. Kohn, see L.L. Snyder (1954) however Kohn appears to have slightly modified his position in his later work (1962).

and insufficient. Traditional dominance here formally transformed itself into state power without undergoing any substantial change. The modern European idiom of secularism, liberal democracy, nationalism etc. were all appropriated to assert what in substance' turned out to be just an updated version of the same old principle of ascription.

In the words of Celestin Bougle,

> The ancient civilisation of the East learns to use all the apparatus of European civilisation, but it is to defend itself; if they change their bodies, it is to protect their souls(C. Bougle 1971: 93).

In Continuity or Break with History   The historic attempt and the failure of the submerged masses—the low caste, Muslim, tribal and other marginalized communities—to emerge as a political nation, the successful re-assertion of the scattered, traditional dominance as nationalism and its transformation into state power, the unfolding of the antagonistic interaction between the two historical blocks of forces, the material and non–material changes that did and did not take place under the pragmatic, largely indirect, hundred year old, British rule: all these in their totality require to be situated within the long and continuous history of the subcontinent's civiliza-tion in order to be viewed and judged in proper perspective. The modern colonial drama, in more senses than usually conceded, is a continuity with the past. The main, collective political actors of the nineteenth and twentieth centuries did not spring up all at once, much less out of nothing; they had been gestating within the womb of a highly diversified and uneven history. The antagonistic com-plementarity of nation and nationalism is but a modern and transformed version of the millennia-old struggle between dominance and resistance passing through several mutations with the passage of time. From within such a long historical perspective, it would hardly appear surprising first, that British rule lasting barely two centuries failed to destroy the particularly resilient old order in the subcontinent. Second, that the kind of colonial modernity it had engendered could so easily be appropriated by the traditional dominance for its re-emergence as the new ideology of nationalism. Third, that the issue of contestation within nation and nationalism largely centred around the old themes—ascriptive superordination, and subordination, culture, religion inheritance etc. And finally, that the outcome itself was a victory for the forces of dominance (nationalism) over those of resistance (nation). The element of break with the past too needs to be recognized. Such a break, our study has revealed, has been more formal than substantial: the politico-juridical recognition of modernity, of modern principles of social and societal interrelationships, as a nation-state within the global system of nation-states constitutes the break. If colonial modernity had substantially empowered and elevated traditional dominance, it had also formally delegitimized traditional subjugation. However, there has been no significant commensurate actualization of these principles within the subcontinent which is still largely a continuity with the past in this sense. The underlying contradiction between the formal and the substantial is what is troubling post-colonial India. Unless and until the formal becomes the substantial, the threat of the potential reversal of the break, modernity will hang like the sword of Democles over the head of the nation-state.[11]

---

[11] B. Moore (1967) p. 415; because 'Within the nation (or nations) there is what Fernando H. Cordoso called the anti-nation' S.K. Ghosh (1989) p. 94. For an alternate, Subalternist version of non-arrival of the nation see R. Guha (1991).

A Consolidated Bibliography
of Books and Articles

Abrams, Philip (1982), *Historical Sociology*, Somerset, Open University Books.

Acharya, Poromesh (1989), Education and Communal Politcs in Bengal: A Case Study, *Economic and Political Weekly (EPW)*, vol. XXIV, no. 30, pp. 81-90.

Ahmed, Aziz (1967), *Islamic Modernism In India and Pakistan 1857-1964*, London, Oxford University Press.

Ahmed, Imtiaz (1971), Caste Mobility Movements in North India, *Indian Economic and Social History Review (IESHR)*, vol. VIII, no. 2, pp. 164-85.

Ahmed, Imtiaz (ed.) (1978), *Caste and Social Stratification among Muslims in India*, New Delhi, Manohar.

Ahmed, Syed Nesar (1991), *Origins of Muslim Consciousness in India: A World System Perspective*, New York, Greenwood Press.

Aiyappan, A. (1965), *Social Revolution in a Kerala Village*, Bombay, Asia Publishing House.

Akzin, Benjamin (1964), *State and Nation*, London, Hutchinson University Library.

Alam, Javeed (1983), Peasantry, Politics and Historiography: Critique of New Trend in Relation to Marxism, *Social Scientist*, vol. XI, no. 2.

Alavi, Hamza (1980), India: Transition from Feudalism to Colonial Capitalism, *Journal of Contemporary Asia*, vol. X, no. 4. pp. 359-99.

Ali, M.M. (1965), *The Bengali Reaction to Christian Activities 1833-1857*, Chittagong, The Mehrub Publications.

All India Congress Committee (1924), *The Indian National Congress (1920-1923)* Allahabad, AICC.

Allen, D., (1992), *Religion and Political Conflict in South Asia*, Delhi, Oxford University Press.

Aloysius, G. (1992), Ideology and Hegemony in the Jharkhand Movement, *Economic and Political Weekly (EPW)*, vol. XXVII, no. 5, pp. 200–3.

—— (1994), The Trajectory of Hindutva, *Economic and Political Weekly (EPW)*, vol. XXIX, no. 24, pp. 1450–52.

Althusser, Louis (1971), *Ideology and Ideological State Apparatus* in *Lenin and Philosophy and other Essays*, London, Verso Editions, pp. 121–77.

Ambedkar, B.R. (1945), *What Congress and Gandhi have done to Untouchables,* Bombay, Thacker & Co.

—— (1970), *Gandhi and Gandhism,* Jullundar, Bheem Patrika Publications.

—— (1982–90), *Collected Works,* vols. 1–8, Bombay, Govt. of Maharashtra.

Anaimuthu, V. (1974), *Thoughts of Periyar* (Tamil) 3 vols. Trichy, Chintaniyalar Kazhagam.

Anderson, Benedict (1983), *Imagined Communities,* London, Verso Editions.

Ansari, Ghaus (1960), *Muslim Caste in Uttar Pradesh,* Lucknow, Ethnographic and Folk Culture Society.

Appadurai, Arjun (1981), *Worship and Conflict under Colonial Rule,* Cambridge, Cambridge University Press.

Argov, Daniel (1966), *Moderates and Extremists: Two attitudes towards British Rule in India,* in S.N. Mukherjee (ed.), *South Asian Affairs,* Oxford: Oxford University Press.

Armstrong, J.A. (1982), *Nations Before Nationalism,* Chapel Hill: University of North Carolina Press.

Arnold, David (1977), *The Congress in Tamil Nadu,* New Delhi, Manohar.

Arnold D. et al (1976), Caste Associations in South India: A Comparative Analysis, *IESHR,* vol. XIII, no. 3, pp. 353–73.

Arnold, D. (1982) *Rebellious Hillmen: The Gudem Rampa Risings,* in R. Guha (ed.) *Subaltern Studies,* vol I, Delhi, Oxford University Press.

Arooran, N.K. (1980), *Tamil Renaissance and Dravidian Nationalism,* Madurai, Koodal Publishers.

—— (1985), *Indians in South Africa with Special Reference to the Tamils,* Thanjavur, Tamil University.

Aurobindo, Sri (1965), *On Nationalism,* Pondicherry, Sri Aurobindo Ashram.

——(1972), *Collected Works*, volumes 1, 2, 14 and 15, Pondicherry, Aurobindo Ashram.

Avineri, Shlomo (1968), *Karl Marx on Colonialism and Modernisation*, New York, Double Day & Co. Inc.

Aziz, K.K. (1987), *A History of the Idea of Pakistan*, 4 vols, Lahore, Vanguard Books.

Babb, Lawrence A. (1972), *The Satnamis—Political Involvement of a Religious Movement*, in M.J. Mahar (ed.), Arizona, The University of Arizona Press, pp. 143-52.

Bald, Suresh Renjen (1982), *Novelists and Political Consciousness*, Delhi, Chanakya Publications.

Balibar, Etienne (1991), *Racism and Nationalism* in E. Balibar and E. Wallerstein, *Race, Nation, Class: Ambiguous Identities*, London, Verso Books.

Baker, C.J. (1976), *The Politics of South India (1920-1937)*, New Delhi, Vikas Publications.

Baker, C.J. & D.A. Washbrook (1976), *South India: Political Institutions and Political Change 1880-1947*, Delhi, MacMillan.

Baker, C.J. (1984), *An Indian Rural Economy 1880-1955. The Tamil Nad Countryside*, Delhi, Oxford University Press.

Baker, D.E.U. (1979), *Changing Political Leadership in an Indian Province: The Central Provinces and Berar: 1919-1939*, Delhi, Oxford University Press.

Banaji, D.R. (1933), *Slavery in British India*, Bombay, D.B. Taraporevala Sons & Co.

Bandyopadhyay, Sekhar (1985), 'Social Mobility in Bengal in the late Nineteenth and the Early Twentieth centuries', Unpublished Ph.D thesis of University of Calcutta.

——(1989), *Social Protest or Politics of Backwardness? The Nama Shudra Movement in Bengal: 1872-1911*, in Basudev Chattopadhyaya and others (eds.), *Dissent and Consensus: Social Protest in Pre-Industrial Societies*, Calcutta, K.P. Bagchi and Co. pp. 170-232.

——(1990), *Caste, Politics and the Raj*, Calcutta, K.P. Bagchi and Co.

Banerjea, S.N. (1925), *A Nation in the Making*, Bombay, Oxford University Press.

Banerjee, Sumanta (1992), Popular Perceptions of Tensions between Regional Identity and Nationalism in the 19th Century Bengali Literature, New Delhi, *I.C.H.R* (Mimeo).

Bardhan, Pranab (1989), The Third Dominant class, *EPW* vol XXIV, no. 3, pp. 155-7.

Barik, R.K. (1987), Primordial Loyalty in Subaltern Politics: A Problem of Understanding the Unrecognized Intelligentsia in Orissa, New Delhi, *NMML* Occasional Papers.

Barnett, M.R. (1976), *The Politics of Cultural Nationalism in South India,* New Jersey, Princeton University Press.

Barrier, N.G. (1968), The Punjab Government and Communalist Politics 1870-1908, *Journal of Asian Studies*, vol. XXVII, no. 3, pp. 523-39.

—— (1985), *Regional Political History: New Trends in the Study of British India,* in Paul Wallace (edit.) *Region and Nation in India,* New Delhi: Oxford & IBH Publishing Co., pp. 111-154.

Basham, A.L. (Papers) (1961), *Modern Historians of Ancient India,* in C.H. Philips (ed.), pp. 260-93.

—— (1967), *The Wonder that was India,* New Delhi, Rupa & Co.

Bates, Crispin (1988), *Congress and the Tribals,* in Shepperdson M. and Simmons C., (eds). *The Indian National Congress and the Political Economy of India (1885-1985)* Aldershot, Gower Press, pp. 231-52.

Baxi, Upendra (1986), *Towards a Sociology of Indian Law,* New Delhi, Satvahan Publishers.

Bayly, C.A. (1990), *Beating the Boundaries: South Asian History, C 1700-1850,* in Sugata Bose (ed.), pp. 27-39.

Bayly, C.A. (1990a), *Indigenous Social Formations and the World System: North India C 1700* in Sugata Bose (ed.), pp. 112-39.

Bearce, George D. (1961), *British Attitudes towards India 1784-1858,* London, Oxford University Press.

Beasant, Annie, n.d., *India: A Nation,* London, T.C & E.C. Jack.

Bendix, Reinhard (1961), *The Lower Classes and the Democratic Revolution* in Gusfield J.R. (ed.) 1970, *Protest, Reform and Revolt,* New York, John Wiley and Sons, pp. 195-213.

Berreman, Gerald D. (1983), *The Evolutionary Status of Caste in Peasant India,* in J.P. Mencher (ed.), pp. 237-50.

Béteille, Andre (1969), *Castes: Old and New,* Bombay, Asia Publishing House.

—— (1974), *Studies in Agrarian Social Structure* Delhi, Oxford University Press.

—— (1980), *The Indian Village: Past and Present* in E.J. Hobsbawm et al. (eds.) *Peasants in History: Essays in Honour of Daniel Thorner,* Delhi, Oxford, University Press, pp. 107-120.

—— (1989), Are the Intelligentsia a Ruling Class, *EPW,* vol. XXIV, no. 3, pp. 151-5.

Bharati, A. (1970), The Hindu Renaissance and its Apolegetic Patterns, *Journal of Asian Studies (JAS)* vol. 29, no. 2, pp. 267-87.

——(1974), *The Language of Modern Hinduism : Cognitive Models and Ethno-Scientific Analysis* in Miller, Roberts (eds.) *Religious Ferment in Asia,* Kansas University Press, pp. 80-103.

Bhat, Chandrasekhar (1984), *The Reform Movement among the Waddars of Karnataka,* in M.S.A. Rao (ed.) 1984, *Social Movements in India,* Delhi, Manohar, pp. 169-90.

Bhatia, B.M. (1965), Growth and Composition of Middle Class in South India in 19th century, *IESHR* vol. II, no. 4, pp. 341-56.

Bhattacharya, Neeladri (1986), *Colonial State and Agrarian Society,* in S. Bhattacharya and R. Thapar (eds.), *Situating Indian History,* Delhi, Oxford University Press, pp. 106-45.

Bhattacharya, P.K. (1991), Rise and Decline of Sankaradeva's Vaish-navism in Fifteenth and Sixteenth Centuries, *EPW,* vol. XXVI, no. 17, pp. 1115-16.

Bhattacharya, Sabyasachi (1983) , 'History from Below', *Social Scientist* vol. II, no. 4, pp. 3-20.

—— (1988), *Swaraj and the Kamgar: The Indian National Congress and the Bombay Working Class 1919-1931,* in R. Sisson and S. Wolpert (eds.), *Congress and Indian Nationalism,* Delhi, Oxford University Press, 223-49.

Biardeau, P. Madeleine (1980), *Hinduism,* Delhi, Oxford University Press.

Birla, G.D. (1968), *In the Shadow of Mahatma,* Bombay, Vakils, Feffers and Simons.

Blum, Jerome (1974), The Condition of European Peasantry on the Eve of Emancipation, *Journal of Modern History,* 46 September 1974, pp. 395-424.

—— (1978), *The End of the Old Order in Rural Europe,* New Jersey, Princeton University Press.

Blumer, Herbert (1969), *Social Movements,* in McLaughlin B. (ed.) *Studies in Social Movements,* New York, Free Press, pp. 8-29.

Bondurant, Joan V. (1988), *Conquest of Violence: The Gandhian Philosophy of Conflict,* New Jersey, Princeton University Press.

Bose, Sugata (1990), *South Asia and World Capitalism*, Delhi, Oxford University Press.

Bougle, Celestin (1971), *Essays on the Caste System*, Cambridge, Cambridge University Press.

Brass, Paul (1974), *Religion, Language and Politics in North India*, Cambridge, Cambridge University Press.

Brasted, Howard (1980), Indian Nationalist Movement and the Influence of Irish Home Rule, *Modern Asian Studies (MAS)* vol. 14, no. 1, pp. 37-63.

Braudel, Fernand (1980), *The Long Duree*, in M. Aymard, and H. Mukhiya, (eds.) *French Studies in History*, vol. I, New Delhi, Orient Longman, pp. 69-101.

Breuilly, John (1982), *Nationalism and the State*, Manchester, Manchester University Press.

Brennan, L. (1970), Social Change in Rohilkhand, 1801-1833, *IESHR* vol. VII, no. 4, pp. 443-65.

Briggs, G.W. (1990) 1920, *The Chamars*, Delhi, Low Price Publications.

Broomfield, J.H. (1966), The Regional Elites: A Theory of Modern Indian History, *IESHR*, vol. II, no. 3, pp. 279-91.

———(1968), *Elite Conflict in a Plural Society: Twentieth Century Bengal*, Bombay, Oxford University Press.

——— (1975), *The Social and Institutional Bases of Politics in Bengal, 1906-1947*, in Van M. Baumer (ed.), *Aspects of Bengali History and Society*, Hawaii, University of Hawaii, pp. 132-46.

Brown, Judith (1969), The Mahatma and Modern India, *MAS*, vol. III, no. 4, pp. 321-42.

———(1972), *Gandhi's Rise to Power*, Cambridge, Cambridge University Press.

——— (1974), Gandhi and India's Peasants, 1917-1922, *Journal of Peasant Studies*, vol. I, no. 4, pp. 462-85.

——— (1977), *Gandhi and Civil Disobedience*, Cambridge, Cambridge University Press.

——— (1984), *Modern India: The Origins of an Asian Democracy*, Delhi, Oxford University Press.

——— (1988), *The Mahatma in Old Age: Gandhi's Role in Indian Political Life 1935-1942*, in R. Sisson and Wolpert (eds.), *Congress and Indian Nationalism*, Delhi, Oxford University Press, pp. 271-304.

Caroll, Lucy (1978) Colonial Perceptions of Indian Society and the Emergence of Caste Associations, *JAS*, vol. 27, no. 2, pp. 233–50.

Carr, E.H. (ed.) (1939), *Nationalism: Report of the Royal Institute for International Affairs*, London, Frank Cass & Co. Ltd.

Cashman, I. R. (1975), *The Myth of Lokmanya: Tilak and Mass Politics in Maharashtra*, Berkeley, University of California Press.

Catanah, I.J. (1966), Agrarian Disturbances in the 19th Century India, *IESHR*, vol. III, no. 1 pp. 65–84.

Chakraborty, Bhaskar (1989), *From Sub-nation to Subaltern: Experiments in the Writing of Indian History*, in Basudev Chattopadhyaya et al. (eds.) *Dissent and Consensus: Social Protest in Pre-industrial Societies*, Calcutta, K.P. Bagchi and Co, pp. 273–99.

Chakravarti, Uma (1987), *Social Dimensions of Early Buddhism*, Delhi, Oxford University Press.

Chakravarty, Dipesh (1985), *Invitation to a Dialogue*, in R. Guha (ed.) *Subaltern Studies IV*, Delhi, Oxford University Press.

Chakravarty, Papia (1992), *Hindu Response to Nationalist Ferment—Bengal 1909-1935*, Calcutta, Subarnarekha.

Chandra, Bipin (1964), Two Notes on the Agrarian Policy of Indian Nationalists (1880-1905), *IESHR*, vol. 1, no. 4, pp. 143–74.

—— (1976), Indian Peasantry and National Integration, *Social Scientist*, vol. V, no. 2, pp. 3–29.

—— (1979), *Nationalism and Colonialism in Modern India*, Delhi, Orient Longman.

—— (1986), *Nationalist Historians' Interpretation of the Indian National Movement*, in S. Bhattacharya and R. Thapar (eds.) *Situating Indian History*, Delhi, Oxford University Press, pp. 194–238.

—— (1984), *Communalism in Modern India*, New Delhi, Vani Educational Books.

Chandra, Bipin et al. (1987), *India's Struggle for Independence*, New Delhi, Viking.

Chandra, Sudhir (1975), *Dependence and Disillusionment: Emergence of National Consciousness in later 19th Century India*, New India, Manas Publications.

—— (1979), *Conflict and Consensus in the Study of Indian Nationalism*, in Devahuti (ed.), *Problems of Indian Historiography*, Delhi, D.K. Publications.

—— (1982), Premchand and Indian Nationalism, *MAS*, vol. 16, no. 4, pp. 601–21.

—— (1982a), Regional Consciousness in 19th Century Hindi Literature, New Delhi, *NMML* Occasional Papers.

—— (1986), Communal Elements in Late 19th Century Hindi Literature, New Delhi, *NMML* Occasional Papers.

—— (1986a), Maithilisharan Gupta and the Idea of Indian Nationalism, *EPW*, vol. 21 no. 51, pp. 2227-30.

—— (1992), *The Oppressive Present: Literature and Social Consciousness in Colonial India*, Delhi, Oxford University Press.

Charlesworth, Neil (1982), *British Rule and the Indian Economy, 1800–1914*, London, MacMillan.

Chatterjee, Bankim Chandra (1969), *Bankim Rachnavali*, Calcutta, Sahitya Sansad.

Chatterjee, Partha (1984), *Gandhi and the Critique of Civil Society*, in R. Guha (ed.) 1984, *Subaltern Studies III*, Delhi, Oxford University Press.

—— (1986), *Nationalist Thought and the Colonial World*, Delhi, Oxford University Press.

—— (1994), *The Nation and its Fragments*, Delhi, Oxford University Press.

Chattopadhyaya, D.P. (1959), *Lokayata*, New Delhi, People's Publishing House.

Chaturvedi, Jayati (1990), *Indian National Movement: A Critical Study of Five Schools*, Agra, M.G. Publishers.

Chintamani, C.Y. (1937), *Indian Politics Since the Mutiny*, Allahabad, Kitabistan.

Chirol, V. (1926), *India*, London, Ernest Ben Ltd.

Coe, John C. (1984), 'Tribe, caste and nationalist politics in Surat District 1920-1935', Unpublished Ph.D thesis submitted to the University of Sydney, Australia.

Cohn, Bernard S. (1970), Society and Social Change Under the Raj, *South Asian Review*, vol. 4, no. 1, pp. 27-49.

—— (1987), *An Anthropologist among Historians and other Essays*, Delhi, Oxford University Press.

Cohn, Stephen P. (1969), The Untouchable Soldier: Caste, Politics and the Indian Army, *JAS*, vol. XXVIII, no. 3, pp. 453-68.

Connor, Walker (1972), Nation-Building or Nation Destroying, *World Politics*, vol. XXIV, no. 3, April 1972, pp. 319-57.

Connor, Walker (1984), *The National Questions in Marxist Leninist Theory and Strategy*, New Jersey, Princeton University Press.

Coomaraswamy, A.K. (1981) 1909, *Essays in National Idealism*, Delhi, Munshiram Manoharlal.

Copland I. (1985), Congress Paternalism: The High Command and the Struggle for Freedom in Princely States (1920-40) *South Asia*, New Series, vol. VIII, no. 1 and 2, pp. 121-40.

Dahrendorf, Ralf (1959), *Class and Class Conflict in Industrial Society*, London, Routledge and Kegan Paul.

Dale, Stephen, Frederich (1980), *Islamic Society on the South Asian Frontier*, Oxford, Clarendon Press.

Dalton, Dennis (1967), *The Gandhian View of Caste and Caste after Gandhi*, in P. Mason (ed.) *India and Ceylon: Unity and Diversity*, Delhi, Oxford University Press, pp. 159-81.

—— (1969), Gandhi: Ideology and Authority, *MAS*, vol. III, no. 4, pp. 377-93.

Das, Arvind N. (1983), *Agrarian Unrest and Socio-Economic Change in Bihar 1900-1980*, Delhi, Manohar Publications.

Das, Binod Sarkar (1987), *Some Aspects of Peasant Resistance Movements in 19th century Orissa*, in C. Palit (ed.) *Revolt Studies*, vol.1, Calcutta, Asiatic Book Agency, pp. 25–45.

Datta, K.K. (1940), *The Santal Insurrection*, Calcutta, University Publications.

De, Amalendu (1974), *Roots of Separatism in 19th Century Bengal*, Calcutta, Ratna Prakashan.

Debray, Regis (1977), Marxism and the National Question, *New Left Review*, no 105, pp. 25-41.

Derrett, J. Duncan (1968), *Religion, Law and the State in India*, New York, Free Press.

Desai, A.R. (1948), *Social Background of Indian Nationalism*, Bombay, Popular Prakashan.

Desai, Mahadev (1953), *The Diary of Mahadev Desai*, Ahmedabad, Navjivan.

De Tocqueville, Alexis (1970), *The Old Regime and the French Revolution*, in J.R. Gusfield (ed.) 1970, *Protest, Reform and Revolt*, New York, John Wiley and Sons, pp. 68-84.

Deutsch, Karl (1953), *Nationalism and Social Communication*, Massachussets, MIT Press.

——(1969), *Nationalism and its Alternatives*. NY, Alfred A. Knopf.

Dev, Bimal J. & Dilip K. Lahiri (1994), *Cosmogony of Caste and Social Mobility in Assam*, Delhi, Mittal Publications.

Dhanagre, D.N. (1975), *Agrarian Movements and Gandhian Politics*, Agra, Agra University.

—— (1983), *Peasant Movements in India 1920-1950*, Delhi, Oxford University Press.

Dhar, Niranjan (1977), *Vedanta and the Bengal Renaissance*, Calcutta, Minerva Associates.

Diehl, Anita (1978), *Periyar E. V. Ramasami*, Bombay, B.I Publications.

Dirks, Nicholas B. (1987), *Hollow Crown*. Cambridge, Cambridge University Press.

Dixit, Prabha (1975), The Political and Social Dimensions of Vivekananda's Ideology, *IESHR*, vol. XII, no. 3, pp. 293–313.

—— (1976), *Modern India and the Bengal School of History: A Critique*, in Devahuti (ed.), *Problems of Indian Historiography*, Delhi, D.K. Publications, pp. 135–47.

—— (1986), *The Ideology of Hindu Nationalism* in T. Pantham and K.L. Deutsch (eds.) *Political Thought in Modern India*, New Delhi, Sage Publications, pp. 122–41.

Douglas, I.H. (1988), *Abdul Kalam Azad—An Intellectual and Religious Biography*, Delhi, Oxford University Press.

Drekmeier, Charles (1962), *Kingship and Community in Early India*, California, Stanford University Press.

Dube, Saurabh (1992), *Myths, Symbols and Community: Satnam Panth of Chattisgarh*, in P. Chatterjee and G. Pandey (eds.), *Subaltern Studies*, vol. VII, Delhi, Oxford University Press, pp. 121–158.

Duby, Georges (1980), *The Three Orders: Feudal Society Imagined*, Chicago, Chicago University Press.

Dumont, Louis, (1970), *Homo Hierarchicus*, Paris, Mouton Publishers.

Dushkin, Lelah (1974), 'Non-Brahmin Movement in the Princely State of Mysore', Unpublished Ph.D thesis University of Pennsylvania.

Dutt, R.C. (1888) 1963, *Early Hindu Civilisation*, Calcutta, Puniti Pusthak.

—— (1888) 1963a, *Late Hindu Civilisation*, Calcutta, Puniti Pusthak.

—— (1901) 1960, *The Economic History of India*, vol. I, New Delhi, Government of India Publications.

—— (1903) 1960a, *The Economic History of India*, vol. II, New Delhi, Government of India Publications.

Dutt, R. Palme, (1970), *India Today*, Calcutta, Manisha.

Edwards, Michael (1986), *The Myth of the Mahatma*, London, Constable.

Embree, Ainslie T. (ed.) (1968), *1857 in India—Mutiny or War of Independence*, Massachusetts, Heath and Company.

—— (1969), *Landholding in India and British Institution* in R.E.

Frykenberg (ed.), *Land Control and Social Structure in Indian History*, Madison, The University of Wisconsin Press, pp. 33–52.

—— (1974), *The Social Role of Religion in Contemporary India*, in R.J. Miller (ed.) *Religious Ferment in Asia*, Kansas University Press, pp. 109–21.

—— (1989), *Imagining India*, Delhi, Oxford University Press.

Emilsen, William W. (1987), Gandhi and Mayo's Mother India, *South Asia*, New Series, vol. X, no. 1, pp. 69-81.

Epstein, S.J.M. (1988), *The Earthy Soil—Bombay Peasants and the Indian Nationalist Movement,* Delhi, Oxford University Press.

Farquhar, J.N. (1967), *Modern Religious Movements in India*, Delhi, Munshiram Manoharlal.

Fiori, G. (1970), *Antonio Gramsci: Life of a Revolutionary*, London, New Left Books.

Foucault, Michael (1990), *The History of Sexuality*, vol. 1, London, Penguin Books.

Forgacs, David (1984), *Formations of Nation and People*, London, Routledge and Kegan Paul.

Forrester, Duncan B. (1980), *Caste and Christianity: Attitudes and Policies on Caste of Anglo-Saxon Protestant Missions in India*, London, Curzon Press.

—— (1991), *The Depressed Classes and Conversion to Christianity (1860–1960)*, in G.A. Oddie (ed.), *Religion in South Asia*, New Delhi, Manohar, pp. 65–94.

Fox, Richard G. (1989), *Gandhian Utopia*, Boston, Beacon Press.

——(1990),*Gandhian Socialism and Hindu Nationalism: Cultural Domination in the World System*, in Sugata Bose (ed.) 1990, pp. 244-61.

Franco, F. Chand and S.V.S. (1989), Ideology as Social Practice—the Functioning of Varna, *EPW*, 25 Nov. 1989, pp. 2601-12.

Frankel, F.R. and M.S.A. Rao, (1989), *Dominance and State Power in Modern India: Decline of a Social Order*, 2 vols. Delhi, Oxford University Press.

Frykenberg, R.E. (1965), *Guntur District (1788-1848) A History of Local Influence and Central Authority in South India*, Oxford, Clarendon Press.

Frykenberg, R.E. (ed.) (1969), *Land Control and Social Structure in Indian History*, Madison, The University of Wisconsin Press.

—— (1978), Reconstructing the History of South India, *MAS*, vol. XII, no. 4, pp. 687–701.

—— (1989), *The Emergence of Modern 'Hinduism' as a Concept and as an Institution: A Reappraisal with special reference to South India*, in G.D. Sontheimer and Hermann Kulke (eds.) *Hinduism Reconsidered*, New Delhi, Manohar, pp. 29–50.

—— (1993), *Hindu Fundamentalism and the Structural Stability of India*, in Martin E. Marty, and R. Scott Appleby (eds.) *Fundamentalism and the State*, Chicago, The University of Chicago Press, pp. 233–55.

Fuchs, Stephen (1965), *Rebellious Prophets: A Study of Messiahnic Movements in Indian Religions*, Bombay, Asia Publishing House.

Fukuyama, Francis (1992), *The End of History and the Last Man*, New York Free Press.

Galanter, Marc (1972), *Untouchability and the Law*, in Michael J. Mahar (ed.) *The Untouchables in Contemporary India*, Tucson, University of Arizona Press, pp. 227-92.

—— (1984), *Competing Equalities*, Delhi, Oxford University Press.

——(1989), *Law and Society in Modern India*, Delhi, Oxford University Press.

Gallagher, et al (eds.) (1973), *Locality, Province and Nation; Essays on Indian Politics, 1870-1940*, London, Cambridge University Press.

Gandhi, M.K. (1922), *Writings and Speeches*, Madras, G.A. Natesan & Co.

—— (1924), *Young India (1919-1922)*, Madras, S. Ganesan.

——(1927), *Young India (1924-1926)* Madras, S. Ganesan.

—— (1935), *Young India (1927-28)*, Madras, S. Ganesan

——(1938), *Hind Swaraj or Indian Home Rule*, Ahmedabad, Navjivan Publishing House.

——(1941), *Constructive Programme: Its Meaning and Place*, Ahmedabad, Navjivan Publishing House.

—— (1947), *India of My Dreams*, Ahmedabad, Navjivan Publishing House.

—— (1954), *The Removal of Untouchability*, Ahmedabad, Navjivan Publishing House.

—— (1962), *Varnashrama Dharma*, Ahmedabad, Navjivan Publishing House.

——(1964), *Caste Must Go and the Sin of Untouchability*, Ahmedabad, Navjivan Publishing House.

—— (1970), *My Theory of Trusteeship*, Bombay, Bharatiya Vidya Bhavan.

Geertz, Clifford (1973), *The Interpretation of Cultures,* New York, Basic Books Inc.

Geetha, V. and S.V. Rajadorai, (1993), Dalit and Non-Brahmin Consciousness in Colonial Tamil Nadu, *EPW*, vol. XXVIII, no. 39, pp. 2091-98.

Gellner, Ernest (1964), *Thought and Change,* Chicago, University of Chicago Press.

—— (1973), Scale and Nation, in Garvie (ed.) *Contemporary Thought and Politics*, London, Routledge and Kegan Paul.

—— (1983), *Nation and Nationalism*, Oxford, Basil Blackwell.

—— (1987), *Culture, Identity and Politics*, Cambridge, Cambridge University Press.

Ghose, Sankar (1967), *The Western Impact on Indian Politics (1885-1919)*, Bombay, Allied Publishers.

Ghosh, Suniti Kumar (1985), *The Indian Big Bourgeosie*, Calcutta, Subarnarekha.

—— (1988), Indian Bourgeosie and Imperialism, *EPW*, vol. XXIII, no. 45-47, pp. 2445-58.

—— (1989), *India and the Raj 1919-1947*, Calcutta, Prachi.

Giueseppe, Flora (1993), The Changing Perception of Mazzini within the Indian National Movement, *NMML* Occasional Papers, New Delhi.

Gold, Daniel (1993), *Organised Hinduisms: From Vedic Truth to Hindu Nation*, in M.E. Marty, and R.S. Appleby (eds.) *Fundamentalisms Observed*, Chicago, University of Chicago Press, pp. 531-93.

Golwalkar, M.S. (1939), *We or Our Nationhood Defined*, Nagpur, Bharat Publications.

Gooptu, Nandini (1993), *Caste and Labour: Untouchable Social Movements in Urban Uttar Pradesh in the Early Twentieth Century*, in P. Robb (ed.) 1993, pp. 277-98.

Gordon, Johnson (1973), *Provincial Politics and Indian Nationalism*, Cambridge, Cambridge University Press.

Gordon, Leonard (1974), *Bengal: The Nationalist Movement (1876-1940)* Delhi, Manohar Book Service.

Gordon, R. (1975), The Hindu Mahasabha and the Indian National Congress 1915-1926, *MAS*, vol. IX, no. 2, pp. 145-203.

Gore, M.S (1993), *Social Context of an Ideology: Ambedkar's Political and Social thought*, New Delhi, Sage Publications.

Gould, Harold A. (1987), *The Hindu Caste System: The Satralisation of a Social Order*, Delhi, Chanakya Publications.

Graham, Reid (1976), 'Arya Samaj as a Reformation in Hinduism with special reference to Caste', Unpublished Ph. D thesis of Yale University.

Gramsci, Antonio (1968), *Modern Prince and Other Writings*, New York, International Publishers.

Gramsci, A. (1971), *Selections from Prison Notebooks*, Quintin Hoare and G.N. Smith (eds.), New York, International Publishers.

Greenfeld, Liah (1996), Nationalism and Modernity, *Social Research*, vol. 63, no. 1, pp. 3-40.

Guha, Ranajit (1982), *On some Aspects of the Historiography of Colonial India* in *Subaltern Studies*, vol. 1, pp. 1-8.

—— (1983), *Elementary Aspects of Peasant Insurgency in Colonial India*, Delhi, Oxford University Press.

Guha, Ranajit (ed.) (1982-88), *Subaltern Studies*, vol. I-VI, Delhi, Oxford University Press.

—— (1989) *Dominance Without Hegemony and its Historiography*, in R. Guha (ed.), *Subaltern Studies*, vol. VI, pp. 210-309.

—— (1991), *A Disciplinary Aspect of Indian Nationalism*, Santa Cruz, Merrill Publications.

Habib, Irfan (1995), *Essays in Indian History*, New Delhi, Tulika.

Hah, Chong-do and J. Martin, (1975) *Towards a Synthesis of Conflict and Integration Theories of Nationalism*, World Politics, vol. 27, no. 3, pp. 361-86.

Haithcox, John Patrick (1971), *Communism and Nationalism in India*, Bombay, Oxford University Press.

Hamid, Abdul (1967), *Muslim Separatism in India*, Lahore, Oxford University Press.

Haq, Jalalul (1992), *Nation and Nation-Worship in India*, New Delhi, Genuine Publications.

Hardgrave, Robert L. (1965), *The Dravidian Movement*, Bombay, Popular Prakashan.

—— (1968), The Breast-Cloth Controversy: Caste Consciousness and Social Change in Southern Travancore, *IESHR*, vol. V, no. 2, pp. 171-87.

—— (1969), *The Nadars of Tamil Nadu*, Berkeley, University of California Press.

Hardiman, David (1981), *Peasant Nationalists of Gujarat*, Delhi, Oxford University Press.

—— (1987), *The Coming of the Devi: Adivasi Assertion in Western India*, Delhi, Oxford University Press.

Hardy, Peter (1971), *Partners in Freedom—and True Muslims: The Political Thought of some Muslim Scholars in British India, 1912–1947*, Copenhagen, Scandinavian Institute of Asian Studies.

—— (1972), *The Muslims of British India*, Cambridge, Cambridge University Press.

Harper, E.B. (1968), *Social Consequences of an Unsuccessful Low Caste Movement*, in J. Silverberg (ed.), *Social Mobility in Caste System in India*, The Hague, Mouton, pp. 36-65.

Hasan, Mushirul (1981), Religion and Politics: The Ulama and Khilafat Movement, *EPW*, vol. 16, no. 20, pp. 903-12.

—— (1986), Pan-Islamism Versus Indian Nationalism: A Reappraisal, *EPW*, vol. 21, no. 24, pp. 1074-9.

—— (1991), *Nationalism and Communal Politics in India, 1885-1930*, Delhi, Manohar.

Hayes, J.H. Carlton (1931), *The Historical Evolution of Modern Nationalism*, New York, Richard R. Smith Inc.

Heberle, R. and J.R. Gusfield, (1968), *Social Movements*, in D.L. Sills (ed.), *International Encyclopaedia of the Social Sciences*, vol. XIV, MacMillan and Free Press, pp. 438-52.

Heehs, Peter (1984), Foreign Influences on Bengali Revolutionary Terrorism 1902-1908, *MAS*, vol. 28, no. 3 pp. 533-56.

Heimsath, Charles H. (1964), *Indian Nationalism and Hindu Social Reform*, New Jersey, Princeton University Press.

—— (1980), The Functions of Hindu Social Reformers—With Special Reference to Kerala, *IESHR*, vol. XV, no. 1, pp. 21-39.

Held, D. (1984), *Political Theory and Modern State*, Oxford, Polity Press.

Henningham, Stephen (1979), Agrarian Relations in North Bihar: Peasant Protest and the Darbanga Raj 1919-20, *IESHR*, vol. XVI, no. 1, pp. 53-83.

—— (1981), Autonomy and Organisation—Harijan and Adibasi Protest Movements, *EPW*, vol. XVI, no. 27, pp. 1153-56.

Herod, C.C. (1976), *The Nation in the History of Marxian Thought*, The Hague, Martinus Nijhoff.

Hettne, Bjorn (1978), *The Political Economy of Indirect Rule (Mysore 1881-1947)*, Copenhagen, Scandinavian Institute of Asian Studies.

Hobsbawm, E. & T. Ranger, (eds.) (1983), *The Invention of Tradition*, Cambridge, Cambridge University Press.

Hroch, Miroslov (1993), From National Movement to Fully Fledged Nation, *New Left Review*, no. 198, pp. 3-20.

Hunter, W.W. (1969), *The Indian Musalmans*, Delhi, Indological Book House.

Husain, S. Abid (1965), *The Destiny of Indian Muslims*, Bombay, Asia Publishing House.

Inden, Roland (1986), Orientalist Construction of India, *MAS*, vol. 20, no. 3, pp. 401-46.

—— (1990), *Imagining India*, Oxford, Basil Blackwell.

Irschick, Eugene F. (1969), *Politics and Social Conflict in South India: The Non-Brahmin Movement and Tamil Separatism, 1916-1929*, Berkeley, University of California Press.

Ishwaran, K. (1968), *Shivapur — A South Indian Village*, London, Routledge & Kegan Paul.

Islam, M.N. (1973), *Bengali Muslim Public Opinion as reflected in the Bengali Press 1801-1930*, Dacca, Bangla Academy.

Jeffrey, Robin (1976), Temple Entry Movement in Travancore (1860-1940), *Social Scientist*, vol. IV, no. 8, pp. 3-27.

Jaffrelot, Christophe (1995), *The Idea of the Hindu Race in the Writings of Hindu Nationalist Ideologies in the 1920s and 1930s: A Concept between two cultures*, in P. Robb (ed.), *The Concept of Race in South Asia* Delhi, Oxford University Press, pp. 327-54.

Jha, Gulab (1990), *Caste and the Communist Movement*, New Delhi, Commonwealth Publishers.

Jha, Hetukar (1977), Lower Caste Peasants and Upper Caste Zamindars in Bihar (1921-1925), *IESHR*, vol. XIV, no. 4, pp. 549-59.

Jha, J.C. (1987), *The Nature of Tribal Unrest on the Chotanagpur Plateau 1831-1833*, in C. Palit (ed.) *Revolt Studies*. vol. 1, Calcutta, Asiatic Book Agency, pp. 49-60.

Jones, Kenneth W. (1973), Hum Hindu Nahin: Arya-Sikh Relations (1877-1905), *JAS*, vol. 32, no. 3, pp. 457-75.

—— (1976), *Arya Dharm: Hindu Consciousness in 19th Century Punjab*, Delhi, Manohar.

—— (1981), *Religious Identity and the Indian Census*, in N. Gerald Barrier (ed.) *The Census in British India*, New Delhi, Manohar, pp. 73-101.

—— (1989), *Socio-Religious Reform Movements in British India*, Cambridge, Cambridge University Press.

—— (ed.) (1992), *Religious Controversy in British India*, New York, State University of New York Press.

Jordens, J.T.F. (1978), *Dayanand Saraswati, His Life and Ideas*, Delhi, Oxford University Press.

——(1981), *Swami Shraddhananda: His Life and Causes*, Delhi, Oxford University Press.

Joshi, V.C. (ed.) (1966), *Lala Lajpat Rai: Writings and Speeches* (2 vols), Delhi, University Publishers.

Juergensmeyer, Mark (1982), *Religion as Social Vision: The Movement against Untouchability in 20th century*, Berkeley, University of California Press.

——(1993), *The Rise of Hindu Nationalism* in N. Smart and S. Thakur (ed.) (1993) *Ethical and Political Dilemmas of Modern India*, New York, St. Martin's Press.

Kamalanathan, T.P. (1985), *Mr. Veeramani Refuted...*, Tirupathur, Ambedkar Self-Respect Movement.

Kannangara, A.P. (1968), Indian Mill Owners and Indian Nationalism before 1914, *Past and Present*, no. 40, pp. 147-64.

Karve, Iravati (1961), *Hindu Society—An Interpretation*, Poona, Deccan College.

Kaushik, Karuna (1984), *Russian Revolution and Indian Nationalism*, Delhi, Chanakya Publications.

Kaviraj, Narahari (1982), *Wahabi and Farazi Rebels of Bengal*, New Delhi, People's Publishing House.

Kavlekar, Kasinath K. (1979), *Non-Brahmin Movement in South India (1873-1949)*, Poona, Shivaji University Press.

Kedourie, E. (1960), *Nationalism*, London, Hutchinson.

Kedourie, Elie (ed.) (1970), *Nationalism in Asia and Africa*, New York, The World Publishing Company.

Keer, Dhananjay (1962), *Dr Ambedkar: Life and Mission*, Bombay, Popular Prakashan.

—— (1964), *Mahatma Jotiba Pooley*, Bombay, Popular Prakashan.

—— (1969), *Lokamanya Tilak*, Bombay, Popular Prakashan.

—— (1973), *Mahatma Gandhi*, Bombay, Popular Prakashan.

Khan, Sir Syed Ahmed (1972), *Writings and Speeches*, edited by S. Mohammed, Bombay, Nachiketa Publications.

Kohn, Hans (1924), *A History of Nationalism in the East*, London, George Routledge and Sons Ltd.

—— (1965), *Nationalism: Its Meaning and History*, London, Van Nostrand: Anvil Books.

—— (1962), *The Age of Nationalism*, New York, Harper Brothers.

—— (1968), *Nationalism*, in David L. Sills (ed.), *International Encyclopaedia of the Social Sciences*, vol. XI, MacMillan and Free Press, pp. 63–70.

Kooiman, Dick (1989), *Conversion and Social Equality in India: The London Missionary Society in South Travancore in the 19th Century*, Delhi, Manohar.

—— (1995), Communalism and Indian Princely States, *EPW*, vol. XXX, no. 34, pp. 2123–33.

Kopf, David (1969), *British Orientalism and the Bengal Renaissance*, Berkeley, University of California Press.

—— (1980), Hermeneutics Versus History, *JAS*, vol. 39, no. 3, pp. 495–506.

—— (1988), *The Brahmo Samaj and the Shaping of the Modern Indian Mind*, New Delhi, Archives Publishers.

Kosambi, Meera (1991), Girl Brides and Socio-Legal Change, *EPW*, 3–10 August 1991, pp. 1857–68.

Koshy, M.J. (1972), *Genesis of Political Consciousness in Kerala*, Trivandrum, Kerala Historical Society Series.

Kothari, Rajni (1970), *Politics in India*, New Delhi, Orient Longman Ltd.

Krishna, Gopal (1966), The Development of Indian National Congress as a Mass Organisation 1918-23, *JAS*, vol. XXV, no. 3, pp. 413–30.

Kshirsagar, R.K. (1994), *Dalit Movements in India and its Leaders*, Delhi, M.D. Publications.

Kumar, Awadesh (1985), *Religious Protest and Status Improvement—A Case Study of Satnamis of Chattisgarh*, in P.N. Pimpley, and S.K. Sharma (eds.) *Struggle for Status*, Delhi, B.R. Publishing Corporation pp. 102–25.

Kumar, Kapil (1983), Peasants' Perception of Gandhi and His Programme: Oudh 1920-22 *Social Scientist*, vol. XI, no. 2, pp. 16–30.

Kumar, Kapil (ed.) (1988), *Congress and Classes: Nationalism, Workers and Peasants*, Delhi, Manohar.

Kumar, Krishna (1991), *Political Agenda of Education*, New Delhi, Sage Publications.

—— (1993), *Hindu Revivalism and Education in North Central India*, in M.E. Marty, & R.S. Appleby (eds.) *Fundamentalism and Society*, Chicago, University of Chicago Press, pp 536–57.

Kumar, Ravinder (1965), Rural Life in Western India on the Eve of the British Conquest, *IESHR*, vol. II, no. 3, pp. 202-20.

—— (1968), *Western India in the 19th Century*, London, Routledge and Kegan Paul.

—— (1969), Class, Community or Nation: Gandhi's Quest for a Popular Consensus in India, *Modern Asian Studies*, vol. III, no. 4, pp. 357-76.

—— (1971), *Political Process in India*, South Asia, no. 1, pp. 91-108.

—— (1983), Nationalism and Social Change, New Delhi, *NMML* Occasional Papers on History and Society (Mimeograph).

Kumar, W.R. Vijaya (1974), *A Historical Survey of Buddhism in India*, in T.S. Wilkinson and M.M. Thomas (eds.) *Ambedkar and the Neo-Buddhist Movement*, Bangalore, Christian Institute for the Study of Religion and Society, pp. 3-32.

Kusuman, K.K. (1973), *Slavery in Travancore*, Trivandrum, Kerala Historical Society.

—— (1976), *The Abstentation Movement*, Trivandrum, Kerala Historical Society.

—— (1977), *The Extremist Movement in Kerala*, Trivandrum, Charitram Publications.

Lal, Deepak (1988), *The Hindu Equilibrium: Cultural Stability and Economic Stagnation*, vol. I, Oxford, Clarendon Press.

Larson, Gerald James 1993, *Discourse About 'Religion' in Colonial and Post-Colonial India*, in Ninian Smart, and Shivesh Thakur (eds.) *Ethical and Political Dilemmas of Modern India*, New York, St. Martin's Press, pp. 181-93.

Latthe, A.B. (1924), *Memoirs of His Highness Shri Sahu Chhatrapati Maharaja of Kolhapur*, 2 vols, Bombay, Times of India Press.

Leopold, Joan (1970), The Aryan Theory of Race, *IESHR*, vol. VII, no. 2, pp. 271-97.

Lieten, G.K. (1983), The Civil Disobedience Movement and the National Bourgeosie, *Social Scientist*, vol. XI, no. 5, pp. 33-48.

Loganathan, I. (1993), *Revival of Buddhism in South India in the Nineteenth Century*, in K.N. Kadam (ed.) *Dr. B.R. Ambedkar, The Emancipator of the Oppressed*, Bombay, Popular Prakashan, pp. 93-102.

Low, A.D. (1968), *Soundings in Modern South Asian History*, Berkeley, University of California Press.

—— (1977), *Congress and the Raj*, London, Arnold–Heinemann.

Ludden, D. (1985), *Peasant History in South India*, Delhi, Oxford University Press.

—— (1990), *World Economy and Village India, 1600–1900: Exploring the Agrarian History of Capitalism*, in Sugata Bose (ed.), pp. 159–77.

Lukes, Stephen (ed.) (1986), *Power*, Oxford, Basil BlackWell.

Lynch, Owen M. (1969), *Politics of Untouchability*, New York, Columbia University Press.

McCully, Bruce Tiebout (1966), *English Education and the Origins of Indian Nationalism*, Massachusetts, Petersmith.

McDonald, Ellen E. et al. (1969), *English Education, Nationalist Politics and Elite Groups in Maharashtra 1885-1915*, Occasional Paper from California University.

McLane, J.R. (1964), Peasants, Moneylenders and Nationalists at the end of the 19th Century, *IESHR*, vol. I, no. 1, pp. 67–73.

—— (1975), *Bengal's Pre-1905 Congress Leadership and Hindu Society*, in Van M. Baumer (ed.) *Aspects of Bengali History and Society*, Hawaii, The University of Hawaii, pp. 147–77.

—— (1977), *Indian Nationalism and The Early Congress*, New Jersey, Princeton University Press.

—— (1988), *The Early Congress, Hindu Populism and the Wider Society*, in R. Sisson and S. Wolpert (eds.), *Congress and Indian Nationalism*, Delhi Oxford University Press, pp. 47–61.

Maddison, Angus (1971), *Class Structure and Economic Growth: India and Pakistan Since Moghuls*, London, George Allen and Unwin Ltd.

Mahar, Michael J. (1972), *The Untouchables in Contemporary India*, Arizona, University of Arizona Press.

Majumdar, B.B. (1965), *Indian Political Associations and Reform of Legislature (1818-1917)*, Calcutta, Firma K.L. Mukhopadhyay.

Majumdar, R.C. (1961), 'Nationalist Historians', in C.H. Philips (ed.), pp. 416–28.

Majumdar, R.C. et al. (1978), *An Advanced History of India*, Delhi, MacMillan.

Malik, F. (ed.) (1971), *Iqbal, Poet-Philosopher of Pakistan*, New York, Colombia University Press.

Manickam, Sundararaj (1977), *The Social Setting of Christian Conversion in South India: The Impact of Wesleyan Methodist Missionaries on the Trichy-Tanjore Diocese with Special reference to Harijan Communities of the Mass Movement Area 1820-1947*, Wiesbaden, Francy Stemer Verlag.

——(1993), *Slavery in the Tamil Country,* Madras, The Christian Literature Society.

Mannheim, Karl (1979), *Ideology and Utopia,* London, Routledge and Kegan Paul.

Manor, James (1977), *Political Change in an Indian State. Mysore 1917-1955,* Delhi, Manohar.

Markovits, Claude (1985), *Indian Business and Nationalist Politics 1931-39,* Cambridge, Cambridge University Press.

——(1988), *The Congress Party and Indian Big Business: Some Salient Features of their Relationship (1920-1947),* in M. Shepperdson and C. Simmons (eds.), *The Indian National Congress and the Political Economy of India 1885-1985,* Brookfield, Avebury, pp. 147-59.

Marriott, McKim (ed.) (1990), *India Through Hindu Categories,* New Delhi, Sage Publications.

Marshall, P.J. (ed.) (1970), *The British Discovery of Hinduism in the 18th Century,* Cambridge, Cambridge University Press.

Mathew, Joseph (1986), *Ideology, Protest and Social Mobility,* New Delhi, Inter-India Publications.

Mehrotra, S.R. (1971), *The Emergence of Indian National Congress,* Delhi, Vikas Publications.

Mencher, Joan P. (ed.) (1983), *Social Anthropology of Peasantry,* Bombay, Somaiya Publications Pvt. Ltd.

Metcalf, Barbara Daly (1992), *Imagining Community: Political Debate in Colonial India,* in Kenneth W. Jones, (ed.).

Mills, C.W. (1959), *The Sociological Imagination,* New York, Oxford University Press.

Minault, Gail (1982), *The Khilafat Movement,* Delhi, Oxford University Press.

Minogue, K.R. (1969), *Nationalism,* London, Penguin.

Misra, B.B. (1961), *The Indian Middle Classes,* London, Oxford University Press.

——(1976), *The Indian Political Parties,* Delhi, Oxford University Press.

——(1990), *The Unification and Division of India,* Delhi, Oxford University Press.

Moffat, Michael (1979), *An Untouchable Community in South India,* New Jersey, Princeton University Press.

Moore, Barrington (1967), *Social Origins of Dictatorships and Democracy,* London, Allen Lane, The Penguin Press.

Morearty, John (1976), *The Two-edged Sword: The Treacherousness of Symbolic Transformation: Ram Mohan Roy, Debendranath, Vivekanand and "The Golden Age"*, in Warren Gunderson (ed.) *Studies in Bengal*, Michigan, Michigan State University, pp. 85-106.

Morris, M.D. *et al* (eds.) (1969), *Indian Economy in the 19th Century: A Symposium*, Delhi, Indian Economic and Social History Association, Delhi School of Economics.

Motyl, A.J. (1992), The Modernity of Nationalism, *Journal of International Affairs*, 45, no. 2, pp. 307-22.

Mouffe, C. (ed.) (1979), *Gramsci and Marxist Theory*, London, Routledge and Kegan Paul.

Mukherjee, Meenakshi (1994), *Realism and Reality: The Novel and Society in India*, Delhi, Oxford University Press.

Mukherjee, Prabhati (1988), *Beyond the Four Varnas: The Untouchables in India*, Shimla, Indian Institute of Advanced Studies.

Mukherjee, Ramakrishna (1979), *Sociology of Indian Sociology*, Bombay, Allied Publishers.

Mukherjee, Rudrashanku (1984), *Awadh in Revolt 1857-1858*, Delhi, Oxford University Press.

Mukhopadyaya, S.K. (1981), *Evolution of Historiography in Modern India 1900-1960*, Calcutta, K.P. Bagchi & Co.

Nagi, Saad Z. (1992), *Nationalism*, in E.F. Borgatta and M.C. Borgatta, (eds.), *Encyclopaedia of Sociology*, New York, MacMillan, pp. 1333-42.

Naidu, Varadharajulu T. (ed.) (1932), *The Justice Movement 1917*, Madras, Dravidar Kazhakam.

Nambudiripad, E M S (1984), *Kerala: Society and Politics*, Delhi, National Book Centre.

Nandy, Ashis (1986), *From Outside the Imperium: Gandhi's Cultural Critique of the West* in R. Roy (ed.) *Contemporary Crisis and Gandhi*, Delhi, Discovery Publishing House, pp. 89-126.

Naoroji, Dadabhai (1901) (1990), *Poverty and Un-British Rule in India*, Delhi, Low Price Publications.

Natarajan, S. (1959), *A Century of Social Reform*, Bombay, Asia Publishing House.

—— (1962), *History of the Press in India*, Bombay, Asia Publishing House.

Nehru, Jawaharlal (1936), *Autobiography*, Delhi, Oxford University Press.

—— (1946) (1992), *The Discovery of India*, New Delhi, Jawaharlal Nehru Memorial Foundation.

Nodia, Ghia (1992), Nationalism and Democracy, *Journal of Democracy*, vol. 3 no. 4, pp. 3–31.

Nossiter, T.J. (1982), *Communism in Kerala*, Delhi, Oxford University Press.

Oddie G.A. (1969), Protestant Missions, Caste and Social Change in India 1850–1914, *IESHR*, vol. VI, no. 3, p. 259–91.

—— (1975), Christian Conversion in the Telugu Country 1860–1900. A Case Study of One Protestant Movement in the Godaveri-Krishna Delta, *IESHR*, vol. XII, no. 1, pp. 61–79.

—— (1979), *Social Protest in India: British Protestant Missionaries and Social Reforms 1850-1900*, Delhi, Manohar.

—— (1991), *Hindu and Christian in South-East India*, London, Curzon Press.

O'Hanlon, Rosalind (1985), *Caste, Conflict and Ideology*, Cambridge, Cambridge University Press.

—— (1988), Recovering the Subject: Subaltern Studies and Histories of Resistance in Colonial South Asia, *MAS*, vol. XXII, no. 1, pp. 189–224.

O'Malley L.S.S. (ed.) (1941), *Modern India and the West*, Oxford, Oxford University Press.

Omvedt, Gail (1976), *Cultural Revolt in a Colonial Society*, Bombay, Scientific Socialist Education Trust.

—— (1982), *Caste and Land Relation*, New Delhi, Delhi University.

—— (1992), *Hinduism, Social Inequality and the State,* in D. Allen (ed.), pp. 17–36.

—— (1994), *Dalits and the Democratic Revolution*, New Delhi, Sage Publications.

Oommen, T.K. (1986), *Insiders and Outsiders in India: Primordial Collectivism and Cultural Pluralism in Nation-building*, International Sociology, vol. I, no. I, pp. 53–74.

—— (1988), Towards an Indian Renaissance: A Sociological Perspective (ed.) in Centre for Research in Rural and Industrial Development (CRRID), *In Search of India's Renaissance*, vol. II, Chandigarh, pp. 43–53.

Pal, Bipin Chandra (1916), *Nationality and Empire*, Calcutta, Yugayatri Prakashan Ltd.

—— (1958), *The Soul of India*, Calcutta, Yugayatri Prakashan Ltd.

——(1959), *Beginnings of Freedom Movement in Modern India*, Calcutta, Yugayatri Prakashan Ltd.

Paliakov, Leon (1974), *The Aryan Myth: A History of Racist and Nationalist Ideas in Europe*, Sussex, University Press.

Pandey, Geethanjali (1984), North Indian Intelligentsia and Hindu Muslim Question: A Study of Premchand's Writings, *EPW*, vol. XIX, no. 38, pp. 1664-70.

Pandey, Gyanendra (1978), *The Ascendency of the Congress in Uttar Pradesh 1926-1934, A Study in Imperfect Mobilisation*, Delhi, Oxford University Press.

—— (1987), Questions of Nationalism and Communalism, *EPW*, vol. 22, no. 25, pp. 983.

Pandian, M.S.S. (1991), 'Colonialism, Nationalism and Legitimation: An essay on Vaikunda Swamy Cult in Travancore', Working Paper, Madras Institute of Development Studies, Madras.

—— (1993), De-Nationalising the Past: Nation in E.V. Ramasamy's Political Discourse, *EPW*, vol. XXVIII, no. 42, pp. 2282–87.

—— (1995), Beyond Colonial Crumbs: Cambridge School, Identity Politics and Dravidian Movement, Mimeo.

Panikkar, K.N. (1986), *The Intellectual History of Colonial India: Some Historiographical and Conceptual Questions*, S. Bhattacharya and R. Thapar (eds.), *Situating Indian History*, Delhi, Oxford University Press, pp. 403-33.

—— (1987), Culture and Ideology: Contradictions in Intellectual Transformation of Colonial Society in India, *EPW*, vol. 22, no. 49, pp. 2115-20.

—— (1989), *Against Lord and State*, Delhi, Oxford University Press.

Pantham, T. (1986), *Proletarian Ideology, Satyagraha and Charisma: Gramsci and Gandhi*, in R. Roy (ed.), *Contemporary Crisis and Gandhi*, Delhi, Discovery Publishing House, pp. 165-89.

Parekh, Bhikhu (1989), *Colonialism, Tradition and Reform*, New Delhi, Sage Publications.

—— (1989a), *Gandhi's Political Philosophy: A Critical Examination*, Houndmills, Macmillan Press.

—— (1991), Nehru and the National Philosophy of India, *EPW*, vol. XXVI, no. 1-2, pp. 35-48.

Parry, Jonathan (1974), Egalitarian Values in a Hierarchical Society, *South Asian Review*, vol. 7, no. 2, pp. 95-121.

Parthasarathy, R. (1989), *Journalism in India*, New Delhi, Sterling Publishers.

Parvathamma, C. (1971), *Politics and Religion: A Study of Historical Interaction between Socio-political Relationships in a Mysore Village*, New Delhi, Sterling Publishers.

Patankar, B. & G. Omvedt, (1979), The Dalit Liberation Movement in Colonial Period, *EPW*, vol. XIV, no. 748, pp. 409-24.

Pathak, Shekhar (1991), The Begar Abolition Movement in British Kumaon, *IESHR*, vol. XXVIII, no. 3, pp. 261-79.

Pati, Biswamoy (1983), Peasants, Tribals and the National Movement in Orissa, 1921-1936, *Social Scientist*, vol. XI, no. 7, pp. 25-49.

—— (1985), Popular Struggles and Indian Nationalism: The Kanika Movement of Orissa (1921-22), *Social Science Probings*, vol. II, no. 2, June 1985, pp. 239-53.

Patnaik, N. (1969), *Caste and Social Change: An Anthropological Study of Three Orissa Villages*, Hyderabad, National Institute of Community Development.

Patwardhan, A. (1983), Gandhi: Film as Theology, *EPW*, vol. XVIII, no. 16-17, pp. 635-7.

Philips, C.H. (ed.) (1961), *Historians of India, Ceylon and Pakistan*, London, Oxford University Press.

Picket, W.J. (1933), *Christian Mass Movements in India:* Cincinnati, The Abingdon Press.

Phule, Jotirao (1991), *Collected Works of Mahatma Jotirao Phule*, vol. II, Bombay, Educational Department, Government of Maharashtra

Pillai, J. Sivashanmugam (1930), *The Life, Select Writings and Speeches of Rao Bahadur M.C. Rajah*, Madras, The Indian Publishing House.

Pillai, P. Chidambaram (1933), *Right of Temple Entry*, Nagereoil, P. Chidambaram.

Pinch, William Ralph (1930), Being Vaishnava Becoming Kshatriya: Culture, Belief and Identity in North India 1800-1840, Unpublished M.A. thesis submitted to University of Virginia.

Pouchepadass, Jacques (1974), Local Leaders and the Intellegentia in the Champaran Satyagraha (1917): A Study in Peasant Mobilisation, *Contributions to Indian Sociology, (New Series)*, no. 8, pp. 67-88.

Pradhan, Sadasiba (1986), *Agrarian and Political Movements in States of Orissa 1931-1949*, New Delhi, Inter-India Publications.

Pyarelal (1932), *The Epic Fast*, Ahmedabad, Gujarat Sahitya Mandir.

Raghavaiah V. (1971), *Tribal Revolts,* 2 vols, Nellore, Admijati Sevak Sangh.

Rajagopal, Indu (1985), *The Tyranny of Caste: The Non-Brahmin Movement and Political Development in South India, (1919-1932),* New Delhi, Vikas Publishing House.

Rajah, M.C. n.d, *The Oppressed Hindu,* Madras, The Huxley Press.

Rajamani, C. (1991), 'The Cult of Muthukutty Swamy', Unpublished M.A. thesis, submitted to Serampore University.

Ram, Mohan (1968), *Hindi Against India: The Meaning of DMK,* New Delhi, Rachna Publications.

Ramusack, Barbara N. (1988), *Congress and the People's Movement in Princely India* in R. Sission and S. Wolpert (eds.) *Congress and Indian Nationalism,* Delhi, Oxford University Press, pp. 377-403.

Ranade, Ramabai (ed.) 1815, (1992), *The Miscellaneous Writings of M.G. Ranade,* New Delhi, Sahitya Academy.

Ranadive, B.T. (1982), *Caste, Class and Property Relations,* Calcutta, National Book Agency.

Rao, M.S.A. (1977), *Themes in the Ideology of Protest Movements,* in Malik S.C. (ed.) *Dissent, Protest and Reform in Indian Civilisation,* Simla, Indian Institute of Advanced Studies, pp. 56-69.

—— (1978),*Social Movements and Social Transformation,* Delhi, Manohar.

—— (ed.) (1984), *Social Movements in India,* Delhi, Manohar.

—— (1986), *Political Philosophy of Social Reform Movements,* in W. Fernandez (ed.) *Inequality, its Bases and Search for Solutions,* New Delhi, Indian Social Institute, pp. 291-303.

Rao, V.N., D. Shulman and Sanjay Subrahmanyam (1992), *Symbols of Substance,* Delhi, Oxford University Press.

Ravindran T.K. (1972), *Asan and Social Revolution in Kerala,* Trivandrum, Kerala Historical Study.

—— (1980), *Eight Furlongs to Freedom,* New Delhi, Light and Life Publishers.

—— (1980a), *Historical Views and Reviews: Collection of Essays* Trivandrum, College Book House.

Ray, Rajat K. (1980), *Interpretations of Indian Nationalism,* in Nanda B.R. (ed.), *Essays in Modern Indian History,* Delhi, Oxford University Press.

Ray, Ratna (1974), Land Transfer and Social Change Under the Permanent Settlement: A Study of Two Localities, *IESHR,* vol. XI, no. 1, pp. 1-45.

Raychaudhuri, T. 1979, Indian Nationalism as Animal Politics, *Historical Journal*, vol. XXII, no. 3, pp. 747-63.

——(1983), *The Mid Eighteenth Century Background* in D.Kumar (ed.), *The Cambridge Economic History of India*, vol II, Cambridge, Cambridge University Press, pp 3-35.

Raychaudhuri, T. and I. Habib (eds.) (1982), *Cambridge Economic History of India*, vol. 1, Cambridge, Cambridge University Press.

Renan, Ernest (1882), *What is a Nation*, in Homi Bhabha (ed.) (1990), *Nation and Narration*, London, Routledge & Kegan Paul.

Richman, Paula (1994), *E.V. Ramasami's Reading of Ramayana*, in P. Richman (ed.), *Many Ramayanas*, Delhi, Oxford University Press, pp. 175-201.

Robb, Peter (1993), *Dalit Movements and the Meanings of Labour in India*, Delhi, Oxford University Press.

Robinson, Francis (1975), *Separatism Among Indian Muslims*, Delhi, Vikas Publications.

Robinson, Ronald 1972, *Non-European Foundations of European Imperialism*, in R. Owen and B. Sutcliffe (eds.), *Studies in the Theory of Imperialism*, London, pp. 117-40.

Rothermund, Dietmar (1970), *The Phases of Indian Nationalism and Other Essays*, Bombay, Nachiketa Publications Ltd.

Rothermund, Indira (1971), Gandhi and Maharastra: Nationalism and National Response, *South Asia*, no. 1, pp. 56-73.

Rowe, William L. (1968), *The New Cauhans: A Caste Mobility Movement in North India*, in Silverberg J. (ed.) *Social Mobility in the Caste System in India*, The Hague, Mouton, pp. 66-77.

Roy, Ajit (1982), 'Revolution' by 'Consent': Indian Case Study *EPW*, vol. XVII, nos. 46-7, pp. 1876-84.

Roy, M.N. (1971), *India in Transition*, Calcutta, Manishæ.

Roy, Ram Mohun (1945), *The English Works of Raja Ram Mohan Roy*, (6 vols) Calcutta, Sadharan Brahmo Samaj.

Rudolph, Lloyd I. & Susanne Hoeber Rudolph, (1967), *The Modernity of Tradition*, Chicago, Unviersity of Chicago Press.

Rudolph, Susanne H. (1971) Gandhi's Lieutenants—Varieties of Fellowship in Power, F. Paul (ed.) *The Meanings of Gandhi*, Hawaii, East-West Centre.

Rudra, Ashok (1981), Against Feudalism, *EPW*, vol. XVI, no. 52, pp. 2133-46.

—— (1989), The Emergence of the Intelligentsia as a Ruling class in India, *EPW*, vol. XXIV, no. 3, pp. 142-50.

Ryerson, Charles (1988), *Regionalism and Religion: The Tamil Renaissance and Popular Hinduism*, Madras, Christian Literature Society.

Sachau, E.C. (ed.) (1914), *Alberuni's India*, London, Kegan Paul, Trench, Trubner.

Sadig, Mohammad (1983), *The Turkish Revolution and the Indian Freedom Movement*, Delhi, MacMillan.

Samuel, V.T. (1977), *One Caste, One Religion, One God*, New Delhi, Sterling Publishers.

Sanyal, S. & Burman, B.K. Roy (eds.) (1970), *Social Mobility Movements Among Scheduled Castes and Scheduled Tribes*, New Delhi, India, Ministry of Home Affairs.

Saradamoni, K. (1980), *Emergence of a Slave Caste: Pulayas of Kerala*, New Delhi, People's Publishing House.

Sarkar, Sumit (1973), *The Swadeshi Movement in Bengal*, Delhi, People's Publishing House.

—— (1975), *Bibliographical Survey of Social Reform Movements in the Eighteenth and Nineteenth Centuries*, New Delhi, Indian Council of Historical Research.

—— (1983), *Modern India 1885–1947*, Delhi, MacMillan.

—— (1983a), *Popular Movements and Middle Class Leadership in Late Colonial India*, Calcutta, Centre for Studies in Social Sciences.

—— (1985), *A Critique of Colonial India*, Calcutta, Papyrus.

—— (1990), *Marxian Approaches to the History of Indian Nationalism*, New Delhi, K.P. Bagchi & Co.

Sarkar, Tanika (1987), Nationalist Iconography: Image of Women in 19th Century Bengali Literature, *EPW*, vol. XXII, no. 47, pp. 2011-15.

—— (1994), Imagining a Hindu Nation: Hindu and Muslims in Bankim Chandra's Later Writings, *EPW*, vol. XXIX, no. 39, pp. 2553-61.

Schwab, Raymond (1984), *The Oriental Renaissance—Europe's Discovery of India and the East, (1680-1880)* New York, Colombia University Press.

Seal, Anil (1968), *The Emergence of Indian Nationalism*, Cambridge, Cambridge University Press.

—— (1973), *Imperialism and Nationalism in India*, in J. Gallagher *et al.* (eds.) *Locality, Province and Nation*, London, Cambridge University Press, pp. 1–28.

Sen, S.P. (1973), *Historians and Historiography in Modern India*, Calcutta, Institute of Historical Studies.

Sengupta, K.K. (1970), The Agrarian League of Pabna–1873, *IESHR*, vol. V, no. 2, pp. 253-69.

Seton-Watson, Hugh (1977), *Nations and States: An enquiry into the Origins of Nations and the Politics of Nationalism*, London, Methuen.

Shah, A.M. (1974), Historical Sociology: a Trend Report, in *ICSSR: Survey of Research in Sociology and Social Anthropology*, vol. I, pp. 432-59.

Shah, Ghanshyam (1974), Traditional Society and Political Mobilisation: the experience of Bardoli Satyagraha (1920-28), *Contributions to Indian Sociology*, no. 8, pp. 89-107.

—— (1990), *Social Movements in India: A Review of the Literature*, New Delhi, Sage Publications.

Sharma, K.K. (1988), Congress, Peasants and the Civil Disobedience Movement in Bihar (1930-1932), *Social Scientist*, vol. XVI, no. 3, p. 47-61.

—— (1989), *Agrarian Movements and Congress Politics in Bihar*, Delhi, Anamika Prakashan.

Sharma, K.L. (1976), The Jharkhand Movement, *EPW*, vol. XI, no. 1-2, pp. 37-43.

Sharma, R.S. (1961), *Historiography of the Ancient Indian Social Order*, in C.H. Philips (ed.) 1961, pp. 102-14.

Sheel, Alok (1986), *Peasant Nationalism in India in the Gandhian Era*, in A.K. Gupta (ed.), *Agrarian Structure and Peasant Revolt in India*, New Delhi, Criterion Publication.

Shinde, J.R. (1985), *Dynamics of Cultural Revolution (19th Century Maharashtra)*, Delhi, Ajanta.

Shraddhanand, Swami (1946), *Inside Congress*, Bombay, Phoenix Publications.

Shulman, David (1985), Reconsidering Hinduism or 'What I might have said (in part) if....', in G.D. Sontheimer and Kulke Hermann (eds.), *Hinduism Reconsidered*, New Delhi, Manohar, pp. 7-10.

Silverberg, J. (ed.) (1968), *Social Mobility in the Caste System in India*, The Hague, Mouton.

Singh, Khushwant (1977), *A History of the Sikhs* vol. 2: 1839-1974, Delhi: Oxford University Press.

Singh, K.S. (1966), *Dust Storm and Hanging Mist*, Calcutta, Firma L. Mukhopadhyaya.

Singh, K.S. (1977), *From Ethnicity to Regionalism: A Study in Tribal Politics and Movements in Chotanagpur from 1900-1975*, in S.C.

Malik (ed.) *Dissent, Protest and Reform in Indian Civilisation*, Simla, Institute of Advanced Studies, pp. 317-44.

Singh, K.S. (1978), *Colonial Transformation of the Tribal Society in Middle India*, New Delhi, Government of India.

—— (1982), *Tribal Movements in India*, 2 vols. Delhi, Manohar.

Singh, Yogendra (1977), *Social Stratification and Change in India*, Delhi, Manohar.

—— (1986), *Modernisation of Indian Tradition*, Jaipur, Rawatt Publications.

Sinha, Sasadhar (1963), *Indian Independence in Perspective*, Bombay, Asian Publishing House.

Sircar, Jadunath (1973), *The History of Bengal, Muslim Period*, Patna, Academia Asiatica.

Smith, Anthony (1981), *The Ethnic Revival*, Cambridge, Cambridge University Press.

——(1983), *Theories of Nationalism*, London, Duckworth and Company Ltd.

—— (1983a), Nationalism and Classical Social Theory, *The British Journal of Sociology*, vol. XXXIV, no. 1, March 83, pp. 19-37.

—— (1986), *The Ethnic Origin of Nations*, London, Basil Blackwell.

—— (1988), The Myth of the Modern 'Nation' and the Myths of Nations, *Ethnic and Racial Studies*, vol. XI, no. 1, Jan. 1988, pp. 1-26.

Smith, D.E. (1963), *India As a Secular State*, Bombay, Oxford University Press.

Snyder, Louis L. (1954), *The Meaning of Nationalism*, Westport, Greenwood Press.

Southard, Barbara (1980), The Political Strategy of Aurobindo Ghosh, The Utilisation of Hindu Religious Symbolism and the Problem of Political Mobilisation in Bengal, *MAS*, vol. XIV, no. 3, pp. 353-76.

Spear, Percival (1969), Mahatma Gandhi, *MAS*, vol. III, no. 4, pp. 291-304.

—— (1973), *History of India*, vol. 2, Middlesex, Penguin Books.

Spodak, Howard (1979), Pluralist Politics in British India: The Cambridge Cluster of Historians of Modern India, *American Historical Review*, vol. LXXXIV, no. 3, pp. 688-707.

Srinivas, M.N. (1962), *Caste in Modern India and Other Essays*, Bombay, Asia Publishing House.

—— (1966), *Social Change in Modern India*, Hyderabad, Orient Longman.

—— (1989), *The Cohesive Role of Sanskritization and Other Essays*, Delhi, Oxford University Press.

Stalin, Joseph, (1913), *Marxism and the National Question*, Moscow, Foreign Language Publishing House.

Stein, Burton (1969), *Integration of the Agrarian System of South India*, in R.E. Frykenberg (ed.), *Land Control and Social Structure in Indian History*, pp. 175–216.

—— (1985), *Peasant State and Society in Medieval South India*, Delhi, Oxford University Press.

Stock, Fredrick and Margaret Stock (1975), *People's Movements in Punjab*, California, William Carrey Library.

Stokes, Eric (1978), *The Peasants and the Raj: Studies in Agrarian Society and Peasant Rebellion in Colonial India*, Delhi, Vikas.

Stokes, Gale (1978), The Underdeveloped Theory of Nationalism, *World Politics*, vol. XXXI, no. 1, Oct. 1978, pp. 150-60.

Suntharalingam, R. (1974), *Politics and Nationalist Awakening in South India (1852-1891)*, Tucson, University of Arizona Press.

—— (1983), *Indian Nationalism: An Historical Analysis*, New Delhi, Vikas.

Swan, Maureen (1985), *Gandhi: The South African Experience*, Johannesburgh, Ravan Press.

Tagore, Rabindranath (1918), *Nationalism*, London, MacMillan.

Talbot, Ian (1988), *Punjab and the Raj 1849-1947*, Delhi, Manohar.

Tara Chand (1976), *History of the Freedom Movement in India*, vol. I, Government of India, Publications Division.

Thapar, Romila (1966), *A History of India*, vol. 1, Middlesex, Penguin Books.

—— (1975), *The Past and Prejudice*, New Delhi, National Book Trust.

—— (1988), Nation-building, Development Process and Communication: Towards Renaissance, in Centre for Research in Rural and Industrial Development Seminar—*In Search of India's Renaissance*, vol. II, Chandigarh, pp. 22–33.

—— (1989), Imagined Religious Communities? Ancient History and the Modern Search For a Hindu Identity, *MAS*, vol. XXIII, no. 2, pp. 209-31.

Thapar, Romila *et al.* (1992), *Communalism and the Writing of Indian History*, New Delhi, People's Publishing House.

Theertha, Swami Dharma (1946), *The Menace of Hindu-Imperialism*, Lahore, Happy Home Publications.

Therbon, Goran (1980), *The Ideology of Power and The Power of Ideology,* London, Verso Editions.

Thompson, E. & G.T. Garratt, (1969), *Rise and Fulfillment of British Rule in India,* Allahabad, Central Book Depot.

Thursby, G.R. (1975), *Hindu-Muslim Relations in British India,* Leiden, E.J. Brill.

Tilak, B.G. (1975), *Samagra Lokmanya Tilak* vols.II and VII, Poona, Kesari Prakashan.

Tinkar, Hugh (1964), 'Magnificent Failure: The Gandhian Ideal in India after Sixteen Years, *International Affairs,* vol. XXXX, no. 2, pp. 262-76.

—— (1967), *Is there an Indian Nation?* in P. Mason (ed.) *India and Ceylon, Unity and Diversity,* London, Oxford, pp. 279-96.

Touraine, Alain (1985), An Introduction to the Study of Social Movements, *Social Forces,* vol. 52, no. 4, pp. 748-87.

Tucker, Richard (1970), From Dharmashastras to Politics, *IESHR* vol. VII, no. 3, pp. 325-45.

—— (1976), Hindu Traditionalism and Nationalist Ideologies in 19th Century Maharashtra, *MAS,* vol. X, no. 3, pp. 321-48.

Tuinman, Hans (1984), Political Economy of Untouchability, Unpublished M.A. Thesis submitted to the University of New South Wales, Sydney.

Turner, Bryan. S. (1983), *Religion and Social Theory,* London, Heinemann Educational Books.

—— (1986), *Citizenship and Capitalism,* London, Allen & Unwin.

—— (1986a), *Equality,* Chicester, Elliswood & London, Tavistock.

—— (1988), *Status,* Stony Stratford, Open University Press.

Upadhyaya, Prakash Chandra (1989), A Celebration of the Gandhian Alternative (Review Article), *EPW,* vol. XXIV, no. 28, pp. 2655-62.

Van der Veer, Peter (1992), *History and Culture in Hindu Nationalism,* in A.W. Van Den Hock *et al.* (eds.) *Ritual, State and History in South Asia,* Leiden, E.J. Brill.

Verma, K.K. (1976), *Changing Role of Caste Associations,* New Delhi, National Publishing House.

Viswanathan, E.S. (1983), *The Political Career of E.V. Ramaswami Naicker,* Madras, Ravi and Vasanth Publishers.

Vivekananda, Swami (1965), *Complete Works Eight Volumes,* Calcutta, Advita Ashram.

Waldron, Arthur N. (1985), Theories of Nationalism and Historical

Explanation (Review Article). *World Politics*, vol. XXXVII, no. 3, pp. 416-33.

Washbrook, David (1976), *The Emergence of Provincial Politics: Madras Presidency (1870-1920)*, New Delhi, Vikas.

—— (1982), *Ethnicity and Racialism in Colonial Indian Society*, in R. Ross (ed.) *Racism and Colonialism*, The Hague, Martinus Nijhoff, pp. 143-182.

—— (1985), *Modern South Indian Political History: An Interpretation*, in R.E Frykenberg and Kolenda (eds.) *Studies of South India*, Madras, New Era Publications, pp. 93-126.

—— (1990), *South Asia, World System and World Capitalism*, in Sugata Bose (ed.), pp. 40-86.

—— (1993), *Land and Labour in Late 18th Century: The Golden Age of the Pariah*, in P. Robb (ed.), pp 68-86.

Weber, Max (1958), *Religion of India: Hinduism and Buddhism* (trans. by H.H. Geith & Don Martindale), Illinois Glencoe.

—— (1978), *Economy and Society*, G. Roth and C. Wittich (ed.), vol. II, Berkeley, University of California Press.

—— (1985), *From Max Weber: Essays in Sociology*, H.H. Gerth and C.W. Mills (eds.), London, Routledge and Kegan Paul.

Webster, John C.B. (1994), *The Dalit Christians*, New Delhi, ISPCK.

Williams, Raymond (1976), *Keywords: A Vocabulary of Culture and Society*, New York, Oxford University Press.

Wink, Andre (1986), *Land and Sovereignty in India*, Cambridge, Cambridge University Press.

Wiser, William Henricks (1958), *The Hindu Jajmani System*, Lucknow, Lucknow Publishing House.

Wolpert, Stanley (1984), *Jinnah of Pakistan*, Oxford, Oxford University Press.

—— (1988), *The Indian National Congress in Nationalist Perspective*, in R. Sisson and S. Wolpert (eds.), *Congress and Indian Nationalism*, Delhi, Oxford University Press, pp. 21-46.

Yang, Anand A. (1989), *The Limited Raj: Agrarian Relations in Colonial India, Saran District 1793-1920*, Delhi, Oxford University Press.

Zelliot, Eleanor (1969), Dr. Ambedkar and the Mahar Movement, Unpublished D. Phil thesis submitted to the University of Pennsylvania.

Zelliot, Eleanor (1970), Mahar and Non-Brahmin Movements in Maharashtra, *IESHR*, vol. VII, no. 3, pp. 397-415.

———(1972), *Gandhi and Ambedkar—A Study in Leadership* in M. Mahar (ed.), pp. 69-96.

——— (1988), *The Congress and the Untouchables 1917-1950*, in R. Sisson and S. Wolpert (eds.), *Congress and Indian Nationalism*, Delhi, Oxford University Press, pp. 182-97.

Zubaida, Sami (1978), *Theories of Nationalism*, in G. Littlejohn *et.al.* (ed.), *Power and the State*, London, Croom Helm, pp. 52-72.

Index